The Novels
of Jack London
A Reappraisal

Jack London. Photograph courtesy of The Huntington Library, San Marino, California.

The Novels of Jack London

A Reappraisal

Charles N. Watson, Jr.

The University of Wisconsin Press

Published 1983

The University of Wisconsin Press
114 North Murray Street
Madison, Wisconsin 53715

The University of Wisconsin Press, Ltd.
1 Gower Street
London WC1E 6HA, England

First printing

Printed in the United States of America

For LC CIP information see the colophon

ISBN 0-299-09300-X

For Betsy
and for Ben and Elizabeth

Contents

Preface   ix
1   An Impassioned Realism   3
2   Manners in the Northland: *A Daughter of the Snows*   17
3   Ghost Dog: *The Call of the Wild*   33
4   Lucifer on the Quarter-Deck: *The Sea-Wolf*   53
5   Redemption of an Outcast: *White Fang*   79
6   Revolution and Romance: *The Iron Heel*   99
7   Art and Alienation: *Martin Eden*   123
8   Three Frontiers: *Burning Daylight*   165
9   Urban Discontents: *The Valley of the Moon*   187
10   A Broken Clock: *The Little Lady of the Big House*   211
Epilogue   235
Notes   247
Chronology of Jack London's Life   287
Books by Jack London   291
Index   295

Preface

This book had its genesis in a course in "American Literary Naturalism" which I taught at Syracuse University in the fall of 1973. Perhaps because as a boy I had unaccountably passed London by, I did not approach him with the condescension that one often retains for the literary enthusiasms of youth. My first acquaintance with his fiction did not come until graduate school, when I read *The Call of the Wild* and *Martin Eden* and found them entirely respectable, even impressive. Hence, though well aware that London was held in low esteem by most critics, I was willing to take a chance and include him in my course along with Crane, Norris, and Dreiser. At that point I read *The Sea-Wolf* for the first time and discovered how strongly it was influenced by *Moby-Dick*. Something, I thought, should be said for a writer who had the good sense to admire Melville at a time when few readers remembered him at all. London would bear looking into.

Since the 1950s, in fact, London has been looked into by a growing number of scholars and critics. Such books as Franklin Walker's *Jack London and the Klondike* (1966), Earle Labor's critical biography *Jack London* (1974), and James I. McClintock's *White Logic: Jack London's Short Stories* (1975) have all, in their different ways, helped to secure London's reputation while preparing the way for the further studies that are sure to come. The present book is written out of a similar conviction that London is a serious and often compelling writer whose reputation has suffered at the hands of critics interested more in advancing a larger thesis than in doing justice to individual writers and works. Those who are fundamentally suspicious of a writer popular in his own time have tended to dismiss London as a talented hack, the author of a few memorable stories for boys. But the danger that he would disappear altogether from the anthologies and literary histories seems lately to have dissolved into something of a London revival.

There are several reasons why I decided to concentrate on London's novels. One is that there is already a good book on the short stories, McClintock's *White Logic*, though doubtless still more work needs to be done on that subject. A second reason is that London himself shared the almost universal prejudice in favor of the great long work over the great short one. The word "great" often connotes size as well as quality, and one need not be reduced to applying a page-count criterion of literary worth in order to recognize that when two works of widely unequal length are compared, some value resides in a writer's ability to sustain his imaginative force over the longer distance. Accordingly, when London began serious writing in the late 1890s, he rapidly became impatient with his apprenticeship in the short story and yearned to attempt a novel. Even after the failure of his first such effort, *A Daughter of the Snows*, he continued to think of his development in terms of the "big work" of novel writing. Later, when his reputation was established, he considered his short stories a potboiling activity to be pursued in the interludes between more important performances in the novels.

The question, of course, is not whether London attempted novels but whether his attempts were successful. Consequently, the most important justification for this study is my inability to accept the conventional wisdom that London was a good short story writer but a poor novelist. It is true that he wrote many excellent short stories, and equally true that he could not always manage the longer fictional forms without losing his grip somewhere in midcourse.

Nevertheless, one might make a case that his reputation rests more securely on his novella *The Call of the Wild* (1903) and his novel *Martin Eden* (1909)—and on his flawed but still impressive *The Sea-Wolf* (1904), *White Fang* (1906), and *The Iron Heel* (1908)—than on any combination of his best short stories. And though such later works as *Burning Daylight* (1910), *The Valley of the Moon* (1913), and especially *The Little Lady of the Big House* (1916) are casually or sometimes scathingly disparaged by nearly all of those few who have bothered to read them, I am convinced that they deserve a place in the second rank of London's novels along with *The Sea-Wolf*, *White Fang*, and *The Iron Heel*.

I decided at an early stage to confine my study mainly to these eight works, arguably the best of his twenty completed novels and novellas. The only deviation from that policy is the inclusion of *A Daughter of the Snows* (1902), which, though weak, sheds light on the development of major themes and on how the apprentice went about learning his craft. Of the works I ruled out, some undeniably have considerable strength, and I omitted them only after deciding that they do not quite merit the extended discussion I planned for the major novels. The early prize-fight novella *The Game* (1905) successfully balances the naive tenderness of a youthful love affair against the fatal brutality of the ring, which becomes, like the Northland, another primitive arena in which the courage and endurance of London's characters can be tested. Still more substantial are the primitive and futurist fantasies *Before Adam* (1907) and *The Scarlet Plague* (1915). In the former, the narrator's racial memory emerges in childhood dreams, allowing him to relive his earlier existence in the Stone Age. Though London was exploiting the contemporary vogue of primitive fantasy, he was also improving on the popular formula, probing the loneliness and insecurity of his protagonist and tracing the evolution of a rudimentary cooperative society out of an earlier anarchic individualism. *The Scarlet Plague* takes an opposite direction, plunging its protagonist not backward in time but forward, after a plague has destroyed an overrefined, self-indulgent civilization and returned it to a primitive wilderness. Each of these novels displays narrative skill and psychological penetration, as well as dramatizing the kinds of social conflicts that emerged more notably in *The Iron Heel.*

Another late novel of considerable merit is *The Star Rover* (1915). Though London himself spoke condescendingly of its elements of occult fantasy, it develops great power and convincing verisimilitude in its account of a San Quentin prisoner who, during periods of torture in a straightjacket, masters a process of self-hypnosis that permits him to escape his present body and, like the narrator of *Before Adam*, to reexperience his former selves and lives. Unfortunately, this device leads London to interpolate into the prison framework a variety of narratives ranging from a chivalric romance to an Indian massacre. The novel thus never fully coheres, becoming merely a repository for a group of short stories unrelated in content and uneven in artistry.

Of the other novels, perhaps the most readable is *Adventure* (1911), a tale of a Solomon Islands planter and his uneasy romance with a spirited and independent-minded woman. London himself dismissed this novel rather cryptically as only a skit, and it is certainly not major fiction. Yet it is enlivened by the narrative power that seldom completely deserts him, and it is his only novel to deal with the demonic Melanesian setting that came to represent to him an ultimate form of Conradian horror. Another potboiling adventure-yarn is *The Mutiny of the Elsinore* (1914), whose magazine serial title, *The Sea Gangsters*, accurately signals the gratuitous brutality which, along with considerable racism and glaring artistic flaws, makes this the worst of London's serious novels. The protagonist, a jaded thirty-year-old writer, retains a certain biographical interest, and the novel does offer a number of other clues to London's grim state of mind during his "bad year" of 1913. But as a work of fiction, it well deserves the censure it has usually received. The remaining novels scarcely merit mention. *The Cruise of the Dazzler* (1902) is a juvenile, and the second prizefight novella, *The Abysmal Brute* (1913), based on a plot purchased from Sinclair Lewis, is a dull and half-hearted performance. Of the posthumous works, *Jerry of the Islands* and *Michael, Brother of Jerry* (both 1917) are *mere* dog stories in a way that *The Call of the Wild* and *White Fang* are not, and *Hearts of Three* (1920) is pure hack work, which London himself, according to his wife, considered something of a joke.

Nine books, then, remain for full consideration, and I begin each chapter by examining the novel as a product of a particular constellation of experiences in London's life and reading. This process of grounding the work in its literary and experiential sources has seemed to me not only a matter of scholarly thoroughness but also a means of demonstrating the degree to which London was dependent for his material on personal experience—either of life or of books. He frequently acknowledged his lack of the power of "origination," yet paradoxically he was most inventive when he allowed his imagination to engage his own real experience or the literary experience of someone else. Like other writers before him, he encountered what Harold Bloom has described as the "anxiety of influence," and his struggle to come to terms with such literary "fathers" as Kipling, Conrad, and Melville constitutes an important part of the drama of his imaginative development.

After considering the genesis and sources of each novel, I go on to discuss its qualities as a work of fictive art. This is a task of both interpretation and evaluation. As an interpreter, I have tried to approach London with a minimum of preconceptions and to avoid the reductive distortions that a thesis frequently entails. Thematic patterns or biographical conclusions might emerge from my study, but they were not to be imposed on the novels at the outset. To put the point another way, I have sought what E. D. Hirsch, Jr., has usefully defined as "author's meaning"—if that term is understood to include dimensions of meaning of which the author is not fully conscious. The more problematical task of evaluation, I hope, is more than a matter of subjective taste. It is based on the generic and formal assumptions that lie behind London's own conception of his art—assumptions rooted in the contemporary critical battle between realism and romance.

Admittedly, any method, even one which is thus empirical and somewhat eclectic, is bound to be reductive to some degree. The process of selection—the critic's perceiving in a novel this meaning or merit rather than that, his unconscious tendency to stress one thing and slight another—inevitably reduces the work by confining it within his limited field of vision. Correspondingly, to assert the centrality of any one theme while examining only nine of London's published writings is to oversimplify a complex and to some extent shapeless career. Yet my belief that London poured his most deeply felt experiences and convictions into certain of his novels requires that these works be given a larger prominence in any attempt to discern a figure in the carpet. And a central theme has, indeed, emerged: that London's novels repeatedly dramatize the chief conflict within his own character—the uneasy marriage between the sensitive, bookish aspirant to art and culture and the brash adventurer, the "brain merchant" for whom writing was only another trade. Typically, each of these personae encounters an opposite, or double, and is changed—and sometimes destroyed—by the experience. A fuller explanation of this conflict will be the purpose of the first chapter, which is followed by a chapter on each of the nine novels and an attempt, in a brief epilogue, to summarize and evaluate London's achievement.

During these past several years of research and writing, I have been generously assisted by a number of persons and institutions. My largest debt is to Earle Labor, whose friendly support and expert advice have been helpful to me from virtually the beginning of the project. His careful reading of the manuscript at a semifinal stage has made this a better book than it would otherwise have been. I am grateful, as well, to I. Milo Shepard, executor of the London estate, who kindly showed me the London ranch when I visited Glen Ellen and who later granted me permission to quote passages from London's unpublished papers. Two of my colleagues, John W. Crowley and Walter Sutton, also read the manuscript and made many useful suggestions, though neither they nor Mr. Labor should be held responsible for my occasional inability to profit from good advice.

I owe further thanks to Syracuse University for three research grants that freed me from the necessity of summer teaching and enabled me to spend two months in California at the Henry E. Huntington Library, whose staff was unfailingly helpful. Virginia J. Renner, especially, made my visit pleasant and productive in innumerable ways, and David Mike Hamilton provided expert knowledge of the London collection and kindly permitted me to read his manuscript on the annotated volumes in London's personal library. The Special Collections staff of the Merrill Library at Utah State University aided my research by providing photocopies of materials in their extensive London holdings, and the staffs of the Interlibrary Loan Department and Arents Rare Book Room of Bird Library at Syracuse University have also been continually helpful. The Huntington and Merrill Libraries have both granted me permission to quote from unpublished papers in their collections.

I wish to thank the editors of *Western American Literature* and *American Literature* for permission to reprint in somewhat different form material that first appeared in those journals; and several other friends, colleagues, and London scholars who have replied to my queries or assisted me in other ways: Thomas Atteridge, Arthur W. Hoffman, Bruce N. Johnson, Russ Kingman, Robert Leitz, Jay Martin, Jean Rice, Irving Stone, and Paul Theiner. The perceptive editorial work of Dennis Trudell has greatly improved the final manuscript; and to the early example and guidance of Lawrance Thompson and Arlin Turner, neither of whom lived to see this book completed, I owe more than a bare statement can readily say. Finally, for the assistance and encouragement of my wife, Betsy, my gratitude is lovingly acknowledged in the dedication.

The Novels
of Jack London
A Reappraisal

1

An Impassioned Realism

What can be said in defense of a writer who proclaimed defiantly that he would rather win a water fight than write the great American novel?[1] Throughout his career, Jack London repeatedly insisted that he wrote only for money. He would write "rot," he told his friend Cloudesley Johns in 1899, "if somebody would only pay me for it,"[2] and he was fond of remarking that he actually hated his work. As he told an interviewer in 1912, "I'd prefer to shovel coal for three hours a day, dig ditches or anything else that was good hard manual labor, but the only way that I can get bread and butter is by turning out fiction."[3] A year later, his intensifying interest in the development of his California ranch led him to announce: "I write a book for no other reason than to add three or four hundred acres to my magnificent estate. I write a story with no other purpose than to buy a stallion. To me, my cattle are far more interesting than my profession. My friends don't believe me when I say this, but I am absolutely sincere."[4]

Quite possibly London believed what he said, for he always put great stock in straight-from-the-shoulder sincerity. Yet as his wife acknowledged, his friends' skepticism was justified. "He never ceased to maintain," she observed, "that he hated to write—had to drive himself to it. It made

3

him flare when this was questioned. . . . But his best work was conceived in passion for its own sake, and I think one feels his urge of self-expression, while many were his enthusiasms over what he was doing."[5] Too many readers, uncritically taking him at his own word, have failed to detect in his defensive "flare" a hint of the complex motivation with which he approached the creative act. Certainly a part of him craved material success, even luxury, and at times revolted against the drudgery required to attain it. He knew as well as anyone that writing is hard work, and he bridled at the notion that with a breath of inspiration a book somehow writes itself. Yet in part his revolt was also a pose, though perhaps an unconscious one.

The pose derives, on one hand, from London's reaction against the decadent estheticism of the *fin de siècle*, which exalted beauty and art at the expense of truth and experience. In common with his California contemporary Frank Norris, he shared the preference of the "red-blooded" realist for matter over manner. "What is form?" he wrote in 1900. "What intrinsic value resides in it? None, none, none—unless it clothe pregnant substance, great substance."[6] Behind such statements lies the suspicion that high art, at its more ethereal fringes, is somehow effeminate, and London's rebellion against it becomes a defensive assertion of the masculinity on which he prided himself. In the age of Richard Harding Davis, the prototypical novelist-reporter-adventurer, and of Teddy Roosevelt, apostle of the strenuous life, such posturing was common. But London, more than most, felt a need to convince himself and others that he was no sissy. Just as Faulkner, a half-century later, was fond of comparing his art to carpentry and describing himself as just an ordinary Mississippi farmer who liked to tell stories,[7] London was inclined to speak of himself as an "honest artisan" and his writing as only another bread-and-butter trade. No highfalutin estheticism for him—at least not in public!

Such a stance, after all, constitutes an understandable reaction against the occasional pretentiousness of literary shoptalk. But it also constitutes, as it did for Faulkner, a source of amusement, a kind of game in which London took a mischievous delight in confounding the expectations of his interviewers. The reporter who had just heard him compare writing to coal-shoveling and ditch-digging was moved to suggest skeptically that surely he must have a feeling of "enthusiasm" and "creative joy" when he composed such "warm poetical passages" as the descriptions of the tropical islands and seas in *Martin Eden.* "Obviously delighted with the astonishment of his questioner's manner," London flatly denied that he had any imagination at all, and proceeded to bait the skeptical interviewer with further exaggerations of his literary attitudes and habits, insisting that writing fiction was his fourth choice after poetry, pamphlets, and music; that he "nearly starved once studying music"; that he "reduce[s] everything to an economic basis and to system"; that he "reads six books a day" and is "taking 20,000 volumes" on his voyage around Cape Horn.

Thus, in judging London's ostentatious proclamations of his mercenary motives, one must look carefully at their context and intended audience. Many of his early statements appear in his letters to Cloudesley Johns, with whom he carried on a friendly running quarrel, Johns disclaiming any low financial motive, London flaunting his own lust for cash out of a suspicion of hypocrisy in his friend. As he wrote to Anna Strunsky in 1900,

Saturday night, and a good week's work done—hack work of course. Why shouldn't I? Like any other honest artisan by the sweat of my brow. I have a friend [Johns] who scorns such work. He writes for posterity, for a small circle of admirers, oblivious to the world's oblivion, doesn't want money, scoffs at the idea of it, calls it filthy, damns all who write for it, etc., etc.,—that is, he does all this if one were to take his words for criteria. But I received a letter from him recently. *Munsey's* had offered to buy a certain story of him, if he would change the ending. He had built the tale carefully, every thought tending toward the final consummation, notably, the death by violence of the chief character. And they asked him to keep the tale and to permit that character, logically dead, to live. He scorns money. Yes; and he permitted that character to live.[8]

A few years later, after Johns had been cured of his high-mindedness, London could not resist an I-told-you-so: "So you're going to begin writing for money! Forgive me for rubbing it in. You've changed since several years ago when you placed ART first and dollars afterward. You didn't quite sympathize with me in those days."[9] Others might aspire to the rarefied atmosphere of art-for-art's-sake; London would make a virtue of financial necessity and iconoclastic candor.

Johns's early aversion to the commercial motive reflects not only his dedication to pure art but also his socialism, and many of London's most notorious statements about his hack work must be read in the further light of his sensitivity to the charge by his socialist friends that he had abandoned his principles and sold himself in the bourgeois literary marketplace. In 1905, when he embarked on a socialist lecture tour attended by his Korean valet, and later when he lavished thousands of dollars on his boat and his ranch, many a socialist eyebrow was raised. Hence London's testy insistence that writing was an honest trade and that in any case he regretted this concession to the bourgeoisie and would prefer to be writing unremunerative socialist tracts. As he told his fellow novelist and socialist Upton Sinclair, "I loathe the stuff when I have done it. I do it because I want money and it is an easy way to get it. But if I could have my choice about it I never would put pen to paper—except to write a Socialist essay to tell the bourgeois world how much I despise it."[10]

For a number of reasons, then, London was inclined to be touchy about his way of making a living and quick to correct anyone who attributed to him a motive higher than the cynically commercial. He could best thwart the predatory bourgeoisie, he thought, by relieving it of some of its cash. Yet like many another writer before and after him, he was torn between writing what the public would buy and writing to please himself. "Dollars damn me," Herman Melville lamented in a famous letter to Hawthorne in 1851. "What I feel most moved to write, that is banned,—it will not pay. Yet, altogether, write the *other* way I cannot."[11] Faulkner, in a similar mood, wrote to his publisher in 1932 to plead for an advance so that he would not be forced to "put the novel aside and go whoring again with short stories."[12] Jack London, throughout his career, experienced precisely the same conflict. Though he made more concessions to the marketplace than did Melville or Faulkner, he also valued creativity and strove to write seriously and well. Beneath the hardboiled pose lay his exacting pride in his craft, his dedication to portraying the truth of things as he saw it, and, intermittently, his experience of what can only be called creative ecstasy.

Take, for example, another of his most notorious statements: his unembarrassed declaration of his willingness to be bowdlerized. "I am the everlasting marvel of the magazine-editors of the United States," he wrote in 1910, "because of the fact that I always give them an absolute free fist in blue-penciling my manuscripts. I never have any passions or excitements over interferences and changes in my work."[13] This boast has been widely misunderstood. It is true that as an apprentice writer anxious to break into print at any cost, London permitted the mutilation of such short stories as "A Thousand Deaths" and "An Odyssey of the North." The former, one of the first of his stories to be accepted, was in any case merely well-paid hack work, but the cutting of the latter caused him real pain. "Did you ever write a yarn of, say, twelve thousand words," he wrote to Johns, "every word essential to atmosphere, and then get an order to cut out three thousand of those words, somewhere, somehow? That's what the *Atlantic* has just done to me. Hardly know whether I shall do it or not. It's like the pound of flesh."[14]

Of course London suppressed his qualms and offered up the pound of flesh, for this acceptance from the *Atlantic* constituted an important breakthrough which he could ill afford to sacrifice. But once his reputation was established, his resistance stiffened. In 1906, when *Cosmopolitan* presumed to tamper with an article and a short story, he let out a "regular long wolf-howl" of complaint. "I don't like the way you have taken liberties with my copy," he huffed. "Any tyro can cut a manuscript and feel that he is co-creator with the author. But it's hell on the author." He would submit to the necessity of "truckling to Mrs. Grundy" by changing "go to hell" to "go to blazes," since that was the "mere shell." But he refused to sit still while some assistant editor was violating the idiomatic speech of his characters or "cutting the heart" out of his narrative: "I WEAVE my stuff; you can cut out a whole piece of it, but you can't cut out parts of it, and leave mutilated parts behind. . . . If the whole woven thing—event, narrative, description—is not suitable for your magazine, why cut it out—cut out the whole thing. I don't care. But I refuse to contemplate for one moment that there is any man in your office, or in the office of any magazine, capable of bettering my art, or the art of any other first-class professional writer."[15] Dependent as he was on the magazine outlet, he reluctantly deferred to the "poor young American girl who mustn't be shocked";[16] this was the kind of "blue-penciling" to which he regularly submitted without protest. But he would not abide more extensive acts of editorial butchery.

Almost invariably, moreover, he rejected suggestions for revision, even those made in the interest of larger sales. When his Macmillan editor, George P. Brett, proposed a few changes in the manuscript of *The Iron Heel*, London agreed to make reasonable minor alterations but not to violate his larger sense of form:

My conceptions of artistry may be all wrong. But nevertheless I am the slave of those conceptions; and my slavery makes me think inartistic your suggestion of working into the Foreword, or of putting in at the end, of THE IRON HEEL, a sketch touching ever so lightly the details of the conditions of that far distant time. In fact, in my own austere way—or, rather, in the austere way made necessary by the form of the narrative—I have given many hints and suggestions of that far future time. To give more, I fear, would be overburdening the artistry of it.

Not even Brett's uneasiness about possible legal action moved London to delete one of his footnotes. "The very passage that might be held to be contempt of court is so felicitously phrased," he replied, "that it goes against my heart to cut it out."[17] In later years he rejected a call by the editor of *Cosmopolitan* for more emphasis on a love story in *The Mutiny of the Elsinore* and *The Star Rover*. In the former, he could not see his way "artistically" to making the love story more important than the voyage around Cape Horn: "I am trying to fuse both motives into one, giving each its due place."[18] London's well-known dislike of revision may in part be sheer laziness, but that possibility does not explain his unwillingness merely to leave an offending passage out. His sense of artistry, though often carefully concealed, was unmistakably present.

Indeed, throughout his career London tried to give due place—if not simultaneously, then alternately—to both the demands of the marketplace and the requirements of his imagination. He always distinguished between his hack work and his serious fiction, and more than once he insisted on a two-tiered conception of his best work: the superficial narrative line aimed at the mass audience, and the "deep underlying motif" that would be understood by "only a few."[19] His early essays are full of hardheaded and mildly cynical advice to young writers on how to crack the magazine market, but he does not advise the abandonment of honest craftsmanship. The writer, he believes, should limit his output to a thousand words a day and make them "the very best he has in him." Although "to satisfy the belly-need, the aspirant must often turn his pen to other than excellent work," this concession will do no harm, he insists, so long as it does not kill serious ambition, for "the confirmed hack-writer is a most melancholy spectacle."[20] To be avoided at all cost is the "insanely vapid [fiction] which amuses the commonplace souls of the commonplace public, and the melodramatic messes which tickle the palates of the sensation mongers." Of course such work pays, he admits, "but because we happen to be mercenarily inclined, there is no reason why we should lose our self respect."[21]

In his letters to Johns, he balanced his remarks on the pot-boiling motive with trenchant advice on artistry: "Don't you tell the reader. Don't. Don't. Don't. But HAVE YOUR CHARACTERS TELL IT BY THEIR DEEDS, ACTIONS, TALK, ETC. Then, and not until then, are you writing fiction and not a sociological paper." Strive for "atmosphere," for "breadth and thickness"; and above all, "get your good strong phrases, fresh, and vivid. And write intensively, not exhaustively or lengthily. Don't narrate—paint! draw! build!—CREATE!"[22] Thus, along with Henry James, London believed that the writer should show, not tell; dramatize, not narrate and pontificate. But he also embraced the un-Jamesian conception of language that he had imbibed from Herbert Spencer's *Philosophy of Style* (1871), with its emphasis on force of expression and economy of the reader's attention. The age, he believed, was "concentrative," preferring short sentences and short novels, requiring prose that is "crisp, incisive, terse." The race "tolerates Mr. James," he insisted, "but it prefers Mr. Kipling."[23]

What sets off the true writer from the hack, London argues in an early essay, is originality. And what constitutes originality is "an ordinary working philosophy of life." Though such a phrase, he admits, eludes precise definition, it does not consist of a particular theory or program of beliefs, nor does it imply a "yielding to the didactic impulse." Rather, it involves the writer's attainment, through experience and reading, of "a view of peculiarly his own"; the development of an "individual standard"; the achievement of "*something to say.*"[24] Yet like Melville before him, London found the world "strangely and coldly averse to his exchanging the joy of his heart for the solace of his stomach." While "the discerning" tempt him with the promise that "truth alone endures," a time-serving editor rejects his truths as "too strong," advising him that the magazine audience requires "truth toned down, truth diluted, truth insipid, harmless truth, conventionalized truth, trimmed truth."[25] On one occasion London contested such editorial timidity by arguing that the reading public, while claiming to prefer trimmed truth and happy endings, actually retains an unacknowledged fascination with the "terrible and tragic." The continuing popularity of Poe, he suggests, reveals that "deep down in the roots of the race is fear." Can any story be "really great," he wonders, "the theme of which is anything but tragic or terrible? Can the sweet commonplaces of life be made into anything else than sweetly commonplace stories?" No, even the love motif derives its popularity "not from the love itself, but from the tragic and terrible with which the love is involved. . . . Romeo and Juliet are not remembered because things slipped smoothly along." Why, he asks, can there not be "a magazine such as Poe dreamed of, about which there shall be nothing namby-pamby, yellowish, or emasculated, and which will print stories that are bids for place and permanence rather than for the largest circulation?"[26]

In this essay London blurs the distinction between Poe's Gothic nightmare world and the tragic drama of *Romeo and Juliet*. Yet his fiction, at its best, contains something of both. At the heart of London's sense of life lies a tragic paradox: the moment of almost mystical exultation in which the protagonist sees most intensely into the mystery of being, even as he stares into the mocking face of death. The most famous expression of this moment occurs in *The Call of the Wild*, when Buck experiences "an ecstasy that marks the summit of life"—an emotion that comes also "to the artist" when he is "caught up and out of himself in a sheet of flame."[27] It is the awareness of death (the passage is pervaded with death images) that makes such exalted moments possible but also impermanent. Ultimately they are but powerful illusions, doomed to fade into the chilling insight that London came to call the White Logic, the nihilistic messenger of "truth beyond truth, the antithesis of life, cruel and bleak as interstellar space, pulseless and frozen as absolute zero.''[28] Out of such oppositions—high art and hack work, illusion and reality, spirit and flesh, life and death, being and nothingness—comes the double vision that energizes London's fiction.

Such tensions emerged early in his life, when he created the masks or roles with which to shield himself from pain. Repelled by his mother's spiritual séances, he rejected all metaphysics and declared himself a brass tacks materialist. Depressed by a drab and frequently lonely boyhood, he escaped into the fantasy world of books and the adventurous life of sailing on San Francisco Bay. Experiencing the monotonous drudgery of manual labor and the abysses of human degradation in a New York penitentiary, he embraced ''superman socialism''[29] and fastened on the writer's trade as a way up the economic ladder. Discovering his illegitimate birth and finding that his natural father was unwilling to recognize him, he invented for himself an honorable lineage, venerated ''good stock'' and Anglo-Saxon supremacy, and hoped desperately for a son and heir.

Not that he utterly denied reality and lost himself in fantasy and role-playing. His painful early experiences remained one important pole of his imaginative vision, and for the most part he retained the ability to distinguish between the outer mask and the inner self. In 1899 he unburdened himself to his friend Anna Strunsky:

I, too, was a dreamer, on a farm, nay, a California ranch. But early, at only nine, the hard hand of the world was laid upon me. It has never relaxed. It has left me sentiment, but destroyed sentimentalism. It has made me practical, so that I am known as harsh, stern, uncompromising. It has taught me that reason is mightier than imagination; that the scientific man is superior to the emotional man. It has also given me a truer and a deeper romance of things, an idealism which is an inner sanctuary and which must be resolutely throttled in dealings with my kind, but which yet remains within the holy of holies, like an oracle, to be cherished always but to be made manifest or be consulted not on every occasion I go to market. To do this latter would bring upon me the ridicule of my fellows and make me a failure.[30]

Thus his vaunted materialism and scientific rationalism became part of the armor that enabled a vulnerable ego to confront the world.

This capacity for role-playing was acknowledged most fully in a remarkable letter he wrote to Charmian Kittredge during the early months of their courtship in 1903:

You speak of frankness. I passionately desire it, but have come to shrink from the pain of intimacies which bring the greater frankness forth. Superficial frankness is comparatively easy, but one must pay for stripping off the dry husks of clothing, the self-conventions which masque the soul, and for standing out naked in the eyes of one who sees. I have paid, and like a child who has been burned by fire, I shrink from paying too often. . . .

I wonder if I make you understand. You see, in the objective facts of my life I have always been frankness personified. That I tramped or begged or festered in jail or slum meant nothing by the telling. But over the lips of my inner self I had long since put a seal—a seal indeed rarely broken, in moments when one caught fleeting glimpses of the hermit who lived inside. . . . My child life was uncongenial. There was little responsive around me. I learned reticence, an inner reticence. I went into the world early, and I adventured among different classes. A newcomer in any class, I naturally was reticent concerning my real self, which such a class could not understand, while I was superficially loquacious in order to make my entry into such a class popular and successful. . . .

Ask people who know me to-day, what I am. A rough, savage fellow, they will say, who likes prizefights and brutalities, who has a clever turn of pen, a charlatan's smattering of art, and the inevitable deficiencies of the untrained, unrefined, self-made man which he strives with a fair measure of success to hide beneath an attitude of roughness and unconventionality. Do I endeavor to unconvince them? It's so much easier to leave their convictions alone.

Most of the time, he concludes, "I manage to fool my inner self pretty well"—so much so that he is compelled to wonder whether that inner self will "dry up some day and blow away."[31]

That fate never completely overtook him, yet his capacity to fool his inner self grew stronger with the years, as it certainly succeeded in fooling those of his critics who never saw behind the mask of the hack writer and literary barbarian. His life remained a precarious emotional seesaw, a constant struggle for balance: "I early learned that there were two natures in me. This caused me a great deal of trouble, till I worked out a philosophy of life and struck a compromise between the flesh and the spirit. Too great an ascendancy of either was to be abnormal, and since normality is almost a fetish of mine, I finally succeeded in balancing both natures. Ordinarily they are at equilibrium; yet as frequently as one is permitted to run rampant, so is the other."[32] His wife put the point more worshipfully when she said that "his materialism incarnated his idealism, and his idealism consecrated and transfigured his materialism."[33] But London himself was closer to the mark in recognizing that his double vision was the product of a smoldering and sometimes explosive inner conflict.

Philosophically, this double vision emerges in the lifelong dialogue between his confident scientific rationalism and his lurking suspicion that heaven and earth held more than Comte and Haeckel had dreamt of. He repeatedly declared himself, like Haeckel, a "hopeless materialist" and a "positive scientific thinker" who had "no patience with the metaphysical philosophers."[34] Yet even as he scorned all supernaturalism, he also retained a Spencerian agnosticism, reminding Cloudesley Johns of the "adamantine line" that Spencer had drawn between "the knowable and the unknowable."[35] Indeed, he increasingly went beyond this scientific agnosticism to flirt with the supernatural and the transcendent. Again and again he dramatized in his fiction those moments of mystical rapture that permit one to burst the fetters of materiality; and although he had long since rejected his mother's spiritualism, he continued to be fascinated by the possibility of supernatural experience. His notes for a "Future Story[,] Metaphysical," which he never wrote, seem at least a serious expression of his unanswered questions: "The isolation of the death spirit—new forces, radium, telepathy, etc.—not so very much known. . . .

Work in the confuting of the materialists, etc. Striking testimony of one man who almost died."[36]

This conflict of beliefs also carries over into his theory of fiction, in which he aligned himself with those who sought a middle ground between the more extreme claims of realism and romance. Though he joined with W. D. Howells in deploring the sentimentality and melodrama in which popular fiction was awash, he was impatient with the drawing-room subtleties of Howells and James, and even with the passion for documentary detail that he found in a kindred spirit like Norris. In his otherwise laudatory review of *The Octopus*, he carped at Norris for his "inordinate realism." What does the world care, he grumbled, "whether Hooven's meat safe be square or oblong; whether it be lined with wire screen or mosquito netting; whether it be hung to the branches of the oak tree or to the ridgepole of the barn; whether, in fact, Hooven has a meat safe or not?"[37] In the same vein, the following year he leaped to the defense of his own fiction against an unnamed critic's charge that it lacked sufficient detail: "When I have drawn a picture in few strokes, he would spoil it by putting in the multitude of details I have left out. . . . His trouble is that he does not see with a pictorial eye. He merely looks upon a scene an[d] sees every bit of it; but he does not see the true picture in that scene, a picture which can be thrown upon the canvas by eliminating a great mass of things that spoil the composition, that obfuscate the true beautiful lines of it." What the critic failed to understand, London concluded, is that "mine is not *realism* but is *idealized realism.*"[38]

Throughout his career, London held to this conception of his art. In 1898, fresh from the Klondike, he recommended one of his sketches to an editor on the grounds that he had learned "to grasp the true romance of things,"[39] and in the eighteen years that remained to him he never found a better characterization of his special quality as a writer. Romance, rightly considered, should not shy away from grim realities; on the contrary, it must be "true," it m st be a romance of "things." Sounding an Emersonian note, he wrote in his tribute to Kipling that history will honor only those artists "who have spoken true of us. . . . Half-truths and partial-truths will not do, nor will thin piping voices and quavering lays. There must be the cosmic quality in what they sing. They must seize upon and press into enduring art-forms the vital facts of our existence." The romance of Homer's Greece "is not our romance."[40] When he fictionalized his own apprenticeship as a writer in *Martin Eden*, he combined Martin's "basic love of reality" with an imagination that was "fanciful, even fantastic at times." What Martin struggles to achieve is the union of esthetic idealism and red-blooded realism, the "school of god" and the "school of clod." He seeks "an impassioned realism, shot through with human aspiration and faith."[41]

Inevitably, this double vision pervades London's novels, becoming the principal focus of his characters and their conflicts. The main characters tend to fall into two types: the sheltered, overcivilized young man or woman who must encounter brutal realities, and the untutored barbarian who must encounter the ethical and esthetic influences of civilization. Initially at least, these two worlds often divide along stereotyped sexual lines, the civilized world being conceived as feminine, while the domain of brute power is masculine. Yet the representative of the "masculine" world is not always a man, nor is the representative of the "feminine" world necessarily a woman; sometimes the stereotypes are reversed. But whether man or woman, each character must encounter his or her opposite and face the possibility of change. If the change is accomplished successfully, the result is a mature sexual balance—a blending of the "feminine" impulse toward civilizing domesticity and the anarchic "masculine" will to power.[42] The conflict can also be tragically destructive, the only change the final one of death, the seal of failure. For London, to whom life was preeminently movement and struggle, the clash of opposites remained throughout his career the chief source of his imaginative vitality. His first novel, *A Daughter of the Snows*, reveals with particular clarity his effort to find a dramatic action equal to this central theme.

2

Manners in the Northland
A Daughter of the Snows

When London returned in the summer of 1898 from his year in the Klondike, he brought with him little enough gold. But he had found a veritable mother lode of mining-camp tales and experiences that would provide the basis of his career as a writer. He had, in fact, been trying his hand at writing for several years, between stints as a manual laborer, oyster pirate, ordinary seaman, and cross-country tramp. At seventeen, he had won first prize in an 1893 newspaper contest with "Story of a Typhoon Off the Coast of Japan," based on his seven-month voyage in a seal-hunting schooner, and a year later he published several promising tales in the Oakland *High School Aegis*. By the time he left for the Klondike in 1897, he had accumulated a respectable pile of rejection slips for the poems, stories, essays, and jokes with which he had attempted to perfect his craftsmanship and break further into print. His adventure in the Northland then gave him what he had lacked: a more mature perspective on his raw physical experience. Only four months after his return, he placed his first Klondike story, "To the Man on Trail," in the *Overland Monthly*. Throughout 1899 he worked hard at his short stories, and by the end of the year

17

the acceptance of "An Odyssey of the North" by the prestigious *Atlantic* and the signing of a contract with Houghton Mifflin for a collection to be called *The Son of the Wolf* assured him that he was on the track of literary success. During the next two years he produced two more collections of Klondike stories, *The God of His Fathers* and *Children of the Frost*.[1]

There is every evidence that London considered the short story a respectable fictional form and that he worked hard to perfect it. Yet almost from the beginning, he was eager to move on to bigger things. "So you have completed a novel?" he wrote to Cloudesley Johns in 1899. "Lucky dog! How I envy you! I have only got from ten to twenty mapped out, but God knows when I'll ever get a chance to begin one, much less finish it."[2] London's claim was not much exaggerated. The notebook he kept after his return from the Klondike contains ideas for a number of novels, including *The Iron Heel, Martin Eden*, and *Burning Daylight*. One note, headed "KLONDIKE NOVEL NO. 1," says simply, "Instead of De Wint, St. Vincent."[3] This cryptic hint for the change of a character's name is the only early reference to the plot that did indeed eventuate in London's first Klondike novel, *A Daughter of the Snows*, which was to center on the developing love of Vance Corliss and Frona Welse against the background of the gold rush.

Not until the summer of 1900, however, could he afford to abandon his short stories and take the time to write it. At that point, on the strength of the moderately favorable reception of *The Son of the Wolf*, he persuaded S. S. McClure to send him $125 a month while the novel was in progress. But despite his excitement over this new testimony to the growth of his reputation, there were ominous signs that he was not yet prepared to write a long work of fiction. On July 23 he wrote to Johns to express his delight at the arrangement with McClure, confessing nevertheless that he was "filled with dismay in anticipation."[4] As a result, he procrastinated. A month later he told Johns that he had been "too busy with other things" and had yet to begin the novel. "Yes," he added nervously, "I'll confess the 'have to' part of it will bother me—until I get started."[5] By early September he reported that he was just finishing the first chapter and was "up against it." In this "first attempt," he continued, "I have chosen a simple subject and shall simply endeavor to make it true, artistic, and interesting. But afterwards, when I have learned better how to handle a sustained effort, I shall choose a greater subject."[6] Already his hollow generalities and apologetic tone suggest that the job was proving more intractable than he had hoped; and two months later, as he approached forty thousand words, he confessed himself "damn well sick of it."[7]

Apparently the promise to McClure, along with an unwillingness to abandon a project once it was begun, dictated his persistence in what he knew almost from the beginning was a misguided effort. In mid-February of 1901 he described the book candidly as "a failure," adding that he said so not "in a fit of the blues, but from calm conviction." Yet the prospect was not wholly dark: "I have learned a great deal concerning the writing of novels. On this one which I have attempted, I could write three books of equal size showing wherein I failed, and why, and laying down principles violated."[8] In mid-March, as he was finishing up, he acknowledged that the novel was weak, but he insisted that he would "be able to do a good one yet."[9] McClure, too, was disappointed and decided against publication, though he honored his agreement by selling the rights to the firm of J.B. Lippincott, which brought the book out in October of 1902.

The failure of this novel had many causes, but a principal one was the coincidence of its being written while London was collaborating his with friend Anna Strunsky on *The Kempton-Wace Letters* (1903), a kind of epistolary novel of ideas in which he argued for a scientific view of love while Strunsky defended romantic passion. Despite the strong clash of views, London was deeply influenced by Strunsky, some of whose traits passed over into Frona Welse, the heroine of *A Daughter of the Snows:* a "passion of sincerity and enthusiasm,"[10] a zest for controversy, and an interest in Browning and Ibsen. The intense vitality of both these women emerged in their earnest high-mindedness and florid rhetoric. That London was affected by Strunsky's style can be seen from his private letters to her, as well as those published in *The Kempton-Wace Letters.*[11] Frona's style is similarly contagious. Though the speech of her crusty old pioneer father is ordinarily terse and prosaic, the presence of Frona reduces him to such unlikely effusions as this: "When they said your boat was coming, death rose and walked on the one hand of me, and on the other life everlasting. *Made or marred; made or marred,*—the words rang through my brain till they maddened me. Would the Welse remain the Welse? Would the blood persist? Would the young shoot rise straight and tall and strong, green with sap and fresh and vigorous? Or would it droop limp and lifeless, withered by the heats of the world other than the little simple, natural Dyea world?" (176–77). London's own prose, moreover, is laced with such bookish rhetoric and diction, for in this early novel he abandons the astringent style of his best short stories.[12]

In one early moment the prose comes to life: in the description of the long column of packers ascending toward Chilkoot Pass. The breaking up of a "mighty glacier" has left the trail littered with "stark corpses" and the "rubbish of overthrown tents and caches." Against the gigantic summit, living things, human and nonhuman, fade into insignificance: "The forest had given up the struggle, and the dizzying heat recoiled from the unclothed rock. On either hand rose the ice-marred ribs of earth, naked and strenuous in their nakedness." Above, on "storm-beaten Chilcoot," crawled "a slender string of men. . . . And it went on, up the pitch of the steep, growing fainter and smaller, till it squirmed and twisted like a column of ants and vanished over the crest of the pass" (39). For once the description is effective, signaling the metaphysical dimension of the northern wilderness that emerges so brilliantly in some of the early stories. The dramatic potential of the theme is briefly realized in the drowning of the five Scandinavians, one moment laughing along the trail, seconds later heroic but helpless as their heavy packs drag them one by one under the water.

But elsewhere London loses his mastery of Northland imagery and falls back on self-conscious fine writing: "It was a mid-December day, clear and cold; and the hesitant high-noon sun, having laboriously dragged its pale orb up from behind the southern land-rim, balked at the great climb to the zenith, and began its shamefaced slide back beneath the earth. Its oblique rays refracted from the floating frost particles till the air was filled with glittering jewel-dust —resplendent, blazing, flashing light and fire, but cold as outer space" (145). Here only the ghost of London's true poetic power remains in the final image of the blaze of fire "cold as outer space," while such trite elegance as "pale orb" betrays the insecurity with which throughout this novel he gropes for the proper tone and fails to find it. The depiction of the spring breakup on the Yukon River is intermittently powerful, but its force is dissipated by the continual interruption of less titanic matters, such as the silly antics of Baron Courbertin and the progress of the love affair between Frona and Vance.

The failure is not only stylistic. The novel also lacks a sense of economy and pace. Within the concentrated dimensions of the short story, London had often succeeded by confining himself to a minimum of characters and a spare, lean action, but the effort to adjust to the greater length encouraged his worst faults. "I can't construct plots worth a damn," he admitted in 1899. "But I can everlastingly elaborate. . . . Never did a person need the gift of selection more than I."[13] Many of London's novels were to suffer from this deficiency, though perhaps none more so than *A Daughter of the Snows*. Especially awkward structurally is the overlong dénouement in which Vance, having won Frona's love in the climactic canoe rescue, must remain offstage awaiting the outcome of her relations with Gregory St. Vincent while the latter is being tried for murder.

At times London gives a degree of life to the scenes of Klondike local color, but more often he succeeds merely in cluttering still further an already crowded canvas. The episodic events along the Dyea-to-Dawson trail sometimes read as if he had merely dumped the contents of several notebooks into the first three chapters of his novel. The scramble for the beach at Dyea and the predatory arts of the Indian packers are sketched with some skill, but such authentic Klondike personages as French Louis and Swiftwater Bill are introduced as if merely to be allowed to come forward and take a bow before disappearing permanently into the wings. Nor is there much justification for the chapter on the plight of the Indians, corrupted and displaced by white civilization—a problem real enough but unrelated to the action of the novel.

One measure of London's failure of nerve is his tendency to fall back on literary stereotypes for his principal characters. Though Vance Corliss's sidekick, Del Bishop, is based on an actual Klondike pocket-miner of the same name, his ungrammatical common sense owes at least as much to the long line of comic foils from the dime novel and the early Dickens back to Fielding and Smollett and their antecedent in *Don Quixote*. Vance may have "learned a hell of a lot out of books," vows Del; "but it takes yours truly to get down and read the face of nature without spectacles" (155). Jacob Welse, who was probably modeled on the Yukon trading czar John J. Healy,[14] largely escapes the taint of being excessively literary. But even he is afflicted with eloquence and propriety when in the presence of Frona, and often London can do no better than retreat to the conventions of drawing-room comedy, imposing them incongruously—sometimes ludicrously—on the raw energies of a gold rush boomtown. The depiction of Dawson, in fact, probably owes less to observed realities than to the tame mining camp stereotypes of

Bret Harte. The dancehall is an acknowledged institution, and prostitution is vaguely alluded to, although the gamey attractions of the mining camp whore are kept discreetly in the background.

Yet the social comedy, however incongruous, is thematically important, and it begins on the long trail when Frona arrives in a camp full of men and encounters the priggish Vance. After discovering that she is not the dancehall girl he has assumed her to be, he officiously suggests that she return to respectable civilization. "It is only meet," he pontificates, "that two kinds of women come into this country. Those who by virtue of wifehood and daughterhood are respectable, and those who are not respectable. . . . women who come over the trail must be one or the other" (48). But no sooner has Frona convinced him of her respectability than she again upsets his feminine categories by announcing her intention to bed down for the night. At first Vance protests that so unconventional an arrangement is quite impossible, but Frona ultimately wins the point by holding up Vance's fears to the ridicule they deserve:

"Are *you* afraid?" she asked with just the shadow of a sneer.
"Not for myself."
"Well, then, I think I'll go to bed."
"I might sit up and keep the fire going," he suggested after a pause.
"Fiddlesticks!" she cried. "As though your foolish little code were saved in the least! We are not in civilization. This is the trail to the Pole. Go to bed." (50)

The lines of conflict are thus laid down, and they are continued in a Dawson drawing-room when Del Bishop, in the midst of polite company, indiscreetly rattles on about Vance's hospitality to Frona on the trail. In a later scene, Vance and Del are visited by a rowdy miner and his uninhibited consorts, Caribou Blanche and the Virgin, whose antics give Vance an occasion to reflect wryly on what Frona had called "learning life" and "adding to his sum of human generalizations" (210). When at that point Frona unexpectedly drops in, she is much amused by Vance's embarrassment at being caught in such low company.

Vance and Frona clash more seriously, however, after Frona's chance meeting on the trail with the prostitute Lucile, who is no common whore but a genteel fallen woman to whose beauty, pathos, and culture Frona is intensely attracted, observing that "only by the fast-drawn lines of social caste and social wisdom were they not the same" (97). They quote Browning to each other and exchange tentative confidences, and Frona insists on accompanying her new friend openly as they go back to Dawson. At that point they are noticed by Vance, who, shocked by Frona's violation of social convention, coldly snubs Lucile. Frona, in turn, is enraged by his "smugly sanctimonious air" (101); and though she later concedes that his attitude reflects prevailing social standards ("You simply stood for society" [105]), she will not agree that those standards are just. Vance is moved to apologize to Lucile, acknowledging that he had been "a brute and a coward" (117). Thus both he and Frona have adjusted their perspectives, Frona acknowledging the power of social convention while Vance learns the virtues of spontaneous fellow-feeling. When Lucile marries the respectable Colonel Trethaway, Vance joins in the conspiracy to reconcile the couple with polite society.

Thus, though London occasionally pokes fun at the extremes of social snobbery and rigidity, he takes the distinctions between classes with the utmost seriousness, declaring that there were "two sides" to the social life of Dawson:

Up at the Barracks, at the Welse's [sic], and a few other places, all men of standing were welcomed and made comfortable by the womenkind of like standing. There were teas, and dinners, and dances, and socials for charity, and the usual run of things; all of which, however, failed to wholly satisfy the men. Down in the town there was a totally different though equally popular other side

. . . in the saloons. . . . There all life rubbed shoulders, and kings and dog-drivers, old-timers and *chechaquos,* met on a common level. (93–94)

In the saloons the democratic shoulder-rubbing is thus confined to men, while among women the social division remains absolute. The redemption of Lucile might seem to argue for the penetrability of class lines, but Lucile is a candidate for redemption only because she is genteel to begin with.

Such social values are underscored by London's adherence to the older novelistic convention of employing elevated speech for the upper-class characters and an ungrammatical dialect for those of lesser status. Among serious novelists the rise of realism had eroded this convention, though it lingered on in such popular forms as the historical romance. But the self-consciousness of the young novelist is evident in Vance's stilted apology to Frona for having learned how to swear:

"Oh, I assure you I am not unlearned," he retorted. "No man can drive dogs else. I can swear from hell to breakfast, by damn, and back again, if you will permit me, to the last link of perdition. By the bones of Pharaoh and the blood of Judas, for instance, are fairly efficacious with a string of huskies; but the best of my dog-driving nomenclature, more's the pity, women cannot stand. I promise you, however, in spite of hell and high water—"
"Oh! Oh!" Mrs. Schoville screamed, thrusting her fingers into her ears. (144)

This passage is intended as comedy, of course; and Vance is presented as regarding his new rough edges with amusement. Yet by using such precious terms as "not unlearned," "efficacious," and "nomenclature," he takes care that his excursion into mild profanity will be regarded not as a softening of his class-consciousness but as a kind of verbal slumming, from which he can withdraw at will to a more genteel diction.

A Daughter of the Snows is a conventional and conservative novel, therefore, both artistically and ideologically. Yet there is genuine potential in the variation London plays on the old comic plot of the domestication of the hero through the influence of a good woman. Instead of the wild hero tamed by the genteel lady, the priggish Vance is led to manhood by an independent-minded woman who encourages, instead of carping at, the standard masculine vices of smoking, drinking, swearing, and brawling; and who accompanies the hero on his perilous journey instead of staying behind, teary-eyed, begging him not to go. A more mature comic imagination might have made something of such material, but London, seldom at best in comedy, too often misses the mark. The best he can do is to fall back on one of the popular plots of red-blooded realism, the initiation of the cultured sissy who must earn his manhood through a physical ordeal. The prototype of such novels is Kipling's *Captains Courageous* (1897), which was quickly followed by Frank Norris's *Moran of the Lady Letty* (1898).[15] London would adhere to this plot even more faithfully in *The Sea-Wolf*, but the pattern is already clear enough in *A Daughter of the Snows*.

Yale-educated and hypercivilized, Vance is the type of the urbanite who has remained too long in the "sheltered life" (75). Although he has been brought up to his mother's "prim teas" (76) and burdened with her "puritanical bent" (74), fortunately "some atavism had been at work in the making of him" (76), a propensity also signaled by his graduate degree in the practical field of mining engineering. As a result, he is a likely candidate for initiation into the rigors of the Northland. The easier portion of his ordeal takes the form of the social comedy in which he comes to terms with Frona's unconventionality. Gradually he begins to see in her "the clean sharp tang of the earth he needed" (90) and to value "that comradeship which at first had shocked him." Even her "lack of prudishness" (91) seems less objectionable. He takes up pipe-smoking, learns to tolerate the profanity of other men, and eventually indulges in a mild oath of his own—achievements of which Frona approves. But soon the tests become more dangerous. The blood-ritual of a free-swinging brawl, which provides him with an atavistic "pang of delight" (121), serves as a trial run for the perilous canoe trip in which he and Frona rescue a man trapped by the spring breakup. This climactic ordeal offers him "a new incarnation" (261)—a moment of ecstasy, both spiritual and sexual, such as many of London's protagonists would experience. As he "shake[s] off his limitations and rise[s] above time and space," he finds that the strokes of his paddle become part of a "vast rhythmical movement" (265, 266).

In qualifying for Frona's hand, Vance has thus met two tests. He has suffered a modest diminution of his social snobbery, and he has proved his physical and moral courage. But the social change has two other closely related dimensions: sexual and racial. In each case, Frona herself becomes the agent of Vance's initiation, serving as his mentor, introducing him to new ideas and perspectives which he ultimately accepts as his own.

As she has already demonstrated in her uninhibited behavior on the trail and in her friendship with Lucile, Frona carries with her a mild but genuine aura of sexual freedom. In this respect Richard O'Connor is mistaken in crediting London with a "new conception of the American woman,"[16] for Frona's type was already well established in literature, both in America and abroad. She has roots, to begin with, in the emerging conception of the "new woman." That London had in mind the controversial Ibsen dramas is clear from the fact that Frona plays Nora in a local production of *A Doll's House*; and when she charges Vance with a sexual double-standard, he dismisses her protest as "new-womanish talk. . . . Equal rights, the ballot, and all that." She, in turn, heatedly responds, "You won't understand me; you can't. I am no woman's rights' creature; and I stand, not for the new woman, but for the new womanhood," by which she means a woman who is "natural, and honest, and true."

His misunderstanding, she believes, is the fault of his having known the wrong women, the "hot-house breeds,—
pretty, helpless, well-rounded, stall-fatted little things,
blissfully innocent and criminally ignorant" (111). Here, for
all her Ibsenism, Frona defines herself in American terms,
her livestock metaphor revealing her as the Western heroine, the type of the California woman translated to the new
frontier of the Klondike.

As Henry Nash Smith has shown, the Western version of
the genteel heroine is an outgrowth of her more pallid Eastern counterpart.[17] Finding her prototype in such dime-novel
characters as Calamity Jane and Hurricane Nell, she manages to combine genteel antecedents with the robust vitality
and masculine accomplishments of the plains and mining
camps. By 1900 such heroines had already appeared in the
California novels of Gertrude Atherton, and Frank Norris
had recently created variations on the type in *Blix* (1899)
and *A Man's Woman* (1900).

Motherless since her early years, Frona has imbibed the
twin influences of the unspoiled wilderness and her father's
pioneer strength. William Wasserstrom has noted the perva-
siveness of close father-daughter relationships in the fiction
of this period, and he sees in them one source of the vitalizing of the genteel heroine.[18] For reasons that the writers
only hint at, the paternal endowment is often both financial
and sexual, and it is evidenced by the heroine's richer emotional and physical life. The devoted daughter is implicitly
being prepared to be a more passionate wife, just as the masculine companionship and tutelage of her father prepares
her to compete with men on their own terms. From the beginning, Frona is her father's daughter, embodying his masculine traits tempered by her genteel education. To her old
friend Matt McCarthy, she offers her biceps to be felt, boasting that she can "swing clubs, and box, and fence . . . and
swim, and make high dives, chin a bar twenty times, and—
and walk on my hands" (21). She has managed to combine,
Matt decides, a "prize-fighter's muscles" with "philosopher's brains" (22).

Despite these manly qualities—indeed because of them—Vance finds that Frona's appeal for him resembles "the allurement of sin" (73). What the priggish Vance means by "sin" is, on the surface at least, merely Frona's indifference to propriety. But at a deeper level he senses in her unfettered spontaneity a more disquieting challenge, implicitly sexual. Like an unfallen Eve, she offers the unstated promise of a natural vitality tinged with inviting eroticism. Her short skirt permits the "free movement of her limbs" (15), and "the flush of the morning was in her cheek, and its fire in her eyes, and she was aglow with youth and love. For she had nursed at the breast of nature,—in forfeit of a mother,—and she loved the old trees and the creeping green things with a passionate love" (24). Bridging the old romantic division between the dark and light heroines, she combines sexual allure with the ideals of genteel culture and the comradeship of the Western sidekick.[19]

But to win such a woman as Frona, Vance must unfortunately go one step further. He must be educated in Frona's—and London's—notions of heredity and race. In traditional comedy a boy courts a girl against the opposition of her father and perhaps also a rival suitor, and the girl must resolve the conflict by choosing the most worthy suitor while at the same time reconciling her father to the match. In *A Daughter of the Snows*, this process has fashionable biological overtones: Frona, conscious of her responsibility to perpetuate her father's racial heritage, must decide whether Vance Corliss or Gregory St. Vincent is the fitter mate.[20] Not only for her own happiness but for the good of the race, she must choose the right father for her children.

From beginning to end, Frona never forgets that she is a Welse, and the "pride of her race" (37) is aroused early when the Indian packers scornfully assume she will be afraid to cross a treacherous river on an unsteady log. The source of this pride is Jacob Welse himself, the first of London's portraits of the great individualist, the self-taught superman who dominates men and environment by a combination of physical strength, crude intelligence, and force of will. He is, in fact, the apotheosis of the Spencerian ethic, the social Darwinist's creed of enlightened selfishness: "He was a giant trader in a country without commerce, a ripened product of the nineteenth century flourishing in a society as primitive as that of the Mediterranean vandals. A captain of industry and a splendid monopolist, he dominated the most independent aggregate of men ever drawn together from the ends of the earth. An economic missionary, a commercial St. Paul, he preached the doctrines of expediency and force" (55).[21] These qualities derive from both heredity and environment. Of "sturdy Welsh stock" and inheriting from both sides "the Wanderlust of the blood," he spends his childhood traveling through "a thousand miles of wilderness" (56). Though he initially believes that cities are "effeminate," he later learns that the "commercial battle with social forces" (57) can be as vitalizing as the battle with nature. Like Burning Daylight in a later novel, he has turned from the conquest of nature to the conquest of capital, for he discovers that "the same principles underlaid both. . . . Competition was the secret of creation. Battle was the law and the way of progress. The world was made for the strong, and only the strong inherited it, and through it all there ran an eternal equity" (58).

Frona is in every respect Jacob's child. "Why were you not a boy?" her father laments. "You would have been a splendid one" (179). Far from resenting his disappointment, Frona shares it. "Oh, to be a man!" she exclaims (135), envying Vance his ability to let loose the beast in the Opera House brawl. As she exults in Vance's successful passing of this test of manhood, she also questions him about the performance of St. Vincent, realizing that she has a chance to compare them under something like laboratory conditions. At first she is drawn to St. Vincent, in whom she sees "her idealized natural man and favorite racial type" (133), while Vance is put at a disadvantage by views that London attributes to his inexperience of biological fact. With his "more conservative mind," he believed himself "too large for race egotism and insular prejudice" (82), but Frona convinces him that the Anglo-Saxons are indeed "a race of doers and fighters, of globe-encirclers and zone-conquerors" (83). At a crucial point, she receives support from the captain of police, who knows to a certainty that "the white man is the greatest and best breed in the world" (85). After this harangue, Vance can only meekly wonder, "But why is it?" The captain replies, with unarguable finality: "I do not know why. I only know that it is." Nodding her head "triumphantly" at Vance, Frona urges him to "acknowledge [his] defeat" (86).

Yet behind all of this biological and racial posturing lies a more humane idea: Frona's conception of sexual balance as a union of body and spirit—not in separate persons, a man strong in body and a woman in spirit, but in two persons each of whom is strong in both. Her own "individual ideal" is to see flesh and spirit "go hand in hand. . . . A splendid savage and a weak-kneed poet! She could admire the one for his brawn and the other for his song; but she would prefer that they had been made one in the beginning" (87).

This balanced conception of human personality, though so stridently advocated, is the most important theme to emerge from London's first novel.[22] Related to—indeed derived from—the duality of the city and the wilderness, it pervades London's later fiction, providing him with an ideal of harmony deeply rooted in his own nature and vision. If on the one hand it springs from his dubious (though at the time widely held) notions of race, it also reflects an ability to look critically at sexual stereotypes. And the idea of sexual balance does at least lend a measure of dramatic coherence to the plot, enabling Frona, under the influence of her father, to create in Vance the wholeness she seeks. It even attracts her irresistibly to the prostitute Lucile, whose combination of sexual experience and genteel culture, though anathema to conventional society, Frona is honest enough to respect. But as London himself was well aware, this coherence of idea and action is not matched by a comparable skill in other facets of narrative art. Only in rare moments do the language and characters come fully to life. More often, the pace falters and the novel succumbs to the stale proprieties of routine magazine fiction. These flaws disappeared, however, when London turned, with the luck and instincts of a good pocket-miner, to the novel that was to make him famous.

3

Ghost Dog
The Call of the Wild

By the autumn of 1902, when *A Daughter of the Snows* was published to an indifferent critical reception, London was approaching a crossroads in his career. Having long since anticipated the failure of his novel, he was more excited about the two books he had completed in the interval: *The Kempton-Wace Letters*, written with Anna Strunsky, and *The People of the Abyss* (1903), a vivid account of human misery in the East End of London, where he had spent the previous summer. He had also taken the important step of signing on with the Macmillan Company, and in November he wrote of his heightening ambition in a long letter to his new editor, George P. Brett, who was to treat him with exemplary tact and discernment for nearly all of his career:

In the first place, I want to get away from the Klondike. I have served my apprenticeship at writing in that field, and I feel that I am better fitted now to attempt a larger and more generally interesting field. I have half a dozen books, fiction all, which I want to write. They are not collections of short stories, but novels. I believe I can turn out a novel now. The novel Lippincott's published this fall [*A Daughter of the Snows*] was written by me over two years ago, at the beginning of my writing. At that time the twenty short stories I had written constituted my literary experience. Not only was that novel my first novel, but it was my first attempt at a novel. I have done a great deal of studying and a great deal of thinking in the last two years, and I am confident that I can to-day write something worth while.[1]

But ironically, even as he expressed his desire to "get away from the Klondike," these ambitions were about to take shape in the story that would link his name permanently with red-blooded Northland adventure.

In all of this there was a measure of accident, of sheer luck —both good and bad. Unlike *A Daughter of the Snows*, which he had planned as a novel and struggled to complete, *The Call of the Wild* was begun as only another Klondike short story but grew irresistibly to the length of a novella. "I sat down to write it into a 4000 word yarn," he said, "but it got away from me & I was forced to expand it to its present length."[2] Though London liked the story well enough, he had no inkling of the astonishing success it would become, and he readily agreed to Brett's proposal that Macmillan buy all book rights for $2000 and promote it heavily in hopes of furthering his reputation. This sum, together with the $700 he received from the *Saturday Evening Post* for the serial rights,[3] constituted his sole remuneration for a book that became an immediate best seller and eventually sold in the millions. His prediction to Brett—that Macmillan "may succeed in getting a fair sale out of it"—turned out to be one of the understatements of the century.

The composition of the story, as he recounted it to Brett, was "very rapid." He began it soon after his return from England in mid-November, 1902, and on December 11 he reported that he had several thousand words to go on the still nameless "Klondike story."[4] The work continued at least into mid-January, and by February 12 he was able to report to Brett that the manuscript, now titled *The Call of the Wild*, had been "virtually accepted" by the *Post*.[5] Since neither London nor the *Post* cared much for the title, they temporarily entertained such alternatives as "The Wolf" or

"The Sleeping Wolf." Neither of these, however, struck London as quite right, and two weeks later he confessed a "sneaking preference" for *The Call of the Wild*.[6]

The immediate inspiration for the story had come from two different dogs, one of them real, the other fictional. While in Dawson during the winter of 1898, London had made the acquaintance of two brothers, Marshall and Louis Bond, who had come to the Klondike from the ranch of their father, Judge Bond, near Santa Clara, south of San Francisco Bay. The Bonds brought with them two dogs, one of whom, named Jack, was greatly admired by London and became the original of Buck, just as Judge Bond's ranch, which London visited sometime after returning from the Klondike, became Judge Miller's ranch in the novel.[7]

But while the Bonds' dog suggested the more attractive qualities, Buck's diabolical cunning and ferocity owe something to the canine protagonist of London's 1902 short story "Bâtard."[8] Like Buck, Bâtard can be bent but not broken by his ruthless master, a devilish French Canadian named Black Leclère; and like Buck, he comes of mixed parentage, part husky and part wolf. In the final scene, Bâtard hurls himself with "fiendish levity"[9] at the box on which Leclère stands with a hangman's noose around his neck, much as Buck becomes the "Fiend incarnate"[10] when he avenges the murder of John Thornton by leaping for the throats of the terrified Yeehats. London may have thought he was writing *The Call of the Wild* to "redeem the species" from the grim portrait of Bâtard, as Earle Labor suggests.[11] But these two ferocious and indomitable beasts have more in common than even the author himself may have recognized.

Though *The Call* is the least self-conscious and most nearly original book London ever wrote, it does have literary precursors. Alert readers quickly discovered that he had drawn a number of details of the trail-dog's life from Egerton R. Young's *My Dogs in the Northland* (1902). But as Franklin Walker has succinctly noted, these were merely "available data in a technical field," which "had little effect on plot, less on theme, and none at all on overtones and allegory.''[12] His use of them resembles Melville's borrowings from source books in his early South Seas narratives. Like Melville, London had visited the territory he was describing and had observed much; but there were inevitable gaps in his memory, and there were some facets of Klondike life that he had not experienced at all. Young's book helped fill these gaps and supply a body of realistic detail to counterbalance the drift of the narrative toward pure fable.

Another precursor was that staple of popular fiction, the sentimental animal story. Written mainly for children, this was typically a warm-hearted celebration of the rewards of kindness to a dumb animal, often in contrast to the pathos of mistreatment at the hands of a cruel master. Though London insisted that his tale was "utterly different in subject and treatment from the rest of the animal stories which have been so successful,"[13] *The Call* nevertheless owes something to this genre. Even its episodic structure resembles that of such classic animal stories as Anna Sewell's *Black Beauty* (1877), which depends for its effect on the alternation of kind and cruel masters. Buck, in short, is at the mercy of whoever happens to own him, and London's emphasis on the curative powers of John Thornton's kindness causes the novel for once to veer toward animal-story sentimentality.

Similarly, the scenes of cruelty are always in danger of succumbing to the animal-story variety of didactic pathos. Yet here, too, London's tact is equal to the stringencies of his narrative method, and he rarely overplays his effects. When Buck is beaten by the man in the red sweater, the potentially heart-rending scene is set forth with rigorous objectivity: the incident teaches a lesson to Buck, but it does not preach to the reader. And the man, it turns out, is not such a villain after all. Having taught Buck the futility of rebellion, he speaks to him in a "genial" voice, pats his head, brings water and a "generous meal of raw meat," and cajoles him into eating out of his hand (32). Hal, Charles, and Mercedes, on the other hand, are virtual cartoon figures in their two-dimensional incompetence and selfishness. But as the narrative moves increasingly in its later stages toward the realm of myth, such characters seem less out of place.

Equally important as an influence are the Mowgli stories in Kipling's *Jungle Book* (1894), especially "Mowgli's Brothers" and "Tiger! Tiger!" It is true that in one way Kipling's animals, who speak with human voices and have humanlike thoughts, are closer to the stylized creatures of the traditional animal fable. Yet this difference, at first glance so striking, is relatively superficial. Beneath it lies considerable similarity of vision: of animal-human relations seen from the animal's point of view; and, more specifically, of the primitive roots of the initiation theme in the conflict of generations—that is, in the conflict between an older leader and his younger challenger. At their deepest levels, both Kipling's and London's fables are of age and youth, father and son; the reversion to the wild is the recovery of an ancestral birthright.

Both Mowgli and Buck spend their early years under the protection of a benign family, then are compelled to venture among alien and unpredictable human beings, only to return at last to the wild to hunt with their brothers in the wolfpack. Within this narrative framework, London echoes a number of Kipling's images and actions. His invocation of the "Law of Club and Fang" (in *White Fang* it would be the "Law of Meat") recalls Kipling's repeated references to the "Law of the Jungle," though the Darwinian cast of London's phrases differs from the complex, humanlike code in the Kipling stories. Some of the imagery of Buck's moonlight battle with Spitz, at the center of the circle of dogs, may have been suggested by the circle of the wolves at the Pack Council in "Mowgli's Brothers," which takes place at the full moon and is concerned with a challenge to the leadership of old Akela. When Akela misses his kill, he insists on his right to meet his challengers in single combat. But no climactic fight occurs such as the one between Buck and Spitz; instead Akela is permitted to linger into impotent old age, while his rival, the tiger Shere Khan, becomes the opponent whom Mowgli must meet and kill to establish his right to a place in the pack. In so doing, Mowgli acquires in the eyes of the human villagers a supernatural power like that attributed by the Yeehats to Buck after he has avenged the murder of Thornton.

But the stimulus provided by Kipling's stories should not be permitted to obscure the originality—and superiority—of London's achievement. As it emerges from under Kipling's shadow, *The Call of the Wild* can no more be dismissed as a dog story than *Moby-Dick* can be dismissed as a whale story. Indeed, Alfred Kazin's fine insight—that Melville's Ishmael "sees the whale's view of things,"[14] that he speaks for the primordial, transhuman world of nature—can equally well be applied to London. Both Melville and London attain a kind of double vision, sensing the alien character of the natural world while at the same time feeling a deep kinship with it. This is not a matter of observing, as some critics have done, that the dog story involves a human "allegory," a term implying that Buck is merely a human being disguised as a dog. Rather, the intuition at the heart of the novel is that the processes of individuation in a dog, a wolf, or a human child are not fundamentally different. Somehow, out of the dim memories of his own childhood, London recaptures the groping steps by which the very young deal with the mystifying sensations of their world, learning that snow is cold and fluffy, that fire burns, that some people are kind and others cruel.[15] This is the "primordial vision" that Earle Labor has rightly insisted is a distinctive facet of London's imagination.

But *The Call of the Wild* is about society as well as about the wilderness—or rather, like *A Daughter of the Snows*, it is about the conflict between the two, a conflict that reaches its height in the final chapter, when Buck finds himself unable to choose between the civilizing influence of John Thornton and the increasingly insistent call of his primitive brothers. The conflict is resolved when Thornton dies and Buck leaves civilized life for good, but that departure is only the culmination of a movement toward the wild that has been taking place throughout the book. The movement is not steady; sometimes Buck will advance one step toward the wild only to be cast back again toward civilization. Still, the fundamental movement is clear, and it can be regarded from two seemingly opposite perspectives. Approached from the assumptions of Zolaesque naturalism, it will seem atavistic—a reversion to savagery, a process of degeneration. On the other hand, from the standpoint of romantic primitivism, it will appear to embody the forward movement of an initiation rite, through which Buck attains maturity and even apotheosis as a mythic hero.

Both of these views accurately describe the action of the novel. Indeed, London himself reveals the same ambivalence when he says of Buck: "His development (or retrogression) was rapid" (61). This "divided stream" of American naturalism was first recognized by Charles Child Walcutt, who saw the materialistic thrust of the new naturalism at odds with the strains of transcendental idealism and romantic individualism that continued to exert a strong influence on American fiction.[16] Frank Norris and Jack London offer particularly good examples of this uneasy combination. Norris, in fact, devoted several of his critical essays to promoting the idea that Zola and other naturalists, including himself, were actually romanticists. The result for all of these novelists is a fruitful tension between the naturalistic impulse, with its emphasis on society and environment, and the romantic impulse, which emphasizes the power of the exceptional individual to act on his own. Such a tension, as so many critics have observed, is one of the most fundamental themes of American fiction.

This indigenous American quality can be seen more clearly if one observes the structural parallels between *The Call of the Wild* and *Adventures of Huckleberry Finn*. As the two novels begin, each young protagonist lives in society under the protection of a benevolent foster parent. Each undertakes a journey away from that sheltered world, encountering in his travels several varieties of civilized virtue and folly. Intermittently, however, he feels the counterinflu-

ence of the natural world and the anarchic impulse toward
escape; and when each at the end is nearly adopted by another benevolent foster parent, he instead heeds the call of
the wild and lights out for the Territory.

Despite manifest differences of tone and narrative method
—The Call, for example, lacks the satirical, picaresque qualities of Twain's novel—these structural and thematic parallels suggest that both Huckleberry Finn and The Call are
sustained at least in part by a common vision. What they
share is the perennial American dream of escape and freedom associated with the natural world. As critics of Huckleberry Finn have repeatedly recognized, it is the river itself,
and the life Huck and Jim lead there, that holds the strong-
est fascination for the reader. In this idyllic world, the stirrings of primitive life reassert themselves when the two
fugitives, rejecting the dessicated piety of civilization, rein-
vent a natural mythology as they speculate about the origin
of the stars, wondering "whether they was made, or only
just happened." Jim suggests that "the moon could a laid
them," and Huck allows that "that looked kind of reasonable . . . because I've seen a frog lay most as many, so of
course it could be done."[17] Just as Huck begins to reexperience the world mythopoetically, from the ground up and
from the sky down, London's Buck must discover, in himself and in the wilderness, the primordial sensations that
lead him to reject the conventions of civilized life. Hence it
is no disparagement to say that both of these are "escape
novels," for the impulse toward escape—toward the world
of wish and dream—exists in all of us, and one of the functions of fiction is to fulfill it. There is, no doubt, a higher
function that fiction can serve: to take us not merely away
from our daily realities but into a reality we have not yet experienced or have experienced only imperfectly. The best
"escape fiction"—including Huckleberry Finn and The Call
of the Wild—serves that purpose, too.

During the long middle section of the novel, Buck is at
the mercy of his owners, and the structure of episodes is
governed chiefly by the contrast between two Klondike

types, the hardened sourdough and the ignorant *chechaquo*. Francois and Perrault, with their rough but humane discipline and their hardy devotion to work, contrast sharply with the hapless incapables: the mindlessly vicious Hal and Charles, who club the dogs for failing to perform impossible tasks, and the self-indulgent, sentimental Mercedes, who protests the whipping of the "poor dears" (131) even while insisting that the bone-weary dogs pull her own weight on the already overloaded sled. This trio, in turn, contrasts sharply with Buck's final master, the kindly John Thornton.

But these episodes offer more than a gallery of Klondike types. They also serve to establish the civilized values against which the wilderness must compete, for human society in this novel is not an irredeemable disaster. Indeed, its most attractive virtues serve as a necessary counterweight to the ever more insistent call of the wild. Of central though qualified value is the pride of work, and even more deeply attractive is the value of love. For Buck, both love and work fulfill a profound need, though neither can finally compete with the deepest need of all—the one ecstatically fulfilled in the blood ritual of the hunt.

In his early years on Judge Miller's estate, though no "mere pampered house-dog" (19), Buck resembles Vance Corliss of *A Daughter of the Snows*, living the easy life of a "sated aristocrat" (18), developing his muscles not through work but through play. The abrupt transition to the Northland introduces him to the world of labor. "No lazy, sun-kissed life was this," he finds, "with nothing to do but loaf and be bored" (43). Instead he must perform the tasks that in the Southland were assigned to draft-horses. Yet once he has absorbed this blow to his dignity, he discovers that "though the work was hard . . . he did not particularly despise it" (55). Gradually accommodating himself to the harness, he experiences the "nameless, incomprehensible pride of the trail and trace—that pride which holds dogs in the toil to the last gasp" (80). As it does for Conrad's Marlow in "Heart of Darkness," work constitutes a source of order in the midst of primitive chaos.

Nevertheless, Buck's attitude toward work grows increasingly ambivalent. Part of the reason lies in the nature of the work itself, especially in the cautionary example of two other dogs of the team, Dave and Sol-leks, who seem the very incarnation of passionate devotion to toil. Otherwise uninspired and phlegmatic, they are "utterly transformed by the harness." The labor of the trail seemed "the supreme expression of their being" (55). Under the inspiriting mastership of Francois and Perrault, such devotion seems admirable, almost heroic; but after the team passes into the hands of the "Scotch half-breed," the work gets harder, more routine, and less rewarding. Though Buck continues to take pride in it "after the manner of Dave and Sol-leks" (110), he no longer enjoys it, for it is "a monotonous life, operating with machine-like regularity" (111). The "pride of trail and trace" has become the drudgery of the work-beast— a fate dramatized when Dave wears down in the traces and must be shot. Thereafter the ineptitude of Hal, Charles, and Mercedes reduces what is left of the nobility of labor to meaningless, grinding, and ultimately fatal toil.[18]

The decreasing attractions of the work itself are accentuated by the ever more alluring alternative of the wild. The conflict heightens when the team first reaches Dawson, where in the civilized daylight world it seems "the ordained order of things that dogs should work." But though by day these dogs haul cabin logs and firewood and freight, most of them are of the "wild wolf husky breed" in whose "nocturnal song, a weird and eerie chant," it is "Buck's delight to join" (83–84). On the trail, as well, though the work is "a delight to him," it becomes "a greater delight slyly to precipitate a fight amongst his mates and tangle the traces" (89). This act is more than a momentary imp of the perverse; there is method in it. What Buck seeks as an alternative to order and work is the deeper satisfaction of the irrational, the anarchic, and the demonic, symbolized by the hunt and the kill. Challenging the leadership of Spitz by plunging the team into disorder, he hopes to precipitate the climactic fight that will confirm his devotion to the primordial life.

The trail and the mining camp thus provide halfway stations between the extremes of civilization and savagery, calling forth the values of hardihood, discipline, and devotion. The other civilized value—the value of love—is also associated with contrasting landscapes. The loving-kindness that Buck experiences with Judge Miller and John Thornton is associated with the Southland, and with its central images: fire, sun, daylight, summer, and warmth. The antithesis of this world of love is, of course, the Northland wilderness, whose images are darkness, frost, moonlight, winter, and cold.[19] London weaves these images into the texture of the novel, subtly establishing the natural rhythms of Buck's divided life.

Like work, love is a source of order—not the order of disciplined movement but that of the stability and security of an enclosed space. Its locale is not the trail but the fireside or the sunlit clearing. In the beginning, Buck basks securely on Judge Miller's estate in the "sun-kissed" Santa Clara Valley (16), and "on wintry nights he lay at the Judge's feet before the roaring library fire" (18). The secluded domesticity of the house, "back from the road, half hidden among the trees," as well as the "rows of vine-clad servants' cottages, an endless and orderly array of outhouses, long grape arbors, green pastures, orchards, and berry patches" (16), make the estate an oasis of pastoral serenity, just as the fire in the library suggests an island of civilization in the midst of a wintry darkness.

But though temporarily under the protection of a benevolent owner and the maternal warmth of the Southland, Buck will soon be abducted into a life of wandering orphanhood in the North.[20] A measure of his loss, of his need for an enfolding maternal presence, arises during his first night on the trail when he searches for a warm place to sleep. Seeing the light and warm glow in the tent of Francois and Perrault, he seeks refuge there but is driven back violently into the cold, where, "miserable and disconsolate, he wandered about among the many tents, only to find that one place was as cold as another" (50). At last he learns the trick of burrowing under the snow, discovering paradoxically that the only warmth lies there.

Afterwards, under the firm discipline of the two Frenchmen, his movement toward self-sufficiency is rapid. But the extraordinary kindness of John Thornton soon causes him to regress to the dependency and idealistic devotion of childhood and consequently to experience the foster-child's fear of abandonment: "For a long time after his rescue, Buck did not like Thornton to get out of his sight. From the moment he left the tent to when he entered it again, Buck would follow at his heels. His transient masters since he had come into the Northland had bred in him a fear that no master could be permanent. He was afraid that Thornton would pass out of his life as Perrault and Francois and the Scotch half-breed had passed out. Even in the night, in his dreams, he was haunted by this fear" (165–66).

Yet this regression is temporary. By the time Thornton is killed, Buck has completed his rite of passage into adulthood, and his grief, though deep and genuine, is but the last of his civilized emotions, his farewell to his life as a son. Not even this deeply affectionate relationship can entirely heal the division in Buck's nature, for in spite of its "soft civilizing influence" on him, "the strain of the primitive . . . remained alive and active. Faithfulness and devotion, things born of fire and roof, were his; yet he retained his wildness and wiliness. He was a thing of the wild, come in from the wild to sit by John Thornton's fire, rather than a dog of the soft Southland stamped with the marks of generations of civilization" (166).

Earlier, in camp on the long trail, Buck's ambivalence had been expressed in two fireside dreams. One is of the "Sunland" (112) of his youth, but the other is of a different fire, beside which a hairy man squatted in fear and beyond which, "in the circling darkness, Buck could see many gleaming coals, two by two, always two by two, which he knew to be the eyes of great beasts of prey" (114). The demonic fascination of those glowing eyes will at last become irresistible. Appealing to the inchoate emotions of the nocturnal world, they call forth a response like that evoked by the haunting, glittering landscape of the Northland wilderness:

With the aurora borealis flaming coldly overhead, or the stars leaping in the frost dance, and the land numb and frozen under its pall of snow, this song of the huskies might have been the defiance of life. . . . When he moaned and sobbed, it was with the pain of living that was of old the pain of his wild fathers, and the fear and mystery of the cold and dark that was to them fear and mystery. And that he should be stirred by it marked the completeness with which he harked back through the ages of fire and roof to the raw beginnings of life in the howling ages. (84–87)

At the center lies the fire of warmth and safety; beyond its perimeter are the cold fire of the northern lights, the white glitter of the stars, and the pall of snow. When Buck finally leaves John Thornton, feeling "compelled to turn his back upon the fire and the beaten earth around it" (168–71), he will conclude a movement that has been underway from the beginning—a movement into the world of his "wild fathers."

Psychologically, this countermovement is a rejection of maternal security, which restricts even while it protects. Increasingly Buck seeks out those "wild fathers," who can be cast as opponents and whose potency is signaled by the brandished club, the flashing white fang, and the many-pronged antler. Against them Buck will test his strength and finally, in deadly combat, make their power and independence his own. In two clearly ritualistic acts—the defeat of Spitz and the killing of the old bull moose—Buck establishes first his supremacy over the half-civilized world of the dogteam, and second his right to lead the wolfpack in the wild as the fabled "Ghost Dog" (227).

Into these rituals London weaves one further strand: the evocative Melvillean symbol of whiteness. This symbol, in fact, is a recurrent one in London's writing. It appears in the early story "The White Silence," where the title signals "the ghostly wastes of a dead world," convincing man of his insignificance.[21] It recurs in the eerie terror of the "white death" that Smoke Bellew and Labiskwee encounter during their flight through the mountains in "Wonder of Woman" —a "weird mist" with the "stinging thickness of cold fire."[22] And finally, as the White Logic, it becomes the central image of *John Barleycorn*, where it implies the ultimate reality, the coldly terrifying truth to be found beyond all comforting illusions. In *The Call of the Wild*, it is not only the menace of the frozen landscape; it is also the personification of that landscape in a white beast, whom Buck must hunt, defeat, and displace—whom he must, in a sense, become.

Buck's first crucial rite of passage occurs in the stirring conflict with Spitz. As the lead dog doomed to be deposed by a younger, stronger rival, Spitz is the symbolic father, the incarnation of the demonic white wilderness of Buck's ancestors. Their climactic encounter, with its atmosphere of ghostly whiteness and its impression of ritualistic compulsions, seems an instinctive reenactment of an episode that has taken place since the beginnings of animal life. The fight is preceded and foreshadowed by a ritualistic hunt for a white rabbit, during which Buck and Spitz compete for the honor of the kill. In the "wan white moonlight" the rabbit flashes across the snow "like some pale frost wraith," while Buck, leading the pack and scenting the kill, anticipates the baptismal moment when he will "wash his muzzle to the eyes in warm blood" (90). In this moment of anticipation comes the exaltation of mystical experience:

There is an ecstasy that marks the summit of life, and beyond which life cannot rise. And such is the paradox of living, this ecstasy comes when one is most alive, and it comes as a complete forgetfulness that one is alive. This ecstasy, this forgetfulness of living, comes to the artist, caught up and out of himself in a sheet of flame; it comes to the soldier, war-mad on a stricken field and refusing quarter; and it came to Buck, leading the pack, sounding the old wolf-cry, straining after the food that was alive and that fled swiftly before him through the moonlight. He was sounding the deeps of his nature, and of the parts of his nature that were deeper than he, going back into the womb of Time. He was mastered by the sheer surging of life, the tidal wave of being, the perfect joy of each separate muscle, joint, and sinew in that it was everything that was not death, that it was aglow and rampant, expressing itself in movement, flying exultantly under the stars and over the face of dead matter that did not move. (91)

Employing a familiar romantic conception of inspiration, London here brilliantly evokes those rare instants when the self is dissolved into a transcendent moment of union with the currents of life.[23]

But at this moment of triumphant anticipation, with the "frost wraith of a rabbit still flitting before him, [Buck] saw another and larger frost wraith leap from the overhanging bank into the immediate path of the rabbit. It was Spitz." As Spitz's "white teeth broke its back in mid air," the dogs raised "a hell's chorus of delight" (92) and the inevitable death-struggle was on. Buck "seemed to remember it all,— the white woods, and earth, and moonlight, and the thrill of battle. Over the whiteness and silence brooded a ghostly calm" (93). As the dogs circle around the combatants, waiting for the kill, the aura of ritual intensifies. Near defeat, Spitz sees "the silent circle, with gleaming eyes, lolling tongues, and silvery breaths drifting upward, closing in upon him as he had seen similar circles close in upon beaten antagonists in the past" (98), until finally "the dark circle became a dot on the moon-flooded snow as Spitz disappeared from view" (98–99).

As Maxwell Geismar has noted, this whole scene resembles the rites of sacrifice and succession that J. G. Frazer found among primitive tribes and described in *The Golden Bough*.[24] Even more important is Freud's argument, in *Totem and Taboo*, for a link between such social rituals and the Oedipal conflict. According to such theories, the ritual sacrifice reenacts the primal patricide, in which a son, cast out of the horde by his father, returns at the head of a band of brothers to kill the father and usurp his leadership.

Though London may not have known about such theories from Frazer, and certainly not yet from Freud, his knowledge of Melville's *Moby-Dick* (1851) could have suggested to him a similar cluster of images and rituals centering on the demonic associations of whiteness.

Melville's narrative of the hunt for the fabled white whale must have been on London's mind during the writing of *The Call of the Wild*, as it certainly was a few months later when he wrote *The Sea-Wolf*. He may have recalled, for example, the scene in "The Quarter-Deck" when Captain Ahab and his harpooners swear a diabolic oath to hunt Moby Dick to his death. As the rest of the crew "formed a circle round the group," their "wild eyes met his, as the bloodshot eyes of the prairie wolves meet the eye of their leader, ere he rushes on at their head in the trail of the bison."[25] Just as Melville based his romance in part on a legendary sperm whale, London may have known of a "ghost dog" story then current in Alaskan folklore.[26] Without question, he knew Melville's chapter "The Whiteness of the Whale," in which several images of demonic whiteness are drawn from landscapes of snow. Conjuring up the "eternal frosted desolateness" of snowcapped mountains, Ishmael imagines "what a fearfulness it would be to lose oneself in such inhuman solitudes." Later, he associates the "dumb blankness, full of meaning, in a wide landscape of snows" with the "colorless, all-color of atheism from which we shrink."[27] These images, which Earle Labor has compared to London's description of the ominous landscape in "The White Silence,"[28] are equally pertinent to *The Call of the Wild*, in which the hunt for the white rabbit is climaxed by the death-struggle with the white dog.

London would have been especially alert to Melville's instances of fabulous white beasts of the American wilderness, whose qualities anticipate those of Spitz and, later, of Buck himself. Most notable is Melville's observation that "to the noble Iroquois, the midwinter sacrifice of the sacred White Dog was by far the holiest festival of their theology, that spotless, faithful creature being held the purest envoy they could send to the Great Spirit with the annual tidings of their own fidelity."²⁹ It is precisely such a ritual sacrifice of the totem animal that Freud saw as a symbolic reenactment of the primal crime of patricide, which is so strongly implied in Buck's killing of Spitz.

The final phase of the initiation into the white wilderness occurs when Buck accompanies Thornton in the search for the "fabled lost mine" of the East (193). The journey is explicitly a "quest," the mine "steeped in tragedy and shrouded in mystery" (193). As they penetrate the "uncharted vastness" of the wilderness, they come to a land that London evokes with a haunting lyricism:

They went across divides in summer blizzards, shivered under the midnight sun on naked mountains between the timber line and the eternal snows, dropped into summer valleys amid swarming gnats and flies, and in the shadow of glaciers picked strawberries and flowers as ripe and fair as any the Southland could boast. In the fall of the year they penetrated a weird lake country, sad and silent, where wild-fowl had been, but where then there was no life nor sign of life—only the blowing of chill winds, the forming of ice in sheltered places, and the melancholy rippling of waves on lonely beaches. (195–96)

In such a land, the gold hunt itself takes on an aura of the fabulous. The questors find themselves on a path that "began nowhere and ended nowhere, and it remained mystery" (196). When at last they find gold-diggings of unimagined richness, they toil "like giants" and their days are "like dreams" (197). Yet the men's quest for riches ends, after all, like any merely mundane quest—in death. Just as in *Moby-Dick* the great shroud of the sea covers over the defeated questors, the gold is reclaimed by the wilderness, where, as the years pass, "a yellow stream flows from rotted moose-hide sacks and sinks into the ground, with long grasses growing through it and vegetable mould overrunning it and hiding its yellow from the sun" (228).

But while the men are defeated, Buck succeeds, for he is summoned by a call not to wealth but to mature selfhood and triumphant life. Despite his love for Thornton, he is filled with a "great unrest and strange desires" (199) as a preternatural sixth sense responds to the ever more insistent call of the "mysterious something" (201) lurking beyond the circle of the fire. Discovering his brotherhood with the wolf and drawn increasingly into wild company, he engages in a final initiation ordeal, the stalking and killing of the old bull moose, whose gigantic fourteen-prong antlers advertise his sexual dominance over his herd of cows and his readiness to resist all challenges to his authority. With the coming of winter, "the young bulls retraced their steps more and more reluctantly to the aid of their beset leader." Finally, at twilight "the old bull stood with lowered head, watching his mates—the cows he had known, the calves he had fathered, the bulls he had mastered. . . . He could not follow, for before his nose leaped the merciless fanged terror that would not let him go" (213–14). Here the challenge to the horde, and its basis in sexual rivalry, is even clearer than in Buck's fight with Spitz. Buck is the figurative son, whose defeat of the bull moose prepares him to assume his place not in the mooseherd but in the wolfpack. His assumption of that place, in the dead of winter, completes his initiation into the demonic white wilderness of his ancestors.

The word "demonic" deserves stress, for Buck's selfless exploits with John Thornton may serve to obscure some infernal undercurrents. Almost from the beginning, Buck has been something of a demon. His imprisonment in the crate transforms him into a "raging fiend" (26). As he clashes with the man in the red sweater, he is "truly a red-eyed devil" (27), while to Francois his demonism is multiplied to that of "two devils" (79). In the final chapter, as he leaves the civilizing influence of the camp, he undergoes a "terrible transformation," becoming a "thing of the wild" who can steal along softly, "cat-footed," or "crawl on his belly like a snake" (210). Avenging the murder of Thornton, Buck ravages the Yeehats with such ferocity that he seems to them the "Fiend incarnate" (221), and as he prepares to lead

the wolfpack, the atmosphere of ghostly, demonic whiteness resembles the haunting landscape in which he first tri-
umphed over Spitz. With the coming of night, "a full moon
rose high over the trees into the sky, lighting the land till it
lay bathed in ghostly day" (223). Soon into the moonlit
clearing the wolves "poured in a silvery flood" (224), challenging Buck, one by one, until each is defeated. At length
they draw back, their "white fangs showing cruelly white in
the moonlight," until an "old wolf, gaunt and battle-
scarred" (226), comes forward to howl the pack's admission
of defeat.

There remains only for Buck to pass into Indian legend as
the "Ghost Dog that runs at the head of the pack" (227). If
London remembered a Northland legend of a ghost dog, he
may also have recalled Melville's description of the White
Steed of the Prairies, "with the dignity of a thousand mon-
archs in his lofty, overscorning carriage":

He was the elected Xerxes of vast herds of wild horses, whose pastures in those days were only fenced by the Rocky Mountains and
the Alleghanies. . . . A most imperial and archangelical apparition
of that unfallen, western world, which to the eyes of the old trap-
pers and hunters revived the glories of those primeval times when
Adam walked majestic as a god, bluff-bowed and fearless as this
mighty steed. . . . always to the bravest Indians he was the object of
trembling reverence and awe. Nor can it be questioned from what
stands on legendary record of this noble horse, that it was his spiritual whiteness chiefly, which so clothed him with divineness; and
that this divineness had that in it which, though commanding worship, at the same time enforced a certain nameless terror.[30]

In his combination of divinity and demonism, his "spiritual
whiteness" evoking both "reverence" and "terror," the
White Steed becomes the incarnation of the primeval wilderness precisely as Buck becomes to the Indians both a sign
of the "Evil Spirit" (228) and yet, as the Ghost Dog, the object of a kind of spiritual awe.[31] His ascendancy as father and
leader is signaled by the "change in the breed of timber

wolves," some now being seen with a "rift of white centring down the chest" (227). As the great white whale triumphantly swims away from the sinking *Pequod*, so does Buck elude the desperate Yeehats, "running at the head of the pack through the pale moonlight or glimmering borealis, leaping gigantic above his fellows" (231). His apotheosis as the Ghost Dog of the North is complete.

4

Lucifer on the Quarter-Deck
The Sea-Wolf

Immediately before writing *The Call of the Wild*, London had expressed to George Brett his eagerness to begin one of the half-dozen novels that had been germinating in his mind. One of these, tentatively titled "The Mercy of the Sea," would be "almost literally a narrative of things that happened on a seven-months' voyage I once made as a sailor."[1] According to London's notes, the cast of characters was to include, in addition to "Jack London—American," the actual captain of the *Sophia Sutherland* (the schooner on which London had sailed in 1893) and a largely Scandinavian crew, among whom were a sprinkling of Scots, Irish, Orientals, and other Americans. The central figure would be an incurable landsman, a Missourian called the Bricklayer, who resembled the incapables of many a Northland tale: "He couldn't steer; he couldn't row, and couldn't learn." Taking no part in the life of the crew, "he never caught the rhythm of the sea."[2]

But during the next two months, the creative fervor of *The Call of the Wild* so stimulated London's imagination that he was no longer content with the autobiographical sea narrative he had originally planned. On January 20, 1903, he told Brett that his next novel would not be "The Mercy of the Sea" but something quite different:

I am on the track of a sea story . . . which shall have adventure, storm, struggle, tragedy, and love. The love-element will run throughout, as the man & woman will occupy the center of the stage pretty much of all the time. Also, it will end happily. The *motif*, however, the human motif underlying all, will be what I may call *mastery*. My idea is to take a cultured, refined, super-civilized man and woman, (whom the subtleties of artificial, civilized life have blinded to the real facts of life), and throw them into a primitive sea-environment where all is stress & struggle and life expresses itself, simply, in terms of food & shelter; and make this man & woman rise to the situation and come out of it with flying colors.

The love story, he went on to say, would attract the "superficial reader," while only the "deeper reader" would discover the underlying theme of mastery.[3]

Three weeks later, buoyed up by the *Post*'s quick acceptance of *The Call*, he determined to use the proceeds to pursue one of his long-standing ambitions. After paying off some of his debts, he would "take what is left, engage cabin passage in a sailing vessel for the South Seas, take a typewriter, plenty of paper & ink, and the plot for my sea story along, and thus get the sea atmosphere on which I have during the last several years gone stale."[4] This alluring but impractical plan never materialized. When the money from the *Post* arrived, London found his debts so large and the South Seas voyage so expensive that he was forced to compromise by purchasing a sloop, the *Spray*, and to content himself with getting his sea atmosphere on San Francisco Bay.[5] Composition finally began around the first of May, and a month later he had completed 30,000 words.[6] By late June, however, his three-year-old marriage to Bess Maddern had begun to come apart; and the trauma of leaving his wife and two young daughters, along with the excitement of his fast-developing love affair with Charmian Kittredge, posed a major distraction. Nevertheless, he was able to keep up his daily stint fairly well, announcing by late July that the novel was "about half-done."[7] Two weeks later he sent off the half-completed manuscript along with a synopsis of the remaining chapters, leaving to Brett the task of negotiating the serial rights with Richard Watson Gilder of *The Century*.

Gilder, ever alert for potential indelicacy, worried aloud to Brett about the propriety of having an unmarried couple alone on an island, but London relieved his anxiety by authorizing him to blue-pencil anything he found offensive and assuring him that the unwritten chapters would contain nothing to shock "the American prudes."[8] During the fall the writing progressed steadily, and in December London worked on the final chapters while he and Cloudesley Johns cruised in the *Spray*.[9] Johns, in fact, read the manuscript and suggested numerous revisions, as did Charmian Kittredge and another of London's close friends, the poet George Sterling. The novel was finished shortly before London's departure on January 7 for Korea, where he was to report on the Russo-Japanese War for the San Francisco *Examiner*.[10]

But in transforming "The Mercy of the Sea" into *The Sea-Wolf*, London had not totally abandoned his original narrative. Indeed, he retained several supporting characters and many details of shipboard life. There was a sailor named Johnson among the original crew, as well as a garrulous Nova Scotia Irishman named Louis; and the hunters and boatsteerers are perhaps little altered from their originals except for their names. The "Telegraph Hill boy," Jack Waters, is probably the original of the rebellious George Leach, but the Bricklayer has disappeared and his functions distributed among several new characters, including Humphrey Van Weyden, Thomas Mugridge, and the greenhorn Harrison, who, in a scene originally intended for the Bricklayer, is paralyzed with terror when he is sent aloft. Some of the details of the Bricklayer's funeral, moreover, pass over into the early account of the unceremonious burial of the mate in chapter 6. And hints of the brutality of Captain Wolf Larsen appear in a separate set of notes for "The Mercy" in which a sailor who has spit tobacco juice on a new sail is "beaten to a pulp" by the mate, and a shirker is kicked by the captain "squarely between the eyes."[11]

If a later version of the Bricklayer's story is any guide,[12] in "The Mercy" London himself was to be a relatively faceless member of the crew, present more as an observer and narrator than as a participant. One measure of the transition from "The Mercy" to *The Sea-Wolf* is London's gradual fictionalizing of the narrator until he emerges as the greenhorn and sissy, Humphrey Van Weyden. This new protagonist does, it should be noted, retain some roots in London's own experience. The awkwardness of Humphrey's early days on the *Ghost* doubtless reflects London's memories of his own difficult period of testing on the *Sophia Sutherland*, for London had presumed to sign on as an able-bodied seaman even though his experience had been confined to sailing small boats on the Bay. He had to prove to a skeptical crew his right to a top rating, and at times had to back up his claim with his fists. He also made use of an experience from his days on the Oakland waterfront in the early 1890s, when a drinking binge led him to fall into the water in the Carquinez Straits. Drifting out with the tide, he was fully determined to let himself drown, but the cold water rapidly sobered him up, and he fought the swift currents until he was picked up by a fishing boat on San Pablo Bay.[13] London undoubtedly recalled these sensations as he imagined the opening incident in *The Sea-Wolf*, in which Humphrey's near-drowning results not from a suicide attempt but from a ferryboat accident like the one that had actually occurred on a foggy night on the Bay in 1901.[14] Even Humphrey's essay on Poe "in the current *Atlantic*"[15] reflects the topic of London's own essay "The Terrible and Tragic in Fiction," which appeared in June, 1903, in *The Critic*.

All of this material was further transformed by London's reading of other fiction. In his notes for "The Mercy," for example, when London reminded himself to write "with the intensity and vividness and rush of Stephen Crane," he must have been thinking of Crane's own autobiographical sea story "The Open Boat" (1897), the imagery of which carries over into *The Sea-Wolf* in the description of the "small waves, with spiteful foaming crests" (8). And just as the isolation of the Bricklayer in the aborted "Mercy" recalls that of James Wait in Conrad's *The Nigger of the Narcissus* (1897), the history of Humphrey Van Weyden may owe something to another Conrad novel, *Lord Jim* (1900).[16] Jim's early act of cowardice in jumping from his ship resembles Humphrey's ignominious flight from the threatening fists of Mugridge. Feeling his manhood "smirched and sullied" (34), Humphrey, like Jim, must spend the remainder of the novel recovering his self-respect by immersing himself in the destructive element until he has mastered it. Each man retreats to an island, where the love of a woman helps him to repel his antagonist's invasion, and every act of courage marks a step toward the recovery of his lost manhood.

Still, this kinship remains relatively distant. More decisive was the influence of Kipling's *Captains Courageous* and Norris's *Moran of the Lady Letty*, each of which develops the plot of the overcivilized young man hardened in the crucible of brutal physical experience. London had already made use of the pattern in *A Daughter of the Snows*; and in his juvenile novel *The Cruise of the Dazzler*, he had come even closer to it by telling of the sheltered son of a San Francisco banker who runs away from home and is caught up in dangerous adventures among the oyster pirates of the Bay.[17] Just as Kipling's Harvey Cheyne, son of an American railway tycoon, falls off a fogbound Atlantic steamer and is rescued, half-drowned, by a Gloucester fishing boat, Humphrey is picked up by an outward-bound sealing schooner; and a number of incidents and verbal echoes suggest that London recalled Kipling's early chapters as he planned Humphrey's adventures.

He must also have recalled Norris's Ross Wilbur, who is drugged and shanghaied from the world of San Francisco cotillions, awakening to find himself on a schooner headed for the Pacific. Ross soon encounters a derelict vessel on which the lone survivor is a young woman, Moran Sternersen, whose subsequent adventures with him resemble those of Humphrey and the similarly rescued Maud Brewster. Ross falls in love with Moran, the tyrannical captain is drowned, and the two lovers finally make shore, where they spend a chaste night alone on a deserted beach similar to Humphrey and Maud's virtuous encampment on Endeavor Island. The next day Ross passes the supreme test of manhood in a battle with a band of Chinese pirates, much as Humphrey does when he slaughters the seals. But while Maud Brewster, in her later scenes of physical hardihood, owes something to Norris's Moran, in her earlier scenes, as a genteel poet and spirited controversialist, she more closely resembles Anna Strunsky. Humphrey's blossoming love for Maud no doubt reflects London's earlier love for Strunsky, as well as his more recent passion for Charmian Kittredge.[18]

Wolf Larsen, too, had a complex genesis. His real-life model was Captain Alexander McLean, a tyrannical sea-lord whose exploits in the North Pacific had become legendary. "I never personally laid eyes on Captain Alex. McLean in my life," London wrote in later years, "but I was seal hunting off the coast of Japan and crossed the trail of his schooner many times in 1893. At that time, on the Steamer Alexandria, another seal hunter, was his brother Captain Dan McLean."[19] London had used the McLean brothers' rivalry earlier as the basis of an episode in "An Odyssey of the North" in which Naass boards a sealing schooner to pursue his rival, Axel Gunderson, into the northern seas. In *The Sea-Wolf* the McLean brothers become the models for the feuding Larsens, Wolf and his brother "Death," with the steamer *Alexandria* becoming the *Macedonia*.

Yet like Humphrey, Wolf Larsen is, in the best sense, primarily a literary creation—perhaps London's most fully imagined character. The shaping influence seems to have been London's rereading of *Moby-Dick*, for as others have noticed, Larsen bears a strong resemblance to Captain Ahab.[20] Behind Ahab lies a host of melancholy or demonic figures such as Hamlet, Milton's Satan, and their descendants in the Gothic hero-villains and brooding Byronic wanderers of the romantic era. In the more immediate foreground can perhaps be found traces of Conrad's Kurtz from "Heart of Darkness" and certainly Browning's Caliban and Nietzsche's conception of the superman.[21]

To make these observations is to do more than compile a routine list of influences, for in this, his most ambitious novelistic performance, London found himself struggling with a number of powerful precursors. As he reported to Brett, he had lately been doing a great deal of reading and thinking, and he was now at the height of his powers, ready to write a novel in which he would attempt to resolve the creative tension between himself and his literary fathers. In *The Call of the Wild*, he had contended rather easily with the examples of the sentimental animal story and Kipling's *Jungle Book*; now in *The Sea-Wolf*, he felt able to compete with Kipling, Norris, and Crane—even with Browning and Conrad—on more or less equal terms. But such luminaries as Shakespeare, Milton, Melville, and Nietzsche presented a more formidable challenge.

Of central importance to this novel, as to *The Call*, is the familiar naturalistic theme of atavism, the notion that civilization is but a thin veneer which, when stripped away, permits man's reversion to his intrinsically savage nature. A de-romanticized version of the earlier conception of the Noble Savage, it received a theoretical impetus from Darwin's *The Descent of Man* (1871) and soon became a hallmark of Zola's naturalistic novels as well as those of such imitators as Frank Norris. Moran Sternersen is a particularly blatant example. Preparing for the assault on the Chinese pirates, she lapses "back to the eighth century again—to the Vikings, the sea-wolves, the berserkers." Under this influence Ross Wilbur is inspired to comparable heights of primitive brutality. When he kills his first man, he feels the "joy of battle, the horrid exhilaration of killing, the animal of the race, the human brute suddenly aroused and dominating every instinct and tradition of centuries of civilization."[22]

In *The Sea-Wolf*, London seems to have divided the primitivism of Moran between the Scandinavian sea-wolf Larsen and the newly awakened mate-woman Maud Brewster, each of whom in turn arouses the primitive instincts of Humphrey. Larsen—a "magnificent atavism," an "anachronism in this culminating century of civilization" (70, 55)—insidiously infects Humphrey with his creed of brute strength and nearly provokes him into an act of murder. Later, on Endeavor Island, the presence of Maud goads Humphrey into an orgy of seal slaughtering, during which he becomes "instantly conscious [of his] manhood" and of "the old hunting days and forest nights of [his] remote and forgotten ancestry" (203, 204). Maud herself is soon moved to primitive heroics when she grasps a seal-club to save Humphrey from Wolf's stranglehold, at which point she becomes for Humphrey "my mate-woman, fighting with me and for me as the mate of a caveman would have fought, all the primitive in her aroused, forgetful of her culture" (238).

Yet while London was attracted to such chest-thumping, he was also moved by its subtler counterpart in Conrad's "Heart of Darkness," in which Marlow journeys "back to the earliest beginnings of the world." Marlow's voice, indeed, is clearly echoed in the images and cadences of Humphrey's evocation of "the fog, like the gray shadow of infinite mystery, brooding over the whirling speck of earth; and men, mere motes of light and sparkle, cursed with an insane relish for work, riding their steeds of wood and steel through the heart of the mystery, groping their way blindly through the Unseen, and clamoring and clanging in confident speech the while their hearts are heavy with incertitude and fear" (5). Journeying into the heart of a similar mystery, Marlow encounters Kurtz, who, like Larsen, has taken "a high seat amongst the devils of the land." In the absence of law and conventions, "there was nothing on earth to prevent him killing whom he jolly well pleased." And much as Marlow discovers in himself "just the faintest trace of a response"[23] to the lure of primitive Africa, the savage shipboard life exerts its effect on Humphrey.

This recognition of atavistic impulses appears also in the musings of Ishmael on the "universal cannibalism" of man and nature in *Moby-Dick*. Ishmael knows that beneath the "tranquil beauty and brilliancy of the ocean's skin" lies a "tiger heart,"[24] just as Old Fleece knows that angels and men are nothing more than sharks well governed. Humphrey Van Weyden is no Ishmael, and *The Sea-Wolf* falls far short of the rich language and profound imaginative vision of Melville's masterpiece. Yet though Matthew J. Bruccoli may be literally correct when he insists that *The Sea-Wolf* "is not a re-write of *Moby-Dick*,"[25] it is worth observing that in a period when Melville's epic narrative was nearly forgotten, London read it more creatively than any novelist had yet done, building on its major motifs and absorbing the literary tradition that lies behind it. Both Ishmael and Humphrey embark on symbolic voyages that will cause them to confront the natural world and their inner selves, and each encounters a powerful demonic figure in his ship's captain.

Much of this atmosphere of demonism reflects the conventions of Gothic romance, as embodied in *Moby-Dick* specifically or in any number of other narratives that London would have known, including those of Poe, who is among the authors in Wolf Larsen's library.[26] The essential effect of Gothic fiction is psychological terror, the continual pressure of an atmosphere of nightmarish menace, either natural or supernatural. The terror is frequently heightened by ominous prophecies, the very elements being heavy with portents of disaster. Nor is it too difficult for a wooden schooner to assume the physical configuration of the Gothic castle or mansion; and the central trio of characters in *The Sea-Wolf* is identical to that of the typical Gothic romance— Wolf Larsen especially being an almost perfect type of the Gothic hero-villain.

At the beginning of such narratives, the hero or heroine is

drawn from the ordinary daylight world into a world of terror. This is precisely what happens to the complacent Humphrey in the fine opening chapter as he rides in apparent safety on the ferry-steamer, only to be plunged suddenly into the horrors of the wreck. The ominous fog, that "gray shadow of infinite mystery," portends the disaster, which soon becomes an inferno of human torment, a "tangled mass of women, with drawn, white faces and open mouths . . . shrieking like a chorus of lost souls" (7). The contagion of terror, which soon spreads to Humphrey, seems almost cosmic, for he finds himself "alone, floating, apparently, in the midst of a gray primordial vastness. I confess that a madness seized me, that I shrieked aloud as the women had shrieked, and beat the water with my numb hands" (8). Once rescued by the *Ghost*, he has a nightmare that further magnifies his fearful isolation as he seems "swinging in a mighty rhythm through orbit vastness." A great gong thunders and knells and the "whole sidereal system" seems "dropping into the void" (10). Though he awakes to discover that his nightmare was caused by the ordinary sounds and motions of shipboard life, he soon finds this "hell ship" frightening enough in all reality—itself a "monstrous, inconceivable thing, a horrible nightmare" (24).

Like Ishmael in the portentous early chapters of *Moby-Dick*, Humphrey immediately encounters prophetic incidents, chief among them being the grisly death-throes of the mate, followed by Wolf's torrential blasphemies and the ignominious burial. But London turns more explicitly to Melville for the standard Gothic device of the prophecy. Vowing that the *Ghost* is "the worst schooner ye could iv selected" and that "there'll be more dead men before the trip is done with," the old sailor Louis then drops unnerving hints about the character of the captain:

"Hist, now, between you an' meself and the stanchion there, this Wolf Larsen is a regular devil, an' the *Ghost*'ll be a hell-ship like she's always ben since he had hold iv her. Don't I know? Don't I know? Don't I remember him in Hakodate two years gone, when he had a row an' shot four iv his men? Wasn't I a-layin' on the *Emma L.*, not three hundred yards away? An' there was a man the same year he killed with a blow iv his fist. Yes, sir, killed 'im dead-oh.'' (41)

Louis's words echo the questions asked by the half-crazed prophet Elijah, in *Moby-Dick*, during his cryptic warning to Ishmael:

''What did they *tell* you about [Ahab]? . . . nothing about that thing that happened to him off Cape Horn, long ago, when he lay like dead for three days and nights; nothing about that deadly skrimmage with the Spaniard afore the altar in Santa?—heard nothing about that, eh? Nothing about the silver calabash he spat into? And nothing about his losing his leg last voyage, according to the prophecy?'' (*MD*, 87)

Then for the concluding portion of old Louis's warning to Humphrey, London draws on Ishmael's ominous conversation with Captain Peleg, who declares that Ahab ''ain't Captain Bildad; no, and he ain't Captain Peleg; *he's Ahab*, boy; and Ahab of old, thou knowest, was a crowned king!'' When Ishmael recalls that the biblical King Ahab was a ''very vile one,'' who was slain and his blood licked by dogs, Peleg allows that an old squaw had said ''the name would somehow prove prophetic'' (*MD*, 77). London's prophesying sailor also draws his hints from the Bible: '' 'Tis the beast he is, this Wolf Larsen—the great big beast mentioned iv in Revelation; an' no good end will he ever come to. . . . He's not black-hearted like some men. 'Tis no heart he has at all. Wolf, just wolf, 'tis what he is. D'ye wonder he's well named?'' (42).

A natural symbolic accompaniment to such prophetic utterances is provided by the sea weather. Early in the voyage, old Louis predicts trouble between Wolf Larsen and one of the sailors. ''I can see it brewin' an' comin' up,'' he says, ''like a storm in the sky'' (43). Later, the onset of a typhoon is signaled by a ''sultry and oppressive'' calm. ''There was something ominous about it,'' Humphrey observes, ''and in intangible ways one was made to feel that the worst was about to come. Slowly the whole eastern sky filled with clouds that overtowered us with some black sierra of the infernal regions" (110–11). As he faces the impending typhoon bathed in an apotheosis of light, Wolf Larsen is raised to almost supernatural stature: "In this purplish light Wolf Larsen's face glowed and glowed, and to my excited fancy he appeared encircled by a halo" (112). Like the defiant Ahab in "The Candles," Wolf seems "an earth-god, dominating the storm, flinging its descending waters from him and riding it to his own ends" (118).[27]

Typically the Gothic romance involves a vulnerable young woman who finds herself in a gloomy mansion or castle inhabited by a mysterious man by whom she is alternately (or simultaneously) attracted and repelled. She seeks frantically to escape but finds herself trapped in the prison-like edifice, where she feels physically—often sexually—menaced. Though a sealing schooner may seem at first an unlikely stand-in for a Gothic castle, it is structurally similar. The lofty turrets of the Gothic castle appear as the vertiginous mastheads which so terrify the greenhorn Harrison, while below deck the narrow companionways and the gloomy galley, forecastle, and steerage provide a setting for the chief scenes of psychological terror. The claustrophobic narrowness of such surroundings enforces the sense of entrapment, contributing an extra dimension to the threat, and often the reality, of brutal force. Wolf's beating of Johnson and attempted rape of Maud take place in the cabin; the knife-sharpening duel between Humphrey and Mugridge is confined to the galley; and Wolf's struggle with the crew occurs in the pitch-black forecastle.

Perhaps the most striking example of such Gothic devices is the first night Humphrey spends on the *Ghost*, when he is sent to sleep in the steerage with the savage seal-hunters for bunkmates and the strange noises of the ship and sea to keep his nerves on edge. The wind sounds with a "muffled roar," feet stamp overhead, and an "endless creaking" seems to surround him, the woodwork and fittings "groaning and squeaking and complaining in a thousand keys." Gradually the demonic atmosphere intensifies:

The hunters were still arguing and roaring like some semi-human amphibious breed. The air was filled with oaths and indecent expressions. I could see their faces, flushed and angry, the brutality distorted and emphasized by the sickly yellow of the sea-lamps which rocked back and forth with the ship. Through the dim smoke-haze the bunks looked like the sleeping dens of animals in a menagerie. Oilskins and sea-boots were hanging from the walls, and here and there rifles and shotguns rested securely in the racks. It was a sea-fitting for the buccaneers and pirates of bygone years. My imagination ran riot, and still I could not sleep. And it was a long, long night, weary and dreary and long. (32)

The "racks" on which the hunters guns rest seem almost a hint of the inquisitorial torture-chamber; and as if these specters were not enough, Robert Forrey has gone a step further and suggested that what the effeminate Humphrey really fears (and perhaps subconsciously desires) is homosexual rape.[28]

Forrey's conjecture is not so far-fetched. Since the possibility of rape is a standard source of terror in the Gothic romance, it can plausibly exist when the potential victim is Humphrey, just as it later becomes explicit in the conflict between Wolf Larsen and Maud. Indeed, the central action of the novel—the midpoint of Humphrey's development—involves a crisis of sexual as well as intellectual identity. In this crisis, "masculinity" implies both homosexuality and nihilism (the creed of brute strength), while "femininity" implies heterosexuality and ethical idealism. Emerging from an abnormally prolonged mother-dependency, Humphrey must pass through an intermediate stage of masculine exclusivity before arriving at a final stage of sexual and philosophical adulthood.

At the age of thirty-five, the Humphrey who is rescued by the *Ghost* has yet to cut his ties to a world of overprotective mother-women, as Mugridge immediately recognizes by calling him a "mamma's darling" (34). Indeed, Humphrey himself comes to understand his arrested development. He has never entered into an "amative" relationship with a woman, he says, because "my mother and sisters were always about me, and I was always trying to escape them." Faced now with the disturbing masculinity of Wolf Larsen, however, he regrets the lost feminine solicitude, thinking "how welcome would have been the feel of their presence" (91).

Humphrey's fascination with his captain has homoerotic overtones almost from the beginning. Especially compelling are Larsen's "large and handsome" eyes, through which at times his soul seems "about to fare forth nakedly into the world on some wonderful adventure." These eyes can "brood with the hopeless sombreness of leaden skies" or "snap and crackle points of fire like those which sparkle from a whirling sword." they can "grow chill as an arctic landscape, and yet again . . . warm and soften and be all a-dance with love-lights, intense and masculine, luring and compelling, which at the same time fascinate and dominate women till they surrender in a gladness of joy and of relief and sacrifice" (18–19). The phallic points of fire and whirling sword cast Wolf in the masculine role, and just as clearly it is the effeminate Humphrey who finds him "luring and compelling." In a later scene, when Larsen's figurative nakedness of soul becomes literal nakedness of body, Humphrey's breathless description makes his emotions plain: "I had never before seen him stripped, and the sight of his body quite took my breath away. . . . I must say that I was fascinated by the perfect lines of Wolf Larsen's figure, and by what I may term the terrible beauty of it." Among the other crew members, only Oofty-Oofty, he says, was physically pleasing, though in a way that "I should call feminine." Wolf, on the other hand, was "the man-type, the masculine, and almost a god in his perfectness. As he moved about or raised his arms the great muscles leapt and moved under the satiny skin. . . . His body, thanks to his Scandinavian stock, was fair as the fairest woman's. . . . I could not take my eyes from him" (100–101).

For Humphrey, this intensely physical masculinity constitutes both a challenge and a temptation. On the positive side, it serves to draw him out of his protected, bookish life into "the world of the real" (109) and to awaken his buried sexuality. But it also tempts him to remain in an exclusively masculine and "unnatural" (91) phase of development—a phase embodied not only in Larsen but in the entire crew of the *Ghost*, whose "masculinity, which in itself is of the brute, has been overdeveloped," and whose "other and spiritual side . . . has been dwarfed" (91). With the temptations of philosophical materialism and sexual inversion thus imminent, it is time for the improbable but psychologically essential entrance of Maud Brewster, who will awaken Humphrey's capacity for heterosexual love and reconfirm his ethical idealism. But Maud's victory is not easily won, and Humphrey must first play a pivotal role in a curious triangle in which Wolf lusts after Maud, Maud is irresistibly attracted to Wolf, and Humphrey is drawn alternately to both. With Larsen at hand, Humphrey continues to play the submissive "feminine" role, attending to Maud in "housewifely fashion" (126), enduring the taunts which, in Maud's presence, are plainly sexual: "I was angry with Wolf Larsen. He was challenging my manhood with his slurs, challenging the very legs he claimed to be instrumental in getting for me" (135). After he and Maud escape from the *Ghost*, he begins to recover his "legs," only to find on Endeavor Island that the unexpected return of Larsen again unmans him. In a phallic gesture, he raises his shotgun but is unable to fire. "Hump," says Wolf contemptuously, "you can't do it. You are not exactly afraid. You are impotent. Your conventional morality is stronger than you" (212).

Thus, while London evokes the creaking Gothic atmosphere of entrapment and sexual peril, he also focuses on the dominating figure of Wolf Larsen. Brutal and unscrupulous, Wolf manages through the very largeness of his powers to fascinate his victims even as he preys on them. Such are the ambivalent emotions with which Humphrey and Maud regard him. Wolf "fascinated me immeasurably, and I feared him immeasurably," says Humphrey (122); and he soon finds that Maud is subject to the same conflicting feelings: "I saw her eyes return to his, involuntarily, as though fascinated; then they fell, but not swiftly enough to veil the rush of terror that filled them" (149).

In part, the Gothic hero-villain is so compelling because he represents a version of Faust, that legendary egoist who, not content with the limits of normal humanity, sells his soul to the devil in exchange for the gratification of his appetites for knowledge, power, and sexual pleasure—indeed, for the secret of eternal life. There is a touch of madness in his quest, as well as something of the Renaissance scientist—a delver into arcane lore and possibly an experimenter with human victims. Yet at least in the tragic version of the Faust legend, the price of such gratification must be paid. The prizes sought, though temporarily enjoyed, eventually pall, and the Satanic bargain must still be redeemed. All of these elements are present in the character and history of Wolf Larsen.

Larsen's two most salient traits are his enjoyment of power and his hunger for knowledge; and his ideas, like his fists, are expressions of his strength. As did Faust, he believes that "man is a natural gambler, and life is the biggest stake he can lay" (105). He tests the crew to see how far they will let him go, pressing against the limits of his own power and their capacity for abasement. Like an alchemist searching for the *elixir vitae*, he "probes them with the cruel hand of a vivisectionist, groping about in their mental processes and examining their souls as though to see of what soul-stuff is made." Even his own rages are sometimes merely "experiments" (55). He watches the fight between Leach and Mugridge "with a great curiosity," observing "the play and movement of life in the hope of discovering

something more about it, of discerning in its maddest writh-
ings a something which had hitherto escaped him,—the key
to its mystery, as it were, which would make all clear and
plain" (85). This Faustian quest for the ultimate meaning of
life is visible even in his invention of a new navigational instrument, which is a source both of "creative joy" and also
of power, "the triumph of movement over matter, of the
quick over the dead" (70).

Yet the Faustian drive to transcend human limitations
ends by succumbing to them. Larsen's power over men is
confined to the *Ghost*, and briefly to the captured crew of
his brother's *Macedonia*. He chafes against these limits, insisting that he has "dreamed as greatly as the Corsican" (72)
but that the opportunity for a larger field of dominance has
never come. His philosophical striving leads only to his increasing isolation, his knowledge of life offers no refuge
from an inevitable death, and he finally regrets that he "ever
open[ed] the books" (73). Even his sexual quest ends in frustration. His attempted rape of Maud is forestalled by one of
his headaches, and she soon escapes him altogether. Indeed,
though Larsen himself thinks his mysterious brain malady
may be a tumor, there is good reason to believe that London
had in mind the symptoms of advanced syphilis of which
Nietzsche had died in 1900.[29] But though frustrated and ultimately defeated, Larsen commands the reader's imagination throughout the novel—and dominates the nightmares
of Humphrey and Maud until he reappears, like a specter
that will not down, off the shore of Endeavor Island. If this
force owes something to the Gothic tradition, his gloomy
isolation, brooding melancholy, and intellectual rebellious-
ness derive from Hamlet, from Captain Ahab, and from Milton's Satan.

Though some of the Hamletism of *The Sea-Wolf* undoubtedly comes directly from Shakespeare, it may also in part
have filtered through the medium of *Moby-Dick*, whose
characters and language are imbued with Melville's enthusiasm for Shakespeare's great tragedies, especially *Hamlet*
and *King Lear*. Correspondingly, Hamlet is Larsen's fa-

vorite Shakespearean hero, and the characters and conflicts of the entire play lie in back of *The Sea-Wolf*. In one sense, Humphrey plays Hamlet to Larsen's Claudius. Wolf, who is a Dane, commands a ship named the *Ghost* and is pursued by his unseen brother, "Death" Larsen, with whom he has been feuding for years. Humphrey, like the young prince sicklied o'er by the pale cast of thought, twice tries to summon the resolution to kill Wolf but is held back by his moral scruples.

Yet if Humphrey for a time inherits Hamlet's indecisiveness—his inability to act in a crisis—it is the Dane, Larsen, who shares the prince's "primal melancholy" (68). In the celebrated soliloquy beginning, "To be, or not to be," Hamlet is torn between the pains of life and the uncertainties of death. Who, he wonders, would "grunt and sweat under a weary life" were it not for that "dread of something after death," which "makes us rather bear those ills we have / Than fly to others that we know not of?"[30] Wolf Larsen restates Hamlet's dilemma in order to destroy Humphrey's belief in immortality. The author of Ecclesiastes, he asserts, "preferred the vanity and vexation [of life] to the silence and unmovableness of the grave. And so I. To crawl is piggish; but not to crawl, to be as the clod and rock, is loathsome to contemplate" (76). Though the dilemma is framed in the language of Larsen's materialism, "to crawl" or "not to crawl" is still very much the question.[31] Indeed, the very intensity of Wolf's defense of life seems a defense against his half-conscious desire for its opposite, the nothingness that will bring ease to his tormented mind.

At times, however, it is difficult to separate the Hamletism of Shakespeare from that which comes to *The Sea-Wolf* indirectly from *Moby-Dick*. When we are told that to know Wolf is to "review the old Scandinavian myths with clearer understanding" (68), we may be reminded both of Hamlet and of the fables of the seagoing Vikings; but we may recall that Captain Ahab, too, possesses "a thousand bold dashes of character, not unworthy a Scandinavian sea-king, or a poetical Pagan Roman" (*MD*, 71). Both Ahab and Wolf have emerged from the vicissitudes of ordinary seafaring life, have read and thought with lonely intensity, and are tormented, like Hamlet, by the mysteries of life and death. The constant brooding that produces Wolf's primal melancholy had produced in Ahab "a half wilful over-ruling morbidness" (*MD*, 71). And where Ahab possesses "all the nameless regal overbearing dignity of some mighty woe" (*MD*, 111), Wolf is "torn by some mighty grief" (69). In each novel the characterizing epithets tend to raise the protagonist to larger-than-life proportions, Ahab's "whole high, broad form" seeming "made of solid bronze . . . like Cellini's cast Perseus" (*MD*, 110), just as the "dark bronze" of Wolf's skin bespeaks "struggle and battle" (70). Yet both characters seem finally unfathomable. To Ishmael, Ahab's "larger, darker, deeper part remains unhinted" (*MD*, 161), while Humphrey says of Wolf, "There was no sounding such a spirit" (18).

Though Wolf's colloquies with Humphrey are not so patently Shakespearian as Ahab's soliloquies or colloquies with Starbuck, they serve much the same purpose, giving us glimpses into the agonized mind of the protagonist, which is hidden during his normal intercourse with the crew. For London, the crucial chapters of *Moby-Dick* seem to be "Sunset" and "The Symphony," in each of which Ahab is most human, most poignantly torn between the beauty of life and the reality of death. In "Sunset," gazing at the sea, he responds lyrically to the "ever-brimming goblet's rim" where the "warm waves blush like wine" and "the gold brow plumbs the blue." But now such "loveliness" is but an "anguish" to him, since he can "ne'er enjoy." Gifted with the high perception, he lacks the "low, enjoying power" (*MD*, 147). For Larsen, as well, "the frivolity of the laughter-loving Latins is no part of him" (68). At one point he can still respond ecstatically to the beauty of the sea and sky, feeling himself "filled with a strange uplift" and exclaiming that he can "almost believe in God." But when his thoughts return to the imminence of death, his vanishing ecstasy evokes the same trope with which Ahab's ecstasy began: "The champagne is already flat. The sparkle and bubble has gone out and it is a tasteless drink" (54).

Near the end, in "The Symphony," the tormented Ahab drops a tear into the sea as he recalls the benignities of nature and home but exclaims, "God! God! God!" as he agonizes over the force that drives him on to the completion of his quest (*MD*, 444). At a similar moment in *The Sea-Wolf*, Humphrey discovers Larsen with his head "buried in his hands" and his shoulders "heaving convulsively as with sobs." As Humphrey withdraws, he hears Wolf groaning, "God! God! God!" (69). Ahab can speak only to the Christian Starbuck of his simultaneous contempt for and envy of the "Pagan" crew—those "unrecking and unworshipping things, that live; and seek, and give no reasons for the torrid life they feel" (*MD*, 144). Wolf likewise finds in Humphrey his only refuge from the "piggish" materiality of the crew, whose dreams are only "of grub" (38). Yet Starbuck's piety is alien to Ahab, and Wolf cynically rejects Humphrey's idealism, finding in Ecclesiastes a pessimism equal to his own: "Is not this pessimism of the blackest?—'All is vanity and vexation of spirit'" (76). Melville's Ishmael, too, in one of his darker moods, declares that "Ecclesiastes is the fine hammered steel of woe. 'All is vanity.' ALL" (*MD*, 355).

The continual conflict between Ahab and Starbuck in *Moby-Dick* also has its counterpart in *The Sea-Wolf*, first in the stubbornly courageous opposition of the sailor Johnson, and second in the crippling idealism of Humphrey. The characterization of Starbuck in "Knights and Squires" may have provided hints for this initial description of Johnson: "One was struck at once by his straightforwardness and manliness, which, in turn, were tempered by a modesty which might be mistaken for timidity. But timid he was not. He seemed, rather, to have the courage of his convictions, the certainty of his manhood." With such qualities, as old Louis accurately predicts, "it's to trouble he'll come with Wolf Larsen" (43). After he suffers a brutal beating at

Wolf's hands when he refuses to truckle, Johnson's spirit, like Starbuck's, is broken.

But Starbuck's "incompetence of mere unaided virtue or right-mindedness" (*MD*, 162) is more closely paralleled by the impotence of ethical idealism in Humphrey, who, once Johnson has been forced into the background, must increasingly entertain the possibility of actively opposing the captain. His "Puritan ancestry" seems to be impelling him "toward lurid deeds and sanctioning even murder as right conduct," persuading him that "it would be a most moral act to rid the world of such a monster" (106). Starbuck's will is crippled by the conflict within him between obedience and rebellion, and in his soliloquy at the rail, he also feels the uneasy stirrings of a sympathy with Ahab's skepticism, an awareness of the "latent horror" of life (*MD*, 148). Humphrey, too, gazes into the sea and finds himself "afflicted with Wolf Larsen's repulsive ideas. . . . Where was the grandeur of life that it should permit such wanton destruction of human souls?" (108). In a climactic scene closely resembling the moment in "The Musket" when Starbuck nearly shoots the sleeping Ahab, Humphrey tries to defend himself and Maud by aiming a shotgun at Larsen only to find himself unable to pull the trigger. His "conventional morality," says Wolf, will not let him "kill an unarmed, unresisting man" (212).

Finally, although *The Sea-Wolf* has no white whale, it does contain a symbol of fatality in the person of Wolf's brother, "Death" Larsen. Just as Ahab turns an ordinary whaling voyage into a personal vendetta, ending in the three-day battle in the Pacific somewhere east of Japan, Wolf Larsen steers the seal-hunting *Ghost* toward a rendezvous with his brother, which he predicts will take place "on the Japan coast." This nemesis, who has been feuding with Wolf for years and seems determined to destroy him, is pure "brutishness," a "lump of an animal without any head"—a figure that recalls the enigmatic facelessness of Moby Dick. In one sense, then, as his name signifies, he represents simply that final nothingness that Larsen both fears and longs for. But in another sense, Death is Wolf's double, the brother who has "all my brutishness" yet "can scarcely read or write" (73). As such, he is that unlettered self of Wolf's squalid beginnings, before he "opened the books" —an elemental, almost subhuman self that Wolf is proud of transcending and yet at times wishes, atavistically, to return to. These ambivalent feelings about his fated meeting with his brother "Death" thus embody his Hamlet-like dilemma. To crawl or not to crawl is, once again, the question —a question that is settled for him when his brother and his disease finally overtake him, leaving him marooned and dying on his destroyed vessel, "dismasted" (209) like Ahab.

This image of Larsen bitterly defiant even in abject defeat suggests a final literary prototype: Milton's Satan. Maud's farewell to the dead captain, "Good-by, Lucifer, proud spirit" (255), is but the last of a series of references to Milton's fallen archangel, whom Blake and Shelley considered the unacknowledged hero of *Paradise Lost*. Melville, too, is heir to that tradition of dark romanticism; and Ahab's defiance, especially in "The Quarter Deck" and "The Candles," reflects the wrath of the banished Satan in the first two books of Milton's epic. Thus, once again *Moby-Dick* becomes the conduit for several lines of demonic characterization, though London also knew *Paradise Lost* firsthand.[32] To the romantic imagination, Satan's defiant ego is precisely his strength, even if directed toward evil ends, and this same frustrated but invincible defiance is what Humphrey sees in Wolf Larsen: "The loneliness of the man is slowly being borne in upon me. There is not a man aboard but hates or fears him, nor is there a man whom he does not despise. He seems consuming with the tremendous power that is in him and that seems never to have found adequate expression in works. He is as Lucifer would be, were that proud spirit banished to a society of soulless, Tomlinsonian ghosts" (68). In one revealing trope, Larsen is likened to a "caged leopard" (149), for although Satan-like he goes to and fro in the earth, "stalk[ing] the sea like Destiny" (125), his power is largely confined to his "hell-ship," where he can vent it only in capricious explosions of rage and brutality.

Once Maud Brewster boards the *Ghost*, the Miltonic triangle is complete, for she and Humphrey serve as the new Adam and Eve, wonder-struck at their new-found love and oblivious of the envy their happiness arouses in Wolf when their flood of literary gossip leaves him "stranded and silent" (139). As Humphrey soon realizes, "the chagrin Wolf Larsen felt from being ignored" is certain to "express itself in some fashion" (140), and in due course it results in the towing of Mugridge. But this envy, frustration, and ensuing brutality constitute only the negative side of Larsen's Satanism. The positive side emerges later, when the text of *Paradise Lost* itself becomes the focus of a debate between Wolf and Maud. "If ever Wolf Larsen attained the summit of living," Humphrey remarks, "he attained it then . . . for he was preaching the passion of revolt. It was inevitable that Milton's Lucifer should be instanced, and the keenness with which Wolf Larsen analyzed and depicted the character was a revelation of his stifled genius" (174–75). As Wolf goes on to defend Satan, expounding the anarchic doctrine of the "lost cause" and the "free spirit," his identity merges with that of the character he defends. With a look of "unnamable and unmistakable terror," Maud exclaims: "You are Lucifer" (175). The ecstasy that Buck felt in the throes of the hunt, Larsen feels at this ultimate moment of passionate self-expression.

Though Maud and Humphrey manage to escape from the hell-ship to the apparent safety of Endeavor Island, eventually Larsen again invades their paradise, making a last effort to destroy their happiness before succumbing to his mysterious disease. Here the sexual basis of the conflict reappears. Once again Larsen's dominating masculinity forces Humphrey into a submissiveness that is underscored with almost humorous clarity in the sexual *pas de deux* in which Humphrey struggles to erect the phallic mast on the derelict ship only to have Larsen repeatedly knock it down again. Not until Larsen is dying and powerless can Humphrey finally get his mast raised, and only after Larsen's death are Humphrey and Maud permitted their first passionate kiss. No longer his "mamma's darling," and no longer a captive of his sexual and ideological fascination with Larsen, Humphrey has moved on to a more balanced phase of development in which both he and Maud emerge as mature adults. As a club-wielding mate-woman, Maud is even less convincing than Frona Welse in *A Daughter of the Snows*, who at least had the excuse of a frontier upbringing. Yet once again London has preserved a certain theoretical consistency in choosing a sexual and philosophical equilibrium for the woman as well as the man. Like Vance and Frona, the two are now fit "mates" for each other.[33]

Yet even as Larsen's sexual powers wane and, blind and paralyzed, he nears death, his intellect retains its iconoclastic force. Maud queries him about his possible glimpses of "immortality"; but he remains "sceptical and invincible to the end" (248), and Humphrey's description of his last moment of life is quietly eloquent: "Somewhere within that tomb of the flesh still dwelt the soul of the man. Walled by the living clay, that fierce intelligence we had known burned on; but it burned on in silence and darkness. And it was disembodied. To that intelligence there could be no objective knowledge of a body. It knew no body. The very world was not. It knew only itself and the vastness and profundity of the quiet and the dark" (250). The demonic ego is at last resolved into the darkness from which it came.

To be sure, as a finished work of art *The Sea-Wolf* can hardly be said to rival *Hamlet*, *Paradise Lost*, or *Moby-Dick*. yet at this point in his career London's artistic aspirations were high, and there is no better measure of their height than the conception of Larsen, through whom London projects the dark vision that was the source of much of his best fiction. Ambrose Bierce's early and often-quoted judgment is still fundamentally right: the novel is redeemed from its defects by "that tremendous creation, Wolf Larsen . . . a per-

manent figure in the memory of the reader."[34] Maxwell
Geismar speaks for the opposition when he says that "Larsen is today, of course, through modern eyes, an empty and
inflated figure; without the myth of the superman to bolster
his rhetoric, his original fascination has collapsed."[35] If
Bierce is (as I believe) more convincing than Geismar, perhaps it is because he recognizes that what reverberates in
the reader's memory is not Larsen's ideas but the force inherent in the demonic archetype. It comes from the largeness and vitality of his powers and the consequent largeness
of their frustration and defeat—from the tensions between
his love of life and his fascination with death. The root of
Larsen's appeal, in short, is not ideological but psychological.

Nor will it do to cite London's later insistence that *The
Sea-Wolf* had been misunderstood by the critics, who failed
to see that he had intended the novel as an attack on "Nietzsche and his super-man idea."[36] In 1903 London saw Larsen
as something more than merely a lesson in the perils of
Nietzscheism. When R. W. Gilder proposed that the novel
be called "The Triumph of the Spirit," presumably to em-
phasize Humphrey's reconversion to idealism, London was
not pleased. "Frankly," he wrote to George Brett, "I do not
like Mr. Gilder's title at all. . . . It seems to breathe a purpose, an advertisement of a preachment."[37] A year later,
while *The Sea-Wolf* was appearing in *The Century*, he was
still speaking of himself as "unsaved in my materialism,"
and in 1905 he recalled "the black philosophy that I worked
out at that time [1903] and afterwards put into Wolf Larsen's
mouth."[38]

To such an extent, at least, London identified himself not
only with Humphrey's new-found manhood and love but
also—and perhaps more fully—with the magnetic Satanism
of Larsen. Though he continued to defend the love story as
entirely realistic, its saccharine conventionality unquestionably robs the last third of the novel of much of its
power. Only the reappearance of Larsen in the final chapters

restores some of the lost tension, for his menacing vitality remains strong almost to the end. He belongs, surely, among the great hero-villains of American fiction, serving as a link between Ahab's metaphysical rebellion and the amoral striving of Faulkner's Thomas Sutpen. This demonic heroism, first depicted in *The Call of the Wild*, would be given another expression two years later in *White Fang*, where, as in *The Sea-Wolf*, it would succumb at the end to the forces of civilization.

5

Redemption of an Outcast
White Fang

After returning in early July, 1904, from his six-month stint as a war correspondent in Korea, London spent a relatively desultory and unproductive year. The immediate success of *The Sea-Wolf* in the fall, following the popularity of *The Call of the Wild* a year earlier, had made him a famous man; but the money seemed to go out as fast as it came in, and he was depressed by the complications of his divorce and the vicissitudes of his affair with Charmian Kittredge. This was the period of illness and despondency that he referred to as his Nietzschean "long sickness." By December he had completed a prizefight novella, *The Game*, though Brett worried that it was not long enough for a book and urged London to expand it. Such expansion, London replied, was "the hardest kind of work to do,"[1] but he promised to try, and eventually he did send off a revised manuscript, only to find Brett complaining that it still did not approach the desired 15,000 words.

Meanwhile his enthusiasm revived over a new idea for a book that would be not a sequel but "a companion" to *The Call of the Wild*. "I'm going to reverse the process," he wrote to Brett. "Instead of the devolution of decivilization of a dog, I'm going to give the evolution, the civilization of a dog—development of domesticity, faithfulness, love, morality, and all the amenities and virtues." With *The Call* as a "forerunner," he declared, the new book "should make a hit."[2] Brett's initial reaction was cool, for what indeed could sound less promising than the story of a dog who develops "amenities and virtues." But as he reflected on the distinction between a sequel and a companion, Brett was won over to a more favorable view. On February 21 London reported that he was "just starting in *White Fang*,"[3] but on June 7 he wrote to Cloudesley Johns that he still had not begun the new novel because he was "writing some short stories in order to get hold of some immediate cash."[4] By this time, too, he was excited by the prospect of buying a ranch near Glen Ellen in Sonoma County, where, away from the competition of his Bay Area friends, his courtship of Charmian seemed to prosper. When he finally began writing on June 26, he was happier than he had been in well over a year, and the new novel reflected his belief that the blackest despair could be cured by love. Composition therefore proceeded smoothly throughout the summer until the novel was completed on October 10.[5]

As London planned his account of White Fang's early development, he was particularly careful to adhere to the established facts of the wolf's life cycle. On the basis of an encyclopedia article, he jotted down the following chronology:

> White Fang
>   Feb. 1st.
> is conceived ~~January 30th~~
> " born April 3rd.
> is blind for 21 days
> Finishes suckling by June 5th.
> Had begun to eat meat by May 3rd.
> He quit his mother for good in December.
> Was full grown in three years.
> Lived 15 years.[6]

He also worked out White Fang's coloring with an eye to his mixed lineage and the typical color patterns of his species:

"The gray wolf commonly sports reddish and blackish individuals. Maybe the mother of White-Fang had a moderately red tinge; his father was the regular gray wolf. White-Fang himself was gray, but with reddish tints and glints in his full coat."[7]

Looking for ways to dramatize White Fang's development, London found usable material in the natural history narratives of Charles G. D. Roberts. In *The Kindred of the Wild* (1902), London paid particular attention to Part Two, "Wild Motherhood," in which he underscored a number of sentences, notably this one: "In the wolf's cave in the great blue and white wall of plaster-rock, miles back beside the rushing of the river, there was famine."[8] Even more to his purpose was Roberts's *Red Fox* (1905), which began serial publication in the June issue of *Outing Magazine* a month before London wrote the first chapter of *White Fang*.[9] The maturation of Red Fox, the largest pup in his brood, parallels that of White Fang in a number of particulars. The mother fox is depicted in her cave with her puppies after her mate has left, and Red Fox, like White Fang, learns gradually from painful experience. He observes his weaker siblings fall prey to a hawk and a lynx, and he learns to catch a brooding partridge much as White Fang gets his first wild meal after stumbling into a nest of ptarmigans. Further lessons come from the young fox's mother; from encounters with a bee, a skunk, and another lynx; and later from the first bewildering experience of ice and snow. In this instance London seems to have escaped the perennial charge of plagiarism, but as in *The Call of the Wild*, he was taking his material wherever he found it, adapting it as always to his own purposes.

These purposes naturally included the desire to capitalize on the phenomenal success of *The Call*. At times London later even claimed to prefer *White Fang* to its more famous predecessor,[10] although critical opinion has unanimously disagreed. There has been no clear consensus, however, on the extent to which the second book falls short of the original. Charles Child Walcutt, for example, finds *White Fang* "perhaps not as bare, tense, and gripping" but nevertheless "a powerful book,"[11] while to Earl Wilcox it is "hack work in its artistry and uninspiring in its philosophy"—a book in which London "seems almost intent upon cheapening the effect which *The Call of the Wild* had had on his reputation." But Wilcox's preoccupation with literary naturalism prevents him from seeing *White Fang* as anything more than a tired reiteration of the "familiar story of a survival-of-the-fittest animal . . . in a bleak and pessimistic setting."[12] This theme is indeed familiar and persistent, but its presence need not condemn the book as hack work. Artistically, *White Fang* is an uneven novel, but at its best, as Walcutt has insisted, it is a powerful one.

Some of this power can, in fact, be explained by London's adherence to the plot, point of view, psychology, and symbolism of *The Call.* Although he may not have realized how much he was repeating himself, some of the repetition actually strengthens the new novel, recapturing the gritty intensity of the original. London himself insisted that while *White Fang* would be thematically the "complete antithesis" of its predecessor, it would also be a *"proper* companion-book—in the same style, grasp, concrete way."[13] London did not achieve those effects consistently, but he did so often enough to raise *White Fang* well into the middle rank of his novels.

The structural similarities between the two stories become clearer when one realizes that Part One, in which Bill and Henry are stalked by the wolf pack, does not belong in the novel at all. To say this is not to deny that Part One is compelling. As a narrative of life and death on the long trail, it ranks with some of the finest of the short stories.[14] The skill with which London captures the mounting horror of the inexorably closing pack provokes comparison with such masterpieces of psychological terror as Poe's "The Pit and the Pendulum." The plight of Poe's prisoner, who struggles to escape the descending blade and constricting walls but is rescued at the eleventh hour, resembles that of Henry and

Bill, who confront the encircling wolves while "the wall of darkness . . . presse[s] about them from every side."[15] In London's story, the terror is augmented by a number of fine touches. The dogs, for example, disappear silently, lured one by one to their deaths by the cunning of the siren she-wolf. Equally chilling are the ring of eyes in the darkness, reflecting the firelight with an almost supernatural lustre; the death of Bill, all the more terrifying because it occurs out of sight and must be imagined; and the desperation with which Henry, now alone, fends off the wolves by hurling brands from the fire. Another striking psychological touch is Henry's sudden appreciation of the details of his own body when he realizes he will soon become the wolves' next meal. Readers may debate whether London was right to permit Henry his chance rescue. Possibly he would have done better to end this story as he ended "The Law of Life," in which old Koskoosh resigns himself to death as the wolves close in.

Part One does, moreover, establish a few important symbols, some of which, as in *The Call*, are reminiscent of *Moby-Dick*. In the two London novels, for example, the oasis of the campfire is surrounded by the sinister darkness of the wild. This image is a microcosm of the larger landscape: the Northland wilderness opposed by the verdant estate in the Santa Clara Valley—the "Southland of life," in which "human kindness was like a sun" (305). Melville had similarly contrasted an island or port, implicitly feminine and domestic, with the "howling infinite" or the sea. The port, says Ishmael, is "safety, comfort, hearthstone, supper, warm blankets, friends, all that's kind to our mortalities," while in the sea reside "all the horrors of the half known life" (*MD*, 97, 236). For London and Melville, former sailors both, the incarnation of oceanic horror is the shark; and just as Melville can refer almost interchangeably to the "sharkish sea" and the "wolfish world," London can allow Bill to say: "I've hearn sailors talk of sharks followin' a ship. . . . Well, them wolves is land sharks" (29). Later, London may be echoing *Moby-Dick*, rather than Genesis 16:12, when he refers to White Fang's "Ishmaelite life" (193) and writes that "the tooth of every dog was against him, the hand of every man" (146), until he is transformed by the loving hand of Weedon Scott. Melville's misanthropic Ishmael is similarly "redeemed" by the companionship of the "soothing savage" Queequeg, after which his "splintered heart and maddened hand" are no longer "turned against the wolfish world" (*MD*, 53). Even the macabre nonchalence with which Bill and Henry use a coffin as their dinner table recalls the way Queequeg converts his coffin into a sea-chest.

Still, good as it is, the story of Bill and Henry is not effectively integrated with the rest of the novel and should have been published separately. One might argue that London was right to establish at the outset the vast gulf between man and wolf, so as to make clear the distance White Fang travels between his wild beginnings and his final domestication. But the ferocity of the natural world hardly needs more graphic demonstration than it receives in Part Two, and between these first two parts there is a jarring discontinuity. The death of Bill and the narrow escape of Henry have nothing to do with the story of White Fang—the men in fact disappear from the novel altogether—and the two stories differ sharply in narrative method. Except for a few pages after the disappearance of Bill, all of Part One is dramatic, the mounting uneasiness of the two men conveyed chiefly through dialogue. The point of view is that of man—increasingly that of Henry, through whose eyes we see the alien animal world. Part Two, however, shifts to the point of view of the wolves, whose world must of course unfold not through dialogue but through narration. Not until much later do a few brief dramatic scenes occur, and even in these the point of view remains that of White Fang. In some novels—for some novelists—such a juxtaposition might serve a purpose, but in *White Fang* it is discordant and ineffective.

Indeed, setting aside Part One as a separate story and allowing for the different endings, one can see more clearly the parallels between *White Fang* and *The Call of the Wild:*

1. Both Buck and White Fang spend their early days in a sequestered retreat (Buck at Judge Miller's estate, White Fang in the cave).
2. Once launched into the world, each discovers the brutality of nature through encounters with other animals (Buck learns the Law of Fang from the deaths of Curly and Spitz, White Fang learns the Law of Meat in numerous clashes with the creatures of the wild); and each learns to submit to the Law of the Club—the rule of man —by suffering a beating (Buck by the man in the red sweater, White Fang by Gray Beaver).
3. Each learns the discipline of obedience and work when he becomes a team-dog for a stern but fair master (Buck for Francois and Perrault, White Fang for Gray Beaver).
4. Each is sold to a master of extreme cruelty, in whose service he nearly dies (Hal and Charles in *The Call*, Beauty Smith in *White Fang*).
5. At a last desperate moment, each is rescued by a kindly master, from whom he learns selfless love (Buck with John Thornton, White Fang with Weedon Scott).

At this point the two narratives diverge, but their inner cores remain remarkably similar. Such parallels, however, need not require the conclusion that the new novel is a shabby piece of work which merely exploits a previously successful formula. For the most part, the language, characters, and action of *White Fang* are successful in their own right.

Unlike *The Call*, with its excursions into lyrical prose, *White Fang* is written entirely in a plain style. Far from being "over-drawn and padded,"[16] the account of White Fang's early experiences in the wild has the economy, concreteness, and visual precision of London's best short stories. Especially noteworthy is the careful attention to the psychology of infancy. In *The Call*, London had occasionally found the perfect visual expression of bewildering new experiences, as when Buck first encounters snow. In *White Fang*, with its more detailed account of puppyhood, there

are many such scenes, especially in the two fine chapters
"The Gray Cub" and "The Wall of the World." The cub's
inability to distinguish the solid walls of the cave from its
penetrable entrance is brilliantly captured in the image of
the "wall of light" (80), toward which the cub strives and
through which the omnipotent father can magically appear
and disappear. In astringent prose, London sketches the
time of famine, muting the too-easy pathos of the death of
White Fang's siblings (81–82).

Especially moving is the account, in "The Wall of the
World," of White Fang's first venture beyond the cave. Approaching the wall of light, the cub discovers that it is "unlike any other wall with which he had had experience." Indeed, it is the antithesis of the "wall of darkness" that
pressed upon Bill and Henry in Part One, for "this wall
seemed to recede from him as he approached." Whereas the
first wall is death, the wall of light is the orifice of the
womb, the pathway to life:

It was bewildering. He was sprawling through solidity. And ever
the light grew brighter. Fear urged him to go back, but growth drove
him on. Suddenly he found himself at the mouth of the cave. The
wall, inside which he had thought himself, as suddenly leaped back
before him to an immeasurable distance. The light had become
painfully bright. He was dazzled by it. Likewise he was made dizzy
by this abrupt and tremendous extension of space. Automatically,
his eyes were adjusting themselves to the brightness, focussing
themselves to meet the increased distance of objects. At first, the
wall had leaped beyond his vision. He now saw it again; but it had
taken upon itself a remarkable remoteness. Also, its appearance
had changed. It was now a variegated wall, composed of the trees
that fringed the stream, the opposing mountain that towered above
the trees, and the sky that out-towered the mountain. (87–88)

There is tender comedy in this scene as the cub ventures
tentatively forward, innocent of real dangers yet terrified of
the most harmless phenomena. Having "lived all his days
on a level floor" and never having "experienced the hurt of a
fall," he cannot negotiate the passage from the lip of the

cave to the slope beyond. Hence he steps "boldly out upon
the air" and falls head downward: "The earth struck him a
harsh blow on the nose that made him yelp. Than he began
rolling down the slope, over and over. He was in a panic of
terror. The unknown had caught him at last. It had gripped
savagely hold of him and was about to wreak upon him
some terrific hurt. Growth was now routed by fear, and he
ki-yi'd like any frightened puppy." Arriving at the bottom of
the slope undamaged and consoling himself with "one last
agonized yelp and then a long, whimpering wail," he picks
himself up and looks about him "as might the first man of
the earth who landed upon Mars." He has "broken through
the wall of the world" (88–89).

These early episodes offer a remarkably precise account of
psychological and epistemological experience. Such terms
may at first sound too pretentious for a novel often dismissed as a children's story, but the image of the "wall of
the world" draws on a complex symbolic tradition. White
Fang's experiences, for example, strongly suggest Plato's allegory of the cave. This parable, as told by Socrates in the
Republic, illustrates the passage of the mind from a state of
false knowledge, based on the deceptive appearance of the
physical world, to a state of true enlightenment, in which
the mind can penetrate the mask of nature and apprehend
ideal "Forms." Socrates asks his listener to imagine that the
mind in a state of unenlightenment resembles the condition
of men who, "from childhood," have been imprisoned in "a
sort of cavernous chamber underground, with an entrance
open to the light and a long passage all down the cave." To
the benighted prisoners, the shadows on the walls would
seem realities. If, however, one of the prisoners were
"forced suddenly to . . . walk with eyes lifted to the light,"
he would be "too dazzled to make out the objects whose
shadows he had been used to see." But an even greater dis-
orientation would result if "someone were to drag him away
forcibly up the steep and rugged ascent and not let him go
until he had hauled him out into the sunlight." Here he
would "suffer pain and vexation," and "his eyes would be

so full of [the sun's] radiance that he could not see a single one of the things that he was now told were real." Certainly, Socrates adds, "he would not see them all at once" but would need to "grow accustomed before he could see things in that upper world." After much effort, he would be able to "look at the Sun and contemplate its nature, not as it appears when reflected in water or any alien medium, but as it is in itself in its own domain." The sun in the parable, as Socrates goes on to explain, stands for "the essential Form of Goodness," which is perceived last and "only with great difficulty."[17]

It might strain credibility to insist that, by leading White Fang to a final experience of selfless love, London was consciously casting the entire novel in a Platonic mold. But the fact remains that the cub's earliest experiences of appearance and reality capture the epistemological spirit and some of the specific images of Plato's parable. Like Plato's prisoners, the cub is unperturbed by the "dim-lighted" cave because "his eyes had never had to adjust themselves to any other light" (77). Further, the wall of shadows that deceives the prisoners resembles the wall of light that deceives White Fang, and the confusion the cub experiences upon emerging into the sunlight closely approximates that of the prisoners dragged from Plato's cave. Just as Plato's prisoner must learn the reality of the sun itself, not as it is reflected in "water or any alien medium," White Fang must painfully discover that water, which looks "as solid as the earth," is actually "without any solidity at all." Terrified by his first drenching, he conceives "an abiding distrust of appearances," discovering that he must "learn the reality of a thing" before he can "put his faith into it" (97).

Since the mysteriously terrifying "wall of light" is also called the "white wall" (82, 86), London may be thinking of one other representation of the deceptiveness of appearances: the whiteness of the whale in *Moby-Dick*. The inverted Platonism of Captain Ahab leads him to see "all visible objects" as "pasteboard masks," which hide not Plato's ultimate Form of Goodness but a principle of evil. Melville may himself be recalling Plato's cave allegory when Ahab exclaims: "If man will strike, strike through the mask! How can the prisoner reach outside except by thrusting through the wall? To me, the white whale is that wall, shoved near to me" (*MD*, 144). Equally suggestive is Ishmael's later observation on the deceptiveness inherent in the "great principle of light," which, though "white or colorless in itself," lays on the "subtle deceits" of nature's coloring (*MD*, 170). London's image of the white wall of light thus crystalizes, with great imaginative resourcefulness, the problem of White Fang's initiation into the alluring but treacherous phenomena of the natural world.

The psychological authenticity of these early episodes is further augmented by London's understanding of the infant's oral needs and the feeling of abandonment when those needs are not gratified. Initially, White Fang's mother is "a fount of warmth and liquid food and tenderness," whose "gentle, caressing tongue . . . soothed him when it passed over his soft little body" and "impelled him to snuggle close against her and to doze off to sleep" (76–77). But such bliss is short-lived. Significantly, its termination occurs during a time of famine, when "the milk no longer came from his mother's breast" (81) and the father, killed by the lynx, no longer returns with meat. No more is the once-blissful cave merely an extention of the mother's womb, and the cub begins to follow his impulse toward a second birth through the wall of light. But though weened and fatherless, he has not been entirely abandoned. After his mother rescues him from the weasel, he associates his hunger for maternal affection with his craving for meat: "The cub experienced another access of affection on the part of his mother. Her joy at finding him seemed greater even than his joy at being found. She nozzled him and caressed him and licked the cuts made in him by the weasel's teeth. Then, between them, mother and cub, they ate the blood-drinker, and after that went back to the cave and slept" (100).

But if in the wild "the time of a mother with her young is short," in the world of man "it is sometimes even shorter"

(137). When Gray Beaver trades the mother away, the young dog's "grief for [her] loss" combines with a "hungry yearning" (142) for the life of his puppyhood. Now his "Ishmaelite life" begins in earnest. No longer protected from the cruelty of the other dogs, he is driven into a savage independence.[18] Even more than Buck or Wolf Larsen, White Fang becomes the personification of the masculine principle of the demonic wild: "The Outcast" and "The Enemy of His Kind," who is "hated by man and dog" (146) and in turn hates them. Even his name suggests both the demonic white wilderness and the savage Darwinian world governed by the Law of Meat, the Law of the Fang. The essence of parts Three and Four is the portrayal of this deepening estrangement from all living things; and like so much of the writing that emerges from the darker corners of London's mind, these chapters evoke a world bereft of redeeming value—a nihilistic world of violence and hate.

This period of estrangement culminates in White Fang's subjection to the twisted malice of Beauty Smith. Here, more strongly than in *The Call*, London draws on his earlier short story "Bâtard," in which the cruelty of Black Leclère is matched by the cunning of the dog who, like White Fang, is both an orphan ("bâtard") and a demon ("diable").[19] Under the tutelage of Smith (this "mad god"), White Fang becomes "a fiend" (215) whose righteous wrath recalls both Buck's avenging of the murder of Thornton and the implacable hatred of Bâtard for Leclère.

It is the privilege of the storyteller, however, to replace a cruel father with a kind one, as London does when he contrives the fortuitous arrival of Weedon Scott. In another sense, Scott's qualities are maternal, for he provides the kindly nurturing that White Fang has not enjoyed since his puppyhood. Once again these qualities serve an oral need, "a void in his being—a hungry, aching, yearning void that clamored to be filled" (259).[20] In the warm California sun, he finally recaptures the womblike security of the cave. Hence, although consciously and morally he may be maturing, psychologically he is regressing.[21]

In fact, though the ulterior logic of the narrative does call for White Fang's socialization, Part Five is much the weakest section of the book. Its title, "The Tame," seems ironically appropriate, for it is tediously anticlimactic and sentimental. Certainly it suffers in the inevitable comparison with the ending of *The Call*. What would we think of the latter if it had closed with "For the Love of Man," as Buck pulled Thornton's sled to victory? There would be little to choose between the tableau of Thornton falling on his knees to embrace Buck and the picture of White Fang surrounded by his puppies, "drowsing in the sun" (327). Nor is the ending helped by London's gratuitous preaching, in the Jim Hall episode, about an indifferent society and an unjust penal system. What London wishes to imply, apparently, is the similarity between the environment that made a demon of Hall and that which earlier had made a demon of White Fang, the difference being merely the lucky chance of White Fang's encounter with Weedon Scott. Yet the Jim Hall material is too topical and London's treatment of it too didactic; the tone of it here is excessively jarring.[22]

Although the environmental theme is prominent throughout the novel, London's naturalism is not always so strident. Heredity and environment, though important, are not the sole determinants of animal and human behavior. In fact, the crucial movement toward civilization entails, ironically, an act of free choice, and White Fang's "bondage" in the world of men contrasts with his freedom in the wild. What pervades the novel is not so much a pure naturalistic determinism as a more flexible view with the imperatives of heredity and environment tempered by the whims of chance and the recognition of free will. Such a view is perhaps closest to the one Ishmael arrives at in the mat-making episode of *Moby-Dick*, in which he sees "chance, free will, and necessity—no wise incompatible—all interweavingly working together" (*MD*, 185).

The carefully distinguished forces of heredity and environment do, however, play the major role in shaping the life of every character in the novel, especially that of White Fang. In the quiet drama of natural selection, heredity is partly genetics, and White Fang's carefully defined heritage —one-fourth dog, three-fourths wolf—implies the struggle within him between his "feminine" civilized impulses and his "masculine" wild ones. At first glance there seems a contradiction here, for these wild, free impulses are the product of deterministic forces: the hereditary traits of his wolf forebears and the hostile environment of the northern wilderness. But London seems implicitly to reject the extreme of an absolute determinism, which holds that an act of apparent free will is only an illusion, that the "choice" itself is shaped by external forces. In London's world, as in Melville's, necessity and free will are "no wise incompatible."

But White Fang's biological heritage is more than symbolic. The wolf in him quite literally gives him a gray coat like his father's, thus making him different from his siblings —"the fiercest of the litter" (79), the only cub strong enough to survive the first famine. Heredity is also a collection of instincts, which emerge one by one when called forth by some triggering event. The she-wolf's instinctive fear of the father is "the experience of all the mothers of wolves" (68), and old One Eye is obeying an "instinct that had come down to him from all the fathers of wolves" (69) when he goes out on the trail of meat.[23] The cub's education, moreover, is partly a process of discovering his instincts and heeding them. Most of them are instincts of avoidance: fear of the unknown, of death; the instinct of concealment. But there is also a tropistic attraction to the light: "The life of his body . . . had yearned toward this light and urged his body toward it in the same way that the cunning chemistry of a plant urges it toward the sun" (77–78). Later, when White Fang instinctively avoids fighting a female, London carefully insists that his behavior is "not a something acquired by experience in the world" (177). It is not learned but is innate.

In a well-worn metaphor, White Fang's heredity is "likened to clay," which "possessed many possibilities, was capable of being moulded into many different forms." The force that serves "to model the clay, to give it a particular form" (177), is environment, and this favorite ingredient of the naturalistic stew receives continual emphasis. An alternative metaphor, noted above, is that of the plant, which withers in an adverse soil while thriving in a more favorable one. The world of the Indians is "no soil for kindliness and affection to blossom in" (149), whereas in the Southland, under the "sun" of human kindness, White Fang "flourished like a flower planted in good soil" (305). Such tropes are close indeed to Zola's conception of the "experimental novel," in which the novelist-as-observer resembles the physiologist. White Fang is a kind of experimental animal transferred from one environment to another so that his reactions can be observed. He acts one way in the wild, another with the Indians, yet another with Beauty Smith, and a fourth in the warm atmosphere of Weedon Scott and the Southland.[24]

The environmental theme is signaled at the outset in the marvelous description of the frozen Northland. The landscape paradoxically combines a foreboding animism with a sinister desolation, as if the ghostly atmosphere and demonic laughter were meant to suggest a kind of limbo, somewhere between life and death:

Dark spruce forest frowned on either side the frozen waterway. The trees had been stripped by a recent wind of their white covering of frost, and they seemed to lean toward each other, black and ominous, in the fading light. A vast silence reigned over the land. The land itself was a desolation, lifeless, without movement, so lone and cold that the spirit of it was not even that of sadness. There was a hint in it of laughter, but of a laughter more terrible than any sadness—a laughter that was mirthless as the smile of the Sphinx, a laughter cold as the frost and partaking of the grimness of infallibility. It was the masterful and incommunicable wisdom of eternity laughing at the futility of life and the effort of life. It was the Wild, the savage, frozen-hearted Northland Wild. (3)

Transporting a corpse through this landscape of quiet terror, Bill and Henry seem like "undertakers in a spectral world at the funeral of some ghost," and the oppressive silence af-

fects them "as the many atmospheres of deep water affect
the body of the diver" (5), giving them a foretaste of death,
as does White Fang's sudden immersion in water on his
first foray into the outer world. Though such an environment can be stupifyingly passive—"as remote and alien and
pulseless as the abysses of space" (5)—it can also be terrify-
ingly active in its effort to destroy life, which is "movement." It "freezes the water to prevent it running to the
sea" and "drives the sap out of the trees till they are frozen
to their mighty hearts" (4).

The constricted atmosphere of the cave then offers a text-
book example of behaviorist psychology, a laboratory setting
for the cub's responses to reward and punishment, pleasure
and pain. Even before the beginning of his conscious life, the
cub discovers the sharp rebuke of his mother's paw, recoil-
ing "automatically from hurt, as he had crawled automatically toward the light" (79). The sensation of fear, the
"hard obstruction of the cave-wall," and the "hunger unap-
peased of several famines"—these had "borne in upon him
that all was not freedom in the world, that to life there were
limitations and restraints. These limitations and restraints
were laws. To be obedient to them was to escape hurt and
make for happiness" (85). As he moves into more complex
environments, the restraints multiply. The "hostile environment" of the Indian Camp forces him into a "rapid and
one-sided" development, in which the "code he learned was
to obey the strong and to oppress the weak" (149). Later, the
ferocity of Beauty Smith hardens his nature almost beyond
repair.

But at the same time the world of man exerts a different
kind of influence on him: he begins actually to like the
"placing of his destiny in another's hands" (132). Insidiously, "the camp-life, replete with misery as it was, was secretly endearing itself to him" (142), preparing the ground
for his eventual covenant with human law. When he is finally transferred to Weedon Scott's affectionate care, the result is in truth a "revolution," for the new environment
forces him "to ignore the urges and promptings of instinct

and reason, defy experience, give the lie to life itself" (255). Unlearning and reversing his natural responses to pleasure and pain, he now "ofttimes elected discomfort and pain for the sake of his god" (259). From one point of view, he is discovering the satisfactions of the higher moral life; from another, he is encountering civilization and its discontents. Though upon completing the novel London insisted that no one could accuse him of having "humanized the dog,"[25] he had in fact somewhat implausibly abandoned the world of animal instincts for the world of humanistic values and choices.

Thus, from beginning to end, environment shapes White Fang's life. But London grants one aspect of the outer world an independent identity: the sudden impingement of chance. Unlike Melville's "necessity" or London's "heredity and environment," which reflect the broadly conceived force of circumstances or surroundings, chance manifests itself in a discrete moment. In Melville's phrase, it has "the last featuring blow at events" (*MD*, 185). Though old One Eye shies away from a dangerous porcupine, he lingers nearby because "he had long since learned that there was such a thing as Chance, or Opportunity" (69), which might yet send him home with his meat. Similarly, young White Fang on his first hunt experiences the "luck of the beginner" when "by sheer blundering . . . he chanced upon the shrewdly hidden ptarmigan nest" (91). Later, London develops ironies reminiscent of Thomas Hardy's when he insists on the large consequences that follow from apparently insignificant chances. Gray Beaver had intended to camp on the far bank of the Mackenzie River, where White Fang could never have reached him:

But on the near bank, shortly before dark, a moose, coming down to drink, had been espied by Kloo-Kooch, who was Gray Beaver's squaw. Now, had not the moose come down to drink, had not Mitsah been steering out of the course because of the snow, had not Kloo-Kooch sighted the moose, and had not Gray Beaver killed it with a lucky shot from his rifle, all subsequent things would have happened differently. Gray Beaver would not have camped on the near side of the Mackenzie, and White Fang would have passed by and gone on, either to die or to find his way to his wild brothers and become one of them,—a wolf to the end of his days. (155)

But while at times London looks at the events from this detached, ironic perspective, more characteristic is an attitude of terror and awe: "Had the cub thought in man-fashion, he might have epitomized life as a voracious appetite, and the world as a place wherein ranged a multitude of appetites, pursuing and being pursued, hunting and being hunted, eating and being eaten, all in blindness and confusion, with violence and disorder, a chaos of gluttony and slaughter, ruled over by chance, merciless, planless, endless" (108). Like the shark massacre in *Moby-Dick*, this is the nightmare world of the naturalist, a purposeless concatenation of savage forces, unredeemed by any glimmer of hope. Maxwell Geismar has aptly called it "a parable of horrors, a lyric poem of barbarism."[26]

This passage may indeed speak for the darkest and even the deepest side of London's vision. Yet *White Fang* is obviously not without hope. One measure of its escape from an unqualified naturalism is London's recognition of the possibility of choice, which is signaled even in the earliest pages when the vast, silent Northland seems so oppressive. Though the environment laughs at "the futility of life and the effort of life," still "there *was* life, abroad in the land and defiant" (3). Even in the cave, where the cub at first seems little more than a Pavlovian dog, London makes a careful distinction. Initially White Fang recoiled from hurt "automatically"; later he recoiled "because he *knew* that it was hurt." These, London insists, are "conscious actions" (79); in a rudimentary way, they are choices..

But such choices are made within narrow limits, their degree of freedom heavily qualified by the emphasis on heredity and environment. In the crucial Part Three, however, the choices are clearer and more consequential. The first of them occurs when the breakup of the Indian camp gives

White Fang his first "chance for liberty." "Quite deliberately," London tells us, "he determined to stay behind"
(150). But having given White Fang this choice, London
seems to take it away, for the loneliness of the forest soon
frightens the cub back to the village. So much for free will,
it would seem.

But on reaching the campsite and finding it deserted,
White Fang faces another decision, and this time the choice
has permanent consequences. He must decide forever between the call of the wild and the companionship of man,
and "it did not take him long to make up his mind" (153).
He "surrendered himself, voluntarily," to Gray Beaver. "Of
his own choice, he came in to sit by man's fire and to be
ruled by him" (156–57). The "covenant" he makes is, by
definition, an agreement freely entered into, entailing a
willing acceptance of duties and benefits. There is some
irony, to be sure, in London's acknowledgment that for the
"possession of a flesh-and-blood god," White Fang "ex-
changed his own liberty" (170). Yet he makes the exchange
knowingly, and its character is confirmed by another volun-
tary return after a later famine, when he "came out boldly
from the forest and trotted into camp straight to Gray Beaver's tepee" (183). This time his return is not impulsive or
panicky but deliberate, and its importance is made plain:
"The seal of his dependence on man had been set upon him
in that early day when he turned his back on the Wild and
crawled to Gray Beaver's feet to receive the expected beating" (257). By contravening his automatic responses to reward and punishment, White Fang proclaims his ability to
shape his own life.

Earl Wilcox is surely correct, therefore, when he says that
"it is not possible to consider Fang as a typical product of
environment because he quickly becomes a superior type."[27]
But this is not so much an inconsistency as a paradox. It is
London's recognition, resembling Melville's, that life is a
complex and mysterious tapestry, woven of shifting and
often conflicting strands. To read London with the expectation of a consistent naturalism is to invite disappointment.

Though unquestionably influenced by naturalism, he was not confined by it. *White Fang*, like *The Call of the Wild*, is about freedom and bondage. Unlike *The Call*, it insists that civilization, for all its discontents, is a bondage worth settling for.

The contrasting endings of *The Call* and *White Fang* thus offer another expression of London's divided impulses. The outward thrust of *The Call*, which carries Buck away from the fireside into the demonic wilderness, expresses the "masculine" principle of movement, whereas the direction of its companion novel is finally centripetal—a return to the center, to the "feminine" principle of stable domesticity. *White Fang* is a product of the time when London emerged from his "long sickness" and began putting down new roots, buying a ranch and preparing for a second marriage. As Andrew Sinclair has observed, it reflects a "determined effort to tame his appetites and settle."[28] Yet the wild—the dark, demonic side of his vision—would continue to call, albeit more quietly; and he would never seem sure that his choice had been right. In his next major novel, the conflict reappears in his ambivalent vision of socialism.

6

Revolution and Romance
The Iron Heel

With the completion of *White Fang* in late 1905, London had written the novels that established permanently his reputation as a writer of popular adventure stores of the Klondike and the sea. His future thus seeming secure, he felt free to take up anew his passion for militant socialism and to revive his long-delayed plan to write a major socialist novel, which he had described in an early entry in the Post-Klondike Notebook: "Perhaps write a novel, a la Wells, out of idea of wage-slaves, ruled by industrial oligarchs, finally ceasing to reproduce. And either figure out new way of penetrating the future, or begin far ahead of the actual time of the story, by having the writing dug up by the people of a new and very immature civilization." The same notebook contained another entry headed "Novel—CAPTAINS OF INDUSTRY," which was to involve "industrial oligarchs controlling the world, terrible struggles of workmen; some big city center of some scene like the Paris Commune. Read up."[1] By November of 1902, among the novels he proposed to George Brett was one that would "bid for a popularity such as Bellamy received"[2] in his utopian romance, *Looking Backward* (1888).

In different ways, all three of these notes contain germs of *The Iron Heel*. The reference to H. G. Wells suggests that the initial inspiration may have come from the apocalyptic fantasy *When the Sleeper Wakes* (1899), in which Wells borrows Bellamy's device of the mesmeric trance to deliver his hero into the middle of a class war two hundred years in the future. Already, however, London was casting about for a "new way of penetrating the future"—some alternative to the unrealistic device of the trance—and his notion of beginning "far ahead of the actual time" and having the writing "dug up" by the people of a new civilization closely resembles the narrative method he eventually chose. In his second note, his reference to the Paris Commune of 1871, on which he did indeed "read up," establishes the historical model for the Chicago Commune in *The Iron Heel*.[3]

Still, for a number of reasons the socialist novel had to wait. In the early phases of his career, London was content to confine his socialism to lectures and essays, while keeping it out of the fiction in which he was struggling for popular success. He had convinced himself, if not his readers, that *The Sea-Wolf* contained a socialistic message, but he was not yet ready to risk his burgeoning reputation on an overtly socialistic novel. Prior to 1906, his only story even remotely socialistic was a negligible fantasy called "The Minions of Midas," published in 1901. Following the unanticipated success of *The Call of the Wild* in 1903, he channeled his creative energies mainly into the writing of *The Sea-Wolf* and *White Fang*.

But while the plans for *The Iron Heel* had been set aside, London had not forgotten his socialism. In September of 1903 he took enough time away from the writing of *The Sea-Wolf* to assemble a collection of his socialistic essays, which he urged Macmillan to publish under the title "The Salt of the Earth"; and when Brett counseled delay, London wrote again from Korea the following April, noting the "timely importance" of the essays and asking him to reconsider.[4] After returning from the Orient, he resumed his lectures to the Ruskin Club and other Bay Area groups; and after the

November presidential election, he celebrated Eugene Debs's surprisingly large Socialist Party vote with an article for the San Francisco *Examiner*.[5] In January, 1905, he lectured on "Revolution" in Los Angeles, then returned home to complete a preface to "The Salt of the Earth," which Macmillan finally published in the spring under the more militant title of *War of the Classes*. January also brought the first eruption of the Russian Revolution, which, with its general strikes and violent suppressions, combined with what he knew of the Paris Commune to give him a renewed sense of the possibilities and dangers of proletarian revolt.

Throughout the year the pace of his speaking engagements continued strong. During the summer, though preoccupied with *White Fang*, his proletarian energies were stirred by his reading of Upton Sinclair's new novel *The Jungle*, then being serialized in the socialist *Appeal to Reason*. No doubt he was especially flattered to find himself portrayed anonymously in the novel as the young California author who "had been a salmon fisher, an oyster pirate, a longshoreman, a sailor; who had tramped the country and been sent to jail, had lived in the Whitechapel slums, and been to the Klondike in search of gold," but who despite his "genius" as a storyteller "still preached the gospel of the poor."[6] The two writers soon began a correspondence, Sinclair helping with some of the arrangements for the eastern lecture tour that London put together for the winter and carried forward with sensational publicity. Back home in mid-February, 1906, London returned Sinclair's favor by puffing *The Jungle* in a widely circulated review,[7] and immediately after completing the proletarian story "The Apostate" in late March, he wrote to George Brett that he intended to begin writing *The Iron Heel* in the summer.[8]

On his way back from the East, London had lectured twice in Chicago, where he also toured the noisome stockyards, rapidly becoming notorious in the wake of Sinclair's novel. What were the portents, he must have wondered, for a civilization bound in industrial squalor and class hatred. Did the rising Chicago socialist vote, as Sinclair proclaimed at the end of *The Jungle*, augur a peaceful transition to a co-operative commonwealth? Or did the answer lie back in San Francisco, where two months later on April 18, the devastating earthquake moved London to images of a biblical apocalypse: an "imperial city" destroyed by a "vast conflagration" that seemed to herald "the end of the world"?[9]

Temperamentally, London inclined toward the latter view. Impatient with evolutionary political reform, he had always been more deeply stirred by the militant rhetoric of the socialist left. Though he repeatedly disclaimed the extremes of anarchism and was careful to declare his allegiance to the ballot box, he also rejected the "sweet and beautiful Utopian dream" of a socialism that was considered "respectable" because it was "non-menacing."[10] His own more militant lectures, such as "The Class Struggle" and "Revolution," fairly bristled with the rhetoric of force. The classes, he declared, were "openly at war"; the proletariat aimed to "possess itself of the government" and "destroy present-day society."[11] Though the socialists "love peace," they are "unafraid of war" and are willing to "meet violence with violence."[12] Rousing a crowded and sometimes hostile lecture hall with such phrases was a heady experience, the fulfillment of a fantasy of revolutionary leadership that London projected into the hero of his novel, Ernest Everhard. As he revealingly acknowledged in "Revolution," militant socialism was both "power" and "romance."[13]

The name Ernest Everhard, which one might suppose was invented to suggest indomitable heroism, was actually taken from a Michigan cousin whom London had visited on his tramping venture in 1894, and he selected it only after rejecting less intrepid-sounding names such as Blenheim and Bartholomew.[14] At five feet nine inches, Everhard is somewhat taller than London's five feet seven; and as a former blacksmith, he better represents the quintessential dignity of labor that London himself had not found in the miscellaneous drudgery of the cannery, jute mill, and steam laundry. Despite his proletarian experience, moreover, Ernest is a "descendant of the old line of Everhards that for over two hundred years had lived in America."[15] Though an editorial footnote is meant to take the sting out of this "invidious" social distinction, the description tallies with the characterization of Everhard throughout the novel as a Nietzschean "blond beast," a working-class prodigy who is also a "natural aristocrat" (6). Thus the Jack London of illegitimate birth and scruffy boyhood who made a fortune as a writer of popular fiction is transformed into the *déclassé* gentleman hero who earns only a "meagre living" from his translations and from the "small sales of his own economic and philosophical works" (25).

Everhard, in other words, combines London's own energy and egoism with the self-effacing dedication of such socialist intellectuals as Austin Lewis and Ernest Untermann, John Spargo and Paul Lafargue. London drew freely on the writings of these men—as well as on such muckrakers and social prophets as Lincoln Steffens and W. J. Ghent—for the facts and arguments with which Ernest demolishes his opponents.[16] Untermann, in particular, struck London as an appropriately Lincolnesque model with his self-education, his unpretentious manner, and his dedication to writing translations and "philosophical works from [the] standpoint of [the] working class."[17] At one point London acknowledged that Everhard was a composite portrait of himself, Untermann, and Eugene Debs;[18] and although Debs does not figure in the notes for the novel, his career does in many respects parallel that of Ernest. He had spent six months in prison for his leadership of the 1894 Pullman strike, and in 1905 he played a key role in the organization of the militant I.W.W. An inspiring speaker selflessly devoted to the cause of labor, Debs was in many ways what London would have wished to be if he had devoted himself solely to radical politics.

Thus, armed with other men's facts, figures, and arguments, Ernest becomes invincible in debate. His argument to the middle-class businessmen in chapter 9 is essentially the Marxist theory of surplus value that London had expounded in his essay "The Question of the Maximum,"[19]

and his incendiary address to the Philomaths is extracted almost verbatim from "What Life Means to Me" and "Revolution," the latter having been delivered by London to a
similar group of wealthy and outraged New Yorkers in January of 1906. The opening scene in chapter 1, in which
Avis's father impishly invites Ernest to dinner in hopes of
provoking a clash with the other guests, is based on an incident of early 1905 in which London's friend Ed Winship set
up a dinner meeting between London and a potential antagonist named Cameron. The hoped-for entertainment finally
materialized when London was at last goaded into his typical blunt polemic; and Cameron, initially enraged, was finally won over by Jack's force and charm.[20] Ernest's hostility toward "metaphysicians," in the same chapter, derives
from London's encounters with Edward B. Payne, "a far
older man whom Jack styled 'metaphysician.'" As his wife
later recalled it, London's participation in these exchanges
was somewhat unwilling and the debate not wholly successful, "for the same familiar stumbling-block was encountered that had disrupted earlier discussions whenever Jack
and the metaphysicians locked horns: Jack could not and
would not accept the premise offered."[21] But in the more
flattering arena of the novel, all comes right: London's stub-
born dogmatism becomes the unassailable logic that leaves
Everhard's opponents helpless to reply.

As the novel took shape in the working notes, various
minor characters were suggested by London's reading in
miscellaneous periodicals. Just before beginning to write, he
came across an account of a man named Jackson whose arm
had been mangled when he tried to save a machine from destruction by picking a piece of flint out of it. The company's
conspiracy against him—the perjured testimony, the silence
of the press, the hostility of the managers' wives—closely
parallels the characterization of the rattan-peddlar whose
fate is instrumental in the conversion of Avis.[22] For Bishop
Morehouse the chief model may have been London's elderly
socialist friend Frederick Irons Bamford, whom he called
"the lion-hearted one" and who, "despite an agonizingly

supersensitive nature," was made of "the stuff of martyrs."[23] But for the bishop's anguished *mea culpa* in chapter 7, London relied on a 1901 article by Frank Harris called "The Bishop of London and Public Morality," a satirical piece in which Harris had tried to imagine what the bishop might say if he actually practiced the Christianity he preached. London had read Harris's piece not in its original publication but in an obscure socialist periodical where it had been reprinted, and he was later forced to produce the clipping when Harris publicly charged him with plagiarism. He had been under the impression, he confessed, that he was using the actual words of the Bishop of London as quoted in the press; he had not realized that the speech had been invented by Harris.[24]

One other minor character, the militant socialist rebel Anna Roylston, has a similarly complex origin. She was originally thought to have been modeled on Jane Roulston, a beautiful young socialist friend from London's mid-twenties, and the similarity of surnames is indeed striking. The full characterization, however, owes much more to Louise Michel, a near-legendary heroine of the Paris Commune who was called by her followers the Red Virgin. After her death in early 1905, London clipped an article on her career and preserved it along with a set of his own notes for a lecture on anarchy: "Louise Michel, the Red Virgin. Describe her life, and, after pointing out how illogical, unscientific and impossible is anarchy, hold Louise Michel up as a better type of human than a woman of the bourgeoisie, fat and selfish and dead." The accompanying article tells of her fanatical dedication to revolution—how her "mere presence could electrify the populace" and how she retained her purity of character and purpose even as she lived among "anarchists, revolutionaries, lawbreakers and nondescripts."[25]

Another minor character, the time-serving reporter to whom Avis takes the case of Jackson's arm, resembles an anonymous journalist quoted by W. J. Ghent in *Our Benevolent Feudalism* (1902). Avis's reporter rebuffs her out of fear for his job if he flouts "editorial policy" and the corporate advertisers; and in reply, Avis charges that his function is merely to "twist truth at the command of [his] employers, who, in turn, obey the behests of the corporations" (64). This episode, in close paraphrase, dramatizes the candid confession of the journalist quoted by Ghent. "I am paid," he says, "for keeping honest opinions out of the paper I am connected with. Other editors are paid similar salaries for doing similar things. If I should allow honest opinions to be printed in one issue of my paper, before twenty-four hours my occupation, like Othello's, would be gone." The effect of such an attitude, Ghent observes, is inevitable: "the recoil upon themselves of the character of their tasks does not, to say the least, sharpen the edge of conscience, and the service of a few years is generally believed to be effective in indurating the finest sensibilities."[26] Though Avis's young journalist is "not yet case-hardened," his conscience is already showing signs of atrophy. "I keep square all right with my own conscience," he lamely insists; but he soon admits, "I don't think. . . . One can't kick over the ropes if he's going to succeed in journalism. . . . it comes out all right, don't you see?" (64, 65).

A second cue for the corrupted journalist came from Thorstein Veblen, whom London quoted in his notes for an essay to be titled "The Persistence of the Established." An editor's first duty, Veblen wrote, is to "gauge the sentiments of his readers" and "tell them what they like to believe," and his second duty is to say nothing that might offend his advertisers. The result, Veblen scornfully observes, is that both news and editorial columns are commonly "meretricious in a high degree." The same set of notes suggests that Veblen influenced *The Iron Heel* in yet another way, by serving as a model for Avis's father, who is eased out of his university professorship because of his radical views and associations and who publishes a book on "the persistence of the established" (106). In his notes for the essay, London observes how the "mushy thought of the Established" endures while unpopular thought is banned. He offers as an instance "Prof. Veblen . . . who was fired out of

Chicago University . . . because he is in revolt against the rule of the dead, because he is dynamic rather than static."[27]

As for Avis herself, the circumstances of her family life in the early chapters suggest that London may have modeled her in part after his sprightly young socialist friend Anna Strunsky, with whom he was in love in late 1901 and early 1902. The Strunskys' San Francisco home, like that of the Cunninghams in the novel, had impressed London as a vibrant center of intellectual life and socialist sympathies. By the time Ernest and Avis are ready to marry, however, Avis more clearly resembled London's second wife, Charmian Kittredge. Doubtless the public notoriety and private gossip that surrounded London's divorce from Bess Maddern and his marriage to Charmian—in November, 1905, in Chicago during his lecture tour—contributed to the portrayal of the "organized ostracism" (182) that follows the marriage of the Everhards. For the first time London's radical politics and the marital scandal combined to cause his books to be banned, and he began to fear the specter of declining sales. These feelings of persecution became associated in his mind with the corrosive life of the city, while his rural refuge near Glen Ellen enters the novel as the site of the rebel hideaway at which Ernest and Avis experience their few moments of happiness.

The Iron Heel thus emerged out of the loose ends and purposeful pursuits of London's career as a passionate if erratic socialist. Another line of influence came from fiction. Even London's title, which derives from Wickson's warning to Everhard that "we will grind you revolutionists down under our heel" (97), echoes Upton Sinclair's comment in *The Jungle* on the victimization of Jurgis Rudkus by the tyrannical beef barons, who had "ground him beneath their heel."[28] More pervasively, London drew on the well-established tradition of late nineteenth-century utopian and antiutopian (or dystopian) novels. Bellamy's *Looking Backward*, which had been enormously popular and was still influential, provided London with a model for the double point of view, which enables the reader to contemplate the utopian future at the same time a representative of that future criticizes the unregenerate present. In the two decades since its publication, Bellamy's book had stimulated a spate of imitations, refinements, and "answers"; and as a number of scholars have noted, such novels fall into two groups. The first, typified by *Looking Backward* and such variations as William Morris's *News from Nowhere* (1891) and W. D. Howells's *A Traveler from Altruria* (1894), suggested that the ideal social commonwealth would evolve gradually and peacefully along Christian and democratic lines. The other group, more doubtful of the benevolence of human nature and the willingness of capitalist magnates to relinquish power, held that a just society would come only after a long struggle and a violent cataclysm. In this category belong two novels that strongly influenced *The Iron Heel:* Wells's *When the Sleeper Wakes* and Ignatius Donnelly's *Caesar's Column* (1890).[29]

Like Bellamy's Julian West, Graham, the hero of Wells's dystopian fantasy, falls into a mesmeric trance, though he awakes to find himself not in Bellamy's benign commonwealth but in the middle of a nightmarish clash between the tyrannical Council of oligarchs and a rebel leader, Ostrog. After a period of wild street-fighting, Ostrog deposes the Council only to set himself up as a tyrant in his own right. He is defeated in a climactic battle of airships (called aeropiles), the forces of humanitarianism now being led by Graham himself, who pilots an aeropile in which he destroys Ostrog and becomes king. While this action is developing, there is a general strike, some talk of a Commune, and much description of the wonders of the vast metropolis of the future, suggestive of London's Ardis and Asgard. The latter subject is pursued at greater length in Wells's speculative essays on the nature of future society in *Anticipations* (1902), in which he also proposes that the warfare of the future will involve the use of manned balloons for surveillance and flying-machines that drop explosives.

Some of the same ingredients can be found in *Caesar's Column*, and Donnelly's influence on London was especially strong. *When the Sleeper Wakes* is more of a futurist fantasy than either *Caesar's Column* or *The Iron Heel*, both of which, though set in the future, more closely reflect the social realities of their own time. Donnelly's book, a crazyquilt melodrama of political intrigue and violent revolution in New York in the late twentieth century, is narrated by a visitor from the benign state of Uganda, Gabriel Weltstein, who accidentally falls in with Maximilian Petion, a heroic rebel conspiring to overthrow a ruthless capitalist cabal alternately called the plutocracy and the oligarchy. Two love stories are woven into the action, which, like that of *The Iron Heel*, is rife with conspiracies and disguises, spies and traitors. If the atmosphere of hysteria and paranoia in *The Iron Heel* derives partly from London's own marital and political life, much of the last third of London's novel reflects the influence of *Caesar's Column*.

Like *The Iron Heel*, Donnelly's novel incorporates the socialist commonplace that public institutions were conspiring against the workers. The newspapers, Gabriel learns, are "the hired mouthpieces of power," and the courts "the merest tools of the rich." Against this entrenched power stands a secret revolutionary organization called the Brotherhood of Destruction, which, with its vast network of insurgents and spies, resembles the Fighting Groups organized by Ernest Everhard. In each novel the revolutionary brotherhood makes a special effort to punish its betrayers. In *Caesar's Column*, a traitor is killed within twenty-four hours, for "if he fled to the uttermost ends of the earth his doom would overtake him with the certainty of fate." In *The Iron Heel*, "from one to a dozen faithful avengers were loosed upon his heels," for "the one thing we could not afford to fail in was the punishment of our own traitors" (249–50). The extreme secrecy in Donnelly's Brotherhood, as in London's Fighting Groups, necessitates the perfection of the art of disguise, and Maximilian lives a "dual life"[30] under two different names much as plastic surgeons change Ernest into virtually "another man" (304).

The art of disguise figures importantly in the first of the central events that London found in Donnelly's novel, the escape and disappearance of Avis after she is released from prison. In a number of details, this incident resembles the escape of Gabriel's sweetheart, Estella, from imprisonment and the threat of concubinage in the mansion of the arch-oligarch, Prince Cabano. Estella escapes disguised as a man, Avis as the pampered daughter of an oligarch; both are escorted by fellow revolutionaries through an intricate series of maneuvers designed to elude their pursuers. Each, moreover, has the important assistance of a faithful revolutionary who doubles as a trusted servant of the arch-oligarch. The intelligence and efficiency of this servant (Rudolph in *Caesar's Column*, John Carlson in *The Iron Heel*) are so impressive that the narrator asks him how he became a revolutionary. In response, each servant provides a brief history of his German birth and youth, conversion to socialism, immigration to America, and gradual rise to a position of trust with a great magnate (Rudolph with Prince Cabano, Carlson with Wickson), from which he can render invaluable service to the revolution.

But London's major debt to Donnelly lies in the climactic holocaust that envelopes the Chicago Commune. Though London omits some of Donnelly's wilder details and shifts the scene from New York to Chicago,[31] he draws the essentials of this episode from the final cataclysm in *Caesar's Column*. In Donnelly's version, a proletarian uprising is planned for New York's financial district, but a spy reveals the plan to the oligarchs, who order the militia to surround the insurgents, trapping them behind their barricades where they can be bombed by dirigiblelike airships before being exterminated by the guns and bayonets of the troops. But when the commander of the airships defects to the revolutionaries and warns them of the impending massacre, the tables are turned: it is the militia that is trapped and destroyed by the bombs and rampaging workers, who soon overrun the mansions of the oligarchs in an orgy of indiscriminate destruction. Eventually they turn against their own leaders, who escape at the last moment in an airship as the whole of New York collapses into barbarism.

In this scene lie all the essentials of London's Chicago Commune. As in *Caesar's Column*, the revolt is betrayed by a spy for the oligarchy, whose militia surround the rebel barricades. But whereas in Donnelly's novel the arrival of the airships alters the course of battle in favor of the rebels, in *The Iron Heel* the rebels' bomb-carrying balloons arrive too late and in insufficient numbers to prevent the slaughter of the insurgent workers, whose corpses pile up into "a heap, a mound, a huge and growing wave of dead and dying" (339), much as Donnelly's giant rebel leader, Caesar Lomellini, orders the corpses piled into a great column as a macabre monument to the revolution. Even the description of the "people of the abyss," so often lamented by London's critics, is little more than a paraphrase of this passage of Donnelly's: "like a huge flood, long dammed up, turbulent, turbid, muddy, loaded with wrecks and debris, the gigantic mass [of the proletariat] broke loose, full of foam and terror, and flowed in every direction. A foul and brutal and ravenous multitude it was, dark with dust and sweat, armed with the weapons of civilization, but possessing only the instincts of wild beasts." Behind this mob come the "criminal classes," a wretched band of "the base, the cowardly, the cruel, the sneaking, the inhuman, the horrible . . . the refuse and outpouring of grog-shops and brothels. . . . They dart hither and thither; they swarm—they dance—they howl—they chatter —they quarrel and battle, like carrion-vultures, over the spoils."[32] This nightmarish "flood" of subhumanity closely resembles London's brutish mob, "an awful river that filled the street . . . mad with drink and wrong, up at last and roaring for the blood of their masters. . . . It surged past my vision in concrete waves of wrath, snarling and growling, carnivorous, drunk with whiskey from pillaged warehouses, drunk with hatred, drunk with lust for blood . . . the refuse and the scum of life, a raging, screaming, screeching, demoniacal horde" (326–27). Though London ordinarily eschewed Donnelly's most flagrant excesses, he was unable to resist the apocalyptic violence and boiling rhetoric of this final scene of revolt.

Thus London built his novel out of a combination of his own experience and his reading in the literature of social conflict. But this material yields a rather different version of London's theme of the conflict between social order and anarchic individualism. The principle of order exists in two versions of society which, ironically, are ideological opponents: the conservative middle class of the early twentieth century and the utopian socialist Brotherhood of Man. Though ideologically antithetical, these societies are psychologically akin, for each represents a realization of stability. Their true antithesis is the spirit of revolution. To this spirit the present state of society is never good enough, while the future society is distant, possibly unattainable— at any rate too dull an affair to be of much interest.

At the heart of this novel, therefore, is the heady atmosphere of social upheaval, the loosing of violent anarchic forces, which are personified by the revolutionary leadership of Ernest Everhard. Yet it is crucial that London decided to present Ernest from an "outside" point of view— that is, from the perspective of one of the two stable societies, either that of the past or that of the future. In fact, through the framing device of the "found" manuscript, London's narrative method achieves both. Inside the frame Ernest is viewed from the perspective of Avis Cunningham, whose upper-middle-class attitudes cast her initially as Ernest's foil but who is soon converted to the spirit of revolution. Then from the outside, both Avis and Ernest are subjected to the comments of Anthony Meredith, the "editor" of Avis's manuscript, who views their revolutionary activities from his perspective seven centuries into the utopian future.

This narrative method is fundamentally well conceived, and its consequences, frequently ignored in the past, have been deservedly stressed by recent critics.[33] Yet the method is not wholly successful. The outer editorial frame works well enough, but the inner narrative is seriously flawed. To see why this is so, it is helpful to consider the novel as a *Bildungsroman*, a novel of development or education. As a didactic proletarian novel, it is something of a special case, because the education of its protagonist is a process of radicalization, of awakening to the realities of class conflict. To describe *The Iron Heel* in this way is to suggest that its protagonist is, after all, not Ernest Everhard but Avis Cunningham.[34]

Avis is at the center of the action from beginning to end, not only because she is the narrator but, more important, because her character—her very nature as a person—is at issue. It is true that Ernest is often in her thoughts, especially when he is engaged in a debate or speech, and to her he is a hero. His heroism, however, is always putative—always asserted by others but never dramatized. His only observable acts of courage occur when he speaks before hostile audiences at the Philomath Club and in the Congress. Yet we are seldom permitted to forget that his arguments serve to educate Avis even as they dramatize Ernest's talents as an "intellectual swashbuckler" (23). When he lectures the group of middle-class businessmen, for example, Avis too is listening and learning: "It was the first time I had ever heard Karl Marx's doctrine of surplus value elaborated, and Ernest had done it so simply that I, too, sat puzzled and dumfounded" (150). In the most impressive scenes of action— the investigation of Jackson's arm, the escape to the Sonoma hideaway, and the Chicago Commune—Ernest is not even present. He *seems* to dominate the novel because of the powers attributed to him by others, especially by the worshipful Avis; but aside from Avis and Bishop Morehouse, his words change no minds and persuade no one to act, unless it is to harden some in opposition. The small businessmen, seemingly overwhelmed by a parade of fact and theory, nevertheless fail to change their ways and are later crushed between the magnates and the workers. The

Philomaths, effectively warned by Ernest's threats, are mobilized by Wickson into a more determined repressive force.

Furthermore, if Ernest is considered the protagonist, the novel must be said to suffer from a serious disunity. Through the early and middle chapters, Avis keeps Ernest before us; and with his tones of prophecy, he seems to be preparing the reader—even as he is preparing Avis, her father, and himself—for his assumption of the mantle of active heroism at the climax. But this expectation is disappointed. Ernest plays no role whatever in the Chicago scenes, materializing only at the end to escape with Avis. Paul Stein has recently argued that Everhard's disappearance at the crucial juncture is appropriate, because it "diminish[es] the centrality of the individual in history."[35] This may be good social theory, but it is not good narrative art. If Ernest is the true proletarian hero of this novel, then the ending is *Hamlet* without the prince.

The inner narrative, therefore, is the story of Avis. London may have identified himself emotionally with Everhard, just as he did with Wolf Larsen in *The Sea-Wolf*; but Avis is the narrator and true protagonist of her story as much as Humphrey Van Weyden is of his. Earle Labor has argued that the chief problem is Avis's narrative voice, that the novel sounds like "*1984* as it might have been penned by Elizabeth Barrett Browning."[36] To put Labor's point another way, *The Iron Heel* as narrated by Avis is what *The Sea-Wolf* would have been if it had been narrated by Maud Brewster. Humphrey Van Weyden, despite his occasional fatuities, is a more interesting and complex character than Maud, and the earlier novel gains from his conflict with Larsen. *The Iron Heel*, in turn, suffers from the lack of such psychological conflict. After their initial clash over Jackson's arm, Ernest and Avis are in perfect harmony, and the novel must depend on the cruder opposition between the selfless socialists and the villainous oligarchy. Despite editor Meredith's insistence that the story "vividly portray[s] the psychology of the persons that lived in that turbulent period" (x), such psychological penetration is precisely what the story lacks.

Accordingly, the characterization of Avis is most successful in the early chapters, when there is still some tension between her and Ernest. The initial situation is plausible and even promising: a genteel young woman is challenged to find out for herself how the other half lives—and, further, how she herself has unwittingly supported flagrant social injustice. Her pursuit of the dismaying truth about Jackson's arm grows more spirited as she becomes more disillusioned, and she might have become a modestly interesting character if, after her story was refused by the newspapers, she had gone on to publish it in *McClure's* and developed a muckraking career of her own. That, of course, would have been a different novel and not the one London wanted to write; but by having Avis marry Everhard and become a revolutionary, he sacrifices her credibility almost completely. From that point on, her only plausible role is to retreat to the Sonoma refuge and await her reunion with her husband. She tells us that she is a secret agent for the revolution, but we never really see her functioning in that capacity. Although we do see her hiding under a pile of corpses in Chicago, her credibility as a revolutionary, or even as an innocent victim, is somewhat diminished by the fact that as soon as the enemy soldiers drag her out from under the gory heap, she begins primly "fixing up [her] hair . . . and pinning together [her] torn skirts" (334).

Thus the lines of Avis's character are fatally blurred by the incongruous roles she is asked to play, and her narrative voice accordingly drifts in and out of focus. At times she is barely present at all, as when she acts as the recording secretary for Ernest's polemics; and in the Chicago scenes her voice often disappears into the tough-minded reportage and overheated rhetoric of her husband—which is to say of Jack London himself—until a fainting spell or a torn skirt reminds us that the observer of all this carnage is indeed Avis. Elsewhere we are all too well aware that she is having a girlish fling at revolution. The change in her life is an "adventure, and the greatest of all, for it was love-adventure" (182). Her social conscience is on its honeymoon, her new-found radicalism inextricably bound up with her adoration of Ernest. No wonder she herself is so frequently struck by the unreality of her suddenly altered life, marveling that "I, little I, who had lived so placidly all my days in the quiet university town, found myself . . . drawn into the vortex of the great world-affairs" (163).

The gasping reference to "I, little I," is more than conventional modesty. However embarrassingly phrased, it represents a radical questioning of her identity. Later, in the Sonoma hideaway, that questioning becomes more explicit when her disguise—her "other self" (274) as (appropriately enough) a pampered daughter of the upper class—leads her to wonder which of her lives is real:

At times it seemed impossible, either that I had ever lived a placid, peaceful life in a college town, or else that I had become a revolutionist inured to scenes of violence and death. One or the other could not be. One was real, the other was a dream, but which was which? Was this present life of a revolutionist, hiding in a hole, a nightmare? or was I a revolutionist who had somewhere, somehow, dreamed that in some former existence I had lived in Berkeley and never known of life more violent than teas and dances, debating societies, and lecture rooms? (278)

Credibility disintegrates here not because Avis has changed her old self into a new one; that is easier to believe than what London also asks us to accept: the existence of two Avises simultaneously—the fluttery young woman of the love adventure and the hardened revolutionary of the political drama. In one role she is unattractive, in the other unconvincing.

It is this former society girl, one should observe, who is the "author" of the repulsive description of the Chicago proletariat as "the refuse and scum of life." Ernest, in contrast, after his emergence from prison, has become more acceptable to her by adding "a certain nobility of refinement" (287) to his features. These social discriminations are most tellingly dramatized when, near the end of her Chicago ordeal, she encounters a wounded rebel—a "wretched slave," she calls him—tottering along the street: "One hand he held tightly against his side, and behind him he left a bloody trail. His eyes roved everywhere, and they were filled with apprehension and dread. Once he looked straight across at me, and in his face was all the dumb pathos of the wounded and hunted animal. He saw me, but there was no kinship between us, and with him, at least, no sympathy of understanding. . . . All he could hope for, all he sought, was some hole to crawl away in and hide like any animal" (344). The irony of this passage is clear. Having herself suffered nothing worse than a few bruises and a torn dress, Avis, in her self-pity, accuses this "wounded and hunted animal" of having no "sympathy of understanding" to offer *her*. Plainly the stare of nonrecognition, the denial of kinship, though she projects it onto him, is entirely her own. Her "strong class instincts" (5), which earlier were shocked by Ernest's bold sexual force, have never deserted her; and in this respect she is perilously close to the gentility of Ruth Morse, whom London was to characterize so devastatingly in his next novel, *Martin Eden*. Avis represents one more attempt by London to portray a heroine who is both genteel and spirited, but Avis wading in blood on the streets of Chicago is no more convincing than Maud Brewster slaughtering seals on Endeavor Island. Her identity remains as much of a mystery to the reader as it does to her.

In the face of such serious defects, it may seem unlikely that any defense of this novel can be made at all. Yet its power is undeniable, for London at times managed an effective combination of realism and the stylized, larger-than-life qualities of a didactic fable or heroic romance. On the one hand, he said that "from a pseudo-scientific standpoint" he considered the novel "plausible,"[37] a claim tallying with his rejection of many of the melodramatic absurdities and futuristic fantasies of Donnelly and Wells, supporting the impression that he wanted his action to seem a credible projection of events taking place only a few years in the future. This realistic dimension depends heavily on the interplay between Avis's point of view and that of the "editor," for Avis's glorification of her adventures in revolution and romance needs the detached, antiromantic comments of Anthony Meredith to bring it down to earth. Again and again this editorial irony deflates both her romantic flights and her vestiges of class-consciousness. At the outset Meredith prepares us to "smile . . . and forgive Avis Everhard for the heroic lines upon which she modelled her husband. We know to-day that he was not so colossal, and that he loomed among the events of his times less largely than the Manuscript would lead us to believe" (ix). When Avis refers to Ernest as a Nietzschean blond beast, the editor dismisses Nietzsche as a lunatic (6); and her pride in her father's "stout old *Mayflower* stock" is treated with gentle editorial scorn: "Descendants of these original colonists were for a while inordinately proud of their genealogy; but in time the blood became so widely diffused that it ran in the veins practically of all Americans" (177).

But the editorial frame accomplishes more than the deflation of Avis's romanticism. As recent critics have pointed out, it provides the entire inner narrative with an illusion of objective distance and historical inevitability, implying the dialectic of class conflict and the final synthesis of a socialist utopia. London only hints at the nature of that utopia and, unlike Bellamy, seems to have had little interest in describing its details. What interests him much more is the nature of the present conflict, and one of the most impressive aspects of *The Iron Heel* is his dramatization of the forms of intimidation and repression characteristic of the modern totalitarian state: Mr. Cunningham's forced resignation from the university, the suppression of his book, the clandestine seizure of his stock, the forgery and foreclosure of his mortgage, the threat of the asylum, and finally his sudden, unexplained disappearance.

Yet the Marxist critics have also been right in viewing the novel as a didactic fable, in which the characters are flat and the action romantically heightened because, as Trotsky put it, "the form of [*The Iron Heel*] represents only an armor for social analysis and prognosis," its author being interested "not so much in the individual fate of his heroes as in the fate of mankind."[38] London himself took a similar line in his notes, observing that the scenes must be made "striking, to make up for absence of regular novel features." *The Iron Heel* is thus a proletarian fable in the form of a heroic romance, in which life among the dedicated revolutionaries is "lived on the heights, where the air was keen and sparkling, where the toil was for humanity, and where sordidness and selfishness never entered" (187). From this enlarged perspective, the novel is not only framed by the Marxist dialectic but also pervaded by the apocalyptic vision of Christianity and the naturalistic imagery of social Darwinism. All of these perspectives blend into a single teleological view of history, in which unregenerate primitive man moves through a period of transitional crisis to achieve a final secular paradise—a movement not unlike that of White Fang.

The Christian framework involves, for the individual capable of it, a tranforming moment of inspired vision; for the society incapable of such a vision, a providential catastrophe and ultimately the regeneration of society through martyrdom. Images of spiritual rebirth pervade the narrative. At the beginning, Avis feels herself about to witness "a new and awful revelation" (60). In the midst of the Chicago violence, she feels "strangely exalted" (327), and her immersion in the pile of corpses is her "red baptism" (332). Ernest, too, is "transfigured" (79) by his righteous zeal, and under his tutelage Bishop Morehouse sees the light "as Saul saw his on the way to Damascus" (112).

But for those willfully blind to the new revelation, there remains only the cleansing force of catastrophe. In the Sonoma hideaway, the revolution "took on largely the character of religion" (250). The imminent disaster is signaled by the sudden emergence of "wild-eyed itinerant preachers" and the "religious frenzy" of "countless camp-meetings." It was, they claimed, "the beginning of the end of the world" (235). Chicago during the First Revolt is like the earth during the Flood, or like Sodom and Gomorrah destroyed by the wrath of God. As Avis's train approaches the city, the portents increase: "The sky had clouded, and the train rushed on like a sullen thunderbolt through the gray pall of advancing day" (314). Smoke and fire fill the air, and the surge of the maddened workers resembles an "awful river," a "rushing stream of human lava" (326, 327).[39]

Yet through this chaos shines the beacon of martyrdom. The bishop, harrowed by his "journey through hell," has turned consciously Christ-like and "is rushing on to his Gethsemane" (107). Befriending the poor and making his home a haven for prostitutes, he becomes in Avis's eyes "God's hero" (200), and he is last seen among the mangled corpses in Chicago, a martyr of the failed revolt. The bishop's death serves in turn to foreshadow the martyrdom of Ernest, who Avis believes may also be "destined for a cross" (61), and she later notes that "for man he gave his life" and, figuratively, was "crucified" (182). Ernest himself finds among the revolutionaries a spirit of "renunciation" and "martyrdom," envisioning the fulfillment of the future as "Christ's own Grail" (79).[40]

The biblical imagery is also present when Ernest speaks to the middle-class businessmen of the "antediluvian ways of your forefathers" (150). Obliquely, Ernest is prophesying the deluge that will wipe out the sinful capitalists forever. But in the same argument he also speaks of the "tide of evolution" that "flows on to socialism" (141). Unhappily for this metaphor, tides ebb as well as flow, but London's intention is to link the naturalistic image to the biblical and Marxist teleology in order to suggest progress toward some inevitable destiny. Another such naturalistic metaphor is that of organic growth, fruition, and decay. As the "editor" comments retrospectively, "Out of the decay of self-seeking capitalism, it was held, would arise that flower of the ages, the Brotherhood of Man. Instead of which . . . capitalism, rotten-ripe, sent forth that monstrous offshoot, the Oligarchy" (xii–xiii). In the ultimate fulfillment of this cycle, the flower of the socialist commonwealth will grow out of the fertilizing decay of a rotten capitalism.

A related metaphor, which London had employed a few months earlier in the primitive fantasy *Before Adam*, presents the rise of the oligarchy as an event in social evolution. As the "editor" asserts, "primitive communism, chattel slavery, serf slavery, and wage slavery were necessary stepping-stones in the evolution of society. But it were ridiculous to assert that the Iron Heel was a necessary stepping-stone. Rather, to-day, is it adjudged a step aside, or a step backward, to the social tyrannies that made the early world a hell" (xi–xii). In the same vein, Ernest views the "primitive" capitalists of the Philomath Club as "the caveman, in evening dress, snarling and snapping over a bone" (74). The catch-phrases of social Darwinism continually recur. In such a society the "big wolves ate the little wolves" (48); life is a "fang-and-claw social struggle" (126); it is "dog eat dog" (129). The "fiat of evolution," Ernest says, is "the word of God," which dictates that because primitive man was a "combinative beast . . . he rose to primacy over all the animals" (132). Socialism, he insists, is "in line with evolution," and those who "prefer to play atavistic roles . . . are doomed to perish as all atavisms perish" (134).

By thus tying the immediate action to larger myths of cosmic process and purpose, London is following Zola's *Germinal*, where violent class conflict is set against the cyclical processes of nature: germination, growth, and fruition. Though London had read *Germinal* years earlier, a nearer influence may have been Frank Norris's *The Octopus* (1901), itself strongly influenced by *Germinal*. Despite his reservations about the "inordinate realism" of minute detail, London praised and quoted at length from the "broad canvas" and heightened rhetoric of Norris's description of the colossal power of the railroad and the primordial energy of the wheat.[41] Thus, even more than in *The Sea-Wolf*, he directs *The Iron Heel* toward the large effects of the romance, especially the flat characterizations embodying the abstract forces of virtue and villainy, which are thrown into violent conflict in the Armageddon of class warfare. When Avis finds among the socialists nothing but "unselfishness and high idealism" (100), or when Ernest speaks in the stylized platitudes of heroic romance ("To-morrow the Cause will rise again, strong with wisdom and discipline" [351]), we are meant to accept these violations of verisimilitude as appropriate to a didactic fable.[42]

Whether such allowances can in fact be made, however, is a question that will be answered differently by different readers. We can thank recent Marxist criticism for a clearer appreciation of the function of the double point of view and for a proper insistence that *The Iron Heel* cannot be judged solely by the criteria of the realistic novel. Yet these corrections do not dispose of the two inescapable flaws: the unconvincing characterization of Avis, and the absence of the hero at the climax. Ernest's martyrdom, which should have come at the height of the Chicago cataclysm, is instead displaced into the hazy future, where its impact is drastically diminished. Bluntly, if we are to take Ernest seriously, we need to see him die.[43]

With subtler art, with more careful novelistic construction, London might have turned a "minor revolutionary classic"[44] into a major one. Even the most sensitive of the Marxist critics descend at times to special pleading in their defense of a novel that London seems to have written too much out of his heart, too little out of his head. That disproportion is no doubt responsible for the most successful scenes, which depict a society's capacity for vindictive violence and injustice. Unfortunately, it is responsible also for the crippling flaws. In his next novel, *Martin Eden*, a proletarian hero would be presented with greater art.

7

Art and Alienation
Martin Eden

Throughout 1906, while *The Iron Heel* was in progress, London was also busy overseeing the building of his ketch, the *Snark*, in which he and his wife planned to make a seven-year voyage around the world. But the earthquake in April limited the availability of materials and labor, and it was not until April 23, 1907, after interminable frustrations and enormous expenses, that the *Snark* finally sailed through the Golden Gate—only to encounter even more "inconceivable and monstrous" difficulties during the passage to Hawaii.[1] A month later the vessel limped into Honolulu harbor, where London disembarked, settled in, and began grinding out travel sketches and short stories in an effort to recoup some of his losses. Not until early August did he begin the novel in which he would try to put in perspective the two strands of his career as a writer: the serious artist, contemptuous of the values of the marketplace; and the literary entrepreneur, struggling for commercial success before all else.[2] In mid-July, defending the publication of his tramp reminiscences in *The Road* (1907), he foreshadowed indirectly the backward glance he was about to take in *Martin Eden*. "I am still firm in my belief," he wrote, "that my

123

strength lies in being candid, in being true to myself as I am to-day, and also in being true to myself as I was at six, sixteen, and twenty-six. Who am I, to be ashamed of what I have experienced? I have become what I am because of my past.''[3]

Curiously, however, when he wrote this letter the new novel was not even in his mind. Nor apparently had he given it any thought during the outward voyage. On May 28, shortly after his arrival in Honolulu, he wrote to George Brett, pleading for an advance of $5000 and supporting his plea with a list of potential moneymaking book manuscripts completed, in progress, or projected.[4] Three finished manuscripts, he said, were already in Brett's hands, four others were in various stages of completion, and three more were planned, though two of these never materialized. Obviously London was pulling out all the stops, mentioning any book he might conceivably write in order to convince Brett that Macmillan could not lose by sending the money. Nowhere, however, does he so much as hint of *Martin Eden*, though he had every reason to do so if it had been even remotely in his mind. There was still no word of it as late as July 11, when he wrote to thank Brett for the advance.

Thus the impulse to write an autobiographical novel, based on his beginnings as a writer and his early infatuation with Mabel Applegarth, came upon him quite suddenly in late July. Yet the impulse was not new, for among his papers can be found several hints of what he came to call the "struggling writer idea." His Post-Klondike Notebook contains a note for a "Novel on Literary Struggles"; and two related sets of notes, almost certainly composed in 1902 or 1903 during a time of disillusionment with his first marriage, expand the idea in such a way as to foreshadow the main directions of *Martin Eden*. The first set, from the same notebook, emphasizes the gradual destruction of love and artistic idealism by a crassly materialistic society:

Goes into the world—the gradual loss of his art and prostitution of his talent to meet present literary demands, insensibly this works on his ideals and he sees the horny side too much; becomes cynical, pessimistical; her daughter; he loves her; some of their correspondence, she is troubled to see how strained in soul he is, and begs him to not grow bitter (some sort of a misunderstanding arises)[;] his bitter responses; she loves him[,] tries to bring out the best in him. The misunderstanding (no sympathy, he believes)[;] lapse of several years—more than successful but marries the wrong woman. Revisits mountain home again—the passion, he falls face down on Eagle Peak, where he had stood years before with her mother; the truth unveils as it did before, clarified vision, he sees it all—she shows up at this juncture in the hour of her weakness, would surrender all, but his real self is awakened, breaks the bonds, he will not [resume the affair] (though he is astounded at it[)]; reversal of positions, he counsels. We will get rid of his wife somehow.[5]

Next, a roughly contemporary set of notes, headed "Sociological Study," stresses the artist's early struggle with poverty and isolation:

An efficient, rising from the dregs—with all the bitterness. And after all, is it worth the candle? Show the rectitude of purpose of the man—the bitter, bitter struggle—the empty success—remember Grant Allen's advice to the young literary aspirant.

How, looking about him, he chose ultimate instead of immediate happiness.

Burned the midnight oil—shut his ears to sounds of joy—lived an anchorite's existence in the midst of the city's pleasures. Liked pleasure, but crucified himself that he might later have greater pleasure. The isolation he suffered during the struggle—the isolation when success was obtained.

How causeless his suicide seemed to his friends and colleagues. Nobody could understand. There was no reason.

He marries, but not from love. Affection, only, for wife who was good, and affection, only, for the children.

In youth had loved. Meager circumstances had caused him to put the temptation from him. Girl becomes woman and goes on the town. Once, at latter end of her career, a tragic meeting occurs between them (very tragic). Woman in prison, suffers life-imprisonment for some murder in which she was accessory to the fact. It is sometime after this that he deliberately commits suicide.

One further set of notes, of later vintage, is a "PLOT FOR PLAY / TRAGEDY," in which London carries some of the same motifs closer to their final form in the novel:

The struggling writer idea, only make it poetry—perhaps, after all, make it a short-story-writer, or an essayist.
First act—
Splendidly enthusiastic—his attic—landlord demanding rent.
Returned manuscript brought in by landlord (maybe letter-carrier), —Bills, duns.
Feels for watch—in soak [i.e., at the pawnshop]. Typewriter in soak. Overcoat in soak.
Have him cooking some potatoes (nothing more to eat). Also dressed in rags.
Visitors—the Uncle, rich, who will not tolerate his writing, but will give him a good job; otherwise will not allow him to come to his house.
Girl he loves, also does the same, that is, advises him to go to work. Will have nothing to do with him otherwise.
Friend, who advises him to go to work.
SECOND ACT,—complete success. Culmination of success, in love, in everything.
Love-scene—"But why do you love me?"
She talks [of] his fame, etc.
"I am unchanged. All that I have written was already written then—why, why?"
Uncle cannot do too much for him, cannot have him at the house too much. Money, presents, etc.,—but *why*, he demands. . . .
THIRD ACT,—the last scene with the girl he loves, in which he is strangely cold, or else desires to break off the engagement.

Following this scenario, three more pages of notes fill out further details of character and action. The first act was to show the young writer "afire with beauty and the noblest throes of creation," convinced that "everything glorious" lay in the "upper strata of society to which he intends fighting his way." His "stormy youth" would be invoked, "all pitiful and sordid; say a ranch life, or slum life—self-education, etc., etc.,—never the right kind about him, the kind he dreamed of having about him." Toward the end he would encounter a "tramp, a philosopher. Neat and cynical wit of tramp. All drink. He pals with tramp; asks tramp's ambition. Tramp answers, 'Drink,' etc., nothing in women and children nor fight nor fame." The last scene was to end with a toast to the tramp, "Then poison. Dies."

A comparison of these three sets of notes reveals London's gradual refinement of the "struggling writer idea." Each set deals with the clash between an idealistic young writer and an uncomprehending philistine world, and in each case his artistic ambitions are complicated by his love for a young woman. The two earliest plots include versions of London's ill-fated first marriage, though by the time he outlined the plot for the play, that episode had been dropped, along with the plan for a melodramatic climax involving a murder. Two of the plots, including that of the play, end with the protagonist's suicide. The plot for the play, in fact, contains so many elements of *Martin Eden* that it can be considered a transitional draft, standing halfway between the early notes and the final novel. The clearest indication of the transition lies in the character referred to in the play as the rich uncle, "who will not tolerate his writing, but will give him a good job; otherwise will not allow him to come to his house." A vestige of this figure remains in London's initial cast of characters for *Martin Eden*, which includes the "Heroes Uncle [*sic*], Joshua Eden in business firm of Eden & Horsley." At this point the cast also includes Martin's sister, Mrs. Bernard Higginbotham, but not Higginbotham himself. Eventually London dropped the rich uncle altogether, shifting his traits and actions to Higginbotham, who, like the uncle of the play, is contemptuous of Martin's writing, offers him a steady job, forbids him the house when he gains newspaper notoriety, then fawns on him when he becomes successful. The play also contains the germ of Russ Brissenden in the character of the philosophical tramp, who at this point is modeled on London's socialist friend Frank Strawn-Hamilton; and there are suggestions of the hotel room scene in chapter 45 where Martin rebuffs Ruth's move for a reconciliation. A version of that scene also appears in one of the earlier sets of notes above, in which the girl seeks out the protagonist "in the hour of her weakness" and "would surrender all, but his real self is awakened [and] breaks the bonds.".

Thus, once London had decided in late July of 1907 to shape these ideas into a novel, he had behind him nearly a decade of reflections on his early love affair and his struggle for success as a writer. In his voluminous working notes,[6] he sketched characters and scenes, tried out bits of dialogue, and at a fairly early stage set down the following cast of characters:

Hero	Martin Eden
Girl	Ruth Morse
Heroes Uncle	Joshua Eden in business firm of Eden & Horsley
Heroes Sister:	Gertrude Eden
Married sister	Mrs. Bernard Higginbotham
	Marian "

Obviously he soon made some changes in the minor characters. The uncle, Joshua Eden, as I noted earlier, dropped out and was replaced by Bernard Higginbotham, who in the novel is married to Gertrude, not to Marian. At some point London decided to provide Marian with a different husband, Hermann von Schmidt, so that Martin could suffer the hostility of two brothers-in-law instead of one. Gertrude and Marian appear to have been modeled partly on London's own step-sisters, Eliza and Ida.[7]

Other subordinate characters were added elsewhere in the notes. Charles Butler, the successful drudge who serves Martin as a cautionary example, is mentioned briefly, and so is the Portuguese landlady, though she is not yet named Maria Silva. Lizzie Connolly appears several times, and London sketches in considerable detail the cynical esthete who in the novel would be named Russ Brissenden but in the notes is referred to only as George. London more than once acknowledged that Brissenden was modeled chiefly on

George Sterling; but though he had used the actual names of living persons for Martin Eden and Lizzie Connolly, it seems improbable that he ever intended to do so for a figure as well known as Sterling. More likely, he had simply not yet decided on an appropriate fictional name.

Martin Eden, as London was fond of stating, was a version of himself. Yet he took many liberties with the facts of his own life, rearranging some events, omitting others, and compressing the highlights of twelve years into the period of less than three years that separates Martin's first meeting with Ruth from his suicide. He increases the intellectual distance between Martin and Ruth by omitting his semester of college; and for the Klondike gold rush that had interrupted his courtship of Mabel Applegarth, he substitutes an eight-month treasure-hunting voyage to the South Seas. In the novel, less than two years intervenes between Martin's decision to become a writer and the zenith of his career when he has two best sellers in print at once, whereas London required six years after his return from the Klondike in 1898 to achieve the consecutive successes of *The Call of the Wild* and *The Sea-Wolf.* The brief months of depression between Martin's sudden success and his suicide are a telescoped version of London's "long sickness" and the maddening frustrations during the building of the *Snark.* The end of the novel then comes quite literally up to the present, since the description of Martin lowering himself out of the porthole of the *Mariposa* was written immediately after London's return to Tahiti on the same vessel. Though London himself did not slide out that porthole, his depiction of Martin's depression reflects his own state of mind during the return voyage.[8]

Both as an autobiographical novel and as London's most self-consciously literary novel since *The Sea-Wolf, Martin Eden* partakes of two well-established modes of fiction: the novel of success and the novel of education. Though these two patterns often coexist, they need to be distinguished, for they represent the two strands of London's own divided life, which are nicely suggested by London's original title: "Success." The title is ironic, in the manner of *The Rise of Silas Lapham* or *The Education of Henry Adams*.[9] It implies a contrast between the kind of success defined by the marketplace and the kind born of a rebellious creative spirit. According to the latter standard, Martin does succeed, yet his inability to escape the definition of success imposed on him by his society prevents him from savoring his achievement. Increasingly, he internalizes the chasm between financial and artistic success, until at last he is a helplessly divided being, vulnerable to ironies and insults that a healthier mind would deflect. To say this, of course, is to suggest that the novel is fundamentally coherent and its ending both comprehensible and inevitable.

As an ironic novel of success, *Martin Eden* inverts the formula popularized in the fiction of Horatio Alger, Jr. London distills the pluck-and-luck, rags-to-riches story of the Alger hero into the exemplary figure of Charles Butler, who becomes one of the touchstones of Martin's divided life (his opposite being the decadent poet Russ Brissenden). The orphaned son of a consumptive bank cashier, Butler goes to work in a printing office and rises from a salary of $3 a week to one of $30,000 a year. Denying himself "the enjoyments that most boys indulge in" and saving every week out of his meager salary, he works in the daytime and goes to school in the evening, his eyes "fixed always on the future."[10]

The chief proponent of this version of success is Ruth Morse, who discovers in Martin a rough diamond whom she hopes to cut and polish into a fit ornament of her upper-middle-class society. Or, to alter the metaphor, she is a female Pygmalion: "He was clay in her hands immediately, as passionately desirous of being moulded by her as she was desirous of shaping him into the image of her ideal of man" (84). Correcting his grammar and polishing his manners, she urges on him the bourgeois virtues of "renunciation, sacrifice, patience, industry, and high endeavor . . . such abstractions being objectified in her mind by her father, and Mr. Butler, and by Andrew Carnegie, who, from a poor im-

migrant boy had arisen to be the book-giver of the world"
(162-63).[11] She shared the "comfortable middle-class feeling that poverty was salutary, that it was a sharp spur that
urged on to success all men who were not degraded and
hopeless drudges" (209).

Ruth's account of Mr. Butler impresses Martin, but it also
disheartens him. Though he sincerely acknowledges that
Butler is a "great man," something in the story jars his
sense of life: "He could not find an adequate motive in Mr.
Butler's life of pinching and privation. Had he done it for
love of a woman, or for attainment of beauty, Martin would
have understood. God's own mad lover should do anything
for the kiss, but not for thirty thousand dollars a year. He
was dissatisfied with Mr. Butler's career. There was something paltry about it, after all. Thirty thousand a year was all
right, but dyspepsia and inability to be humanly happy
robbed such princely income of all its value" (74). Martin's
repudiation of Butler shocks Ruth, making it clear to her
that "more remodelling was necessary" (74). But for Martin
the Butler story holds a more bitter irony. Though his motives—love of woman and love of beauty—will be different,
he will fall inexorably into the pattern of Butler's meager
life until, trapped by the bourgeois values he has striven to
reject, he succumbs to the fate he had scorned in Butler:
spiritual nausea and human alienation rob his princely income, and even his highest art, of all value.

As an ironic success story, *Martin Eden* has further affinities with such novels as Howells's *The Rise of Silas Lapham*
(1885), Norris's *McTeague* (1899), and Dreiser's *Sister Carrie* (1900), in each of which the protagonist's social and economic advancement comes into conflict with alternative
values. Lapham's moral rectitude forces him to choose
bankruptcy rather than enter into a shabby financial conspiracy; McTeague discovers that his marriage to the mi-
serly Trina has estranged him from the simple pleasures of
his former life; and Carrie Meeber's success as an actress is
tarnished by her awareness that money has not relieved her
poverty of spirit. Though Martin Eden's quest is never

merely for money, he is dragged down when his struggle toward an ideal realm of love and beauty becomes entangled with the values of the marketplace.

In the early chapters London handles deftly the kind of social comedy he seldom attempted with any success.[12] Encountering the formal rituals of the Morses' dining room, Martin resembles the terror-stricken Silas Lapham on his first visit to the Coreys. Much as Silas suffers a last-minute panic over his gloves, Martin "did not know what to do with his cap" and is at the point of "stuffing it into his coat pocket" when Arthur comes to his rescue by taking it for him. Attempting to negotiate a cluttered drawing-room, he is grotesquely out of his element:

The wide rooms seemed too narrow for his rolling gait, and to himself he was in terror lest his broad shoulders should collide with the doorways or sweep the bric-a-brac from the low mantel. He recoiled from side to side between the various objects and multiplied the hazards that in reality lodged only in his mind. Between a grand piano and a centre-table piled high with books was space for a half a dozen to walk abreast, yet he essayed it with trepidation. His heavy arms hung loosely at his sides. He did not know what to do with those arms and hands, and when, to his excited vision, one arm seemed liable to brush against the books on the table, he lurched away like a frightened horse, barely missing the piano stool. (1)

At the dinner table, his shirt is soon "wet with sweat from the exertion of doing so many unaccustomed things at once." He must learn to "handle strange tools, to glance surreptitiously about and learn how to accomplish each new thing." Worst of all, he must cope with the servant, "an unceasing menace, that appeared noiselessly at his shoulder" to propound "puzzles and conundrums demanding instantaneous solution" (15). Throughout this scene London is firmly in control, preserving exactly the right distance, permitting us to sympathize with Martin's plight even as we smile at it, but denying us the more extreme reactions of pity or contempt.

Equally effective is the ensuing scene at the Higginboth-ams', which resembles the early episode in which Dreiser's Carrie Meeber must endure the drab apartment of her sister and sullen brother-in-law, who tolerate her presence for the sake of the board she pays while frowning on the slightest expense for pleasure.[13] But London goes beyond Dreiser in sketching the tawdry details of the Higginbothams' world, and in doing so he makes clear the nature of Martin's revulsion from it. After his first visit to the Morses, Martin reacts with disgust to the people, places, and habits that he had previously accepted without offense; and at first his reactions betray a new class-consciousness. The illusion of Ruth's ethereal purity causes him to take a less flattering view of the young women in his own class: "now it seemed to him that they had always reached out and dragged at him with vile hands. This was not just to them, nor to himself. But he, who for the first time was becoming conscious of himself, was in no condition to judge, and he burned with shame as he stared at the vision of his infamy" (34). The melodramatic language successfully sets the reader at a distance from Martin here; nor are we in doubt of London's awareness that invidious class distinctions underlie Martin's appreciation of the loveliness of Ruth's hand in contrast with his own "calloused palm" with its "dirt that was ingrained in the flesh itself."

Yet Martin cannot deny his understanding of why this difference exists: "He was used to the harsh callousness of factory girls and working women. Well he knew why their hands were rough; but this hand of [Ruth's] . . . It was soft because she had never used it to work with. The gulf yawned between her and him at the awesome thought of a person who did not have to work for a living. . . . He had worked himself; his first memories seemed connected with work, and all his family had worked. There was Gertrude. When her hands were not hard from the endless housework, they were swollen and red like boiled beef, what of the washing." He recalls the "hard palms of his mother as she lay in her coffin" and the "horned growth" on his father's hands, "half an inch thick when he died." At the memory of the calloused hands of Margey, the factory girl in the East End of London, "a great wave of pity welled over him. He saw her yearning, hungry eyes, and her ill-fed female form which had been rushed from childhood into a frightened and ferocious maturity; then he put his arms about her in large tolerance and stooped and kissed her on the lips" (36–37). Though these passages are not without some sentimentality and Dreiserian awkwardness ("what of the washing"; "her ill-fed female form"), they also share Dreiser's poignance and integrity—a profound understanding of the material yearnings of those condemned to dreary lives, coupled with an awareness that the world they desire is as banal as the one it would replace.

Thus Martin's reaction is scarcely at all the snobbery of the *arriviste*, who spurns the people whose poverty he has recently fled. After his first reflex of distaste, Martin is never again ashamed of his antecedents—never despises the poor for their poverty. When he takes Maria Silva and her children to buy them a Christmas treat of new shoes and candy-canes, he encounters Ruth and her mother, who are shocked to find him "at the head of that army of Portuguese ragamuffins." Ruth's "passionate, angry tears" half convince him that "he had been a brute, yet in the soul of him he could not see how or why. It never entered his head to be ashamed of those he knew" (308).

Indeed, Martin's revulsion from poverty, though not wholly untainted by the class-consciousness of the Morses, is primarily esthetic. Freshly dazzled by the beauty of Ruth and her world, he returns to the Higginbothams' to be struck most of all by its dinginess and nerve-shattering cacophony. The chromo on the wall, which he "had always liked," now seems "cheap . . . like everything else in this house" in contrast to "the house he had just left," where "he saw, first, the paintings, and next, Her," Ruth, the very symbol of the ideal beauty he yearns toward (29). Back in his room, his ear is offended by the "screeching" of his bedsprings and his eye by the "dirty brown" stains on the walls; but he blots out this "befouled background" by conjuring up a vision of Ruth, repeating her name over and over, amazed that "a simple sound could be so beautiful. It delighted his ear" (33). The next morning he awakens from his "rosy" dreams of Ruth to be greeted by raw sensory squalor, "a steamy atmosphere that smelled of soapsuds and dirty clothes, and that was vibrant with the jar and jangle of tormented life. As he came out of his room he heard the slosh of water, a sharp exclamation, and a resounding smack as his sister visited her irritation upon one of her numerous progeny. The squall of the child went through him like a knife." Here the "very air" is "repulsive and mean," so different from the atmosphere of "beauty and repose" at the Morses'. Martin is drawing not so much a crude social distinction as a contrast between the "spiritual" and the "meanly material" (39).

Throughout the novel, but especially in the first half, London frequently displays the novelist's special gift for the telling descriptive phrase. Bernard Higginbotham, for example, is deftly summed up by his "beady eyes, sneering, truculent, cowardly . . . the same eyes when their owner was making a sale in the store below" (29). Martin's fellow boarder, Jim, is "a plumber's apprentice whose weak chin and hedonistic temperament, coupled with a certain nervous stupidity, promised to take him nowhere in the race for bread and butter" (41). Or there is Martin's sister, whose nature "seemed taking on the attributes of stale vegetables, smelly soapsuds, and of the greasy dimes, nickels, and quarters she took in over the counter of the store" (40).

An especially poignant piece of social comedy occurs after Martin's first visit to the Morses', when he goes to the public library in search of the passwords to this strange new life but instead finds himself intimidated by the towering stacks, the very embodiment of the barriers of class that conspire to keep him out. As he ventures in, "from every side the books seemed to press upon him and crush him" (43). He searches out the books on etiquette, for "his mind was vexed by a simple and very concrete problem: *When*

*you meet a young lady and she asks you to call, how soon
can you call?* was the way he worded it to himself. But when
he found the right shelf, he sought vainly for the answer. He
was appalled by the vast edifice of etiquette, and lost himself in the mazes of visiting-card conduct between persons
in polite society" (44). The library, both a maze and a closed
edifice, is a bastion of upper-class culture, withholding from
the outsider the key to its inner recesses.

This comedy of manners, though especially prominent in
the early chapters, occurs intermittently throughout the
book—occurs, that is, whenever London detaches himself
sufficiently from Martin's inner life to view in broader perspective the sparks struck by the clash between a settled,
complacent society and an upstart candidate for admission.
Once separated from the Morses, for example, Martin can
casually but acutely observe "the beautiful things that
women wear when they do not have to do their own laundry-
ing" (150). In a later chapter, London makes good comedy of
Martin's brash attack on professors of English and Ruth's
horrified reaction to the sacrilege. "The science professors
should live," Martin grandly declares. "They're really
great. But it would be a good deed to break the heads of nine-
tenths of the English professors—little, microscopic-minded
parrots!" This, the narrator comments with mild irony, was
"rather severe on the professors, but . . . to Ruth [it] was
blasphemy. She could not help but measure the professors,
neat, scholarly, in fitting clothes, speaking in well-modu-
lated voices, breathing of culture and refinement, with this
almost indescribable young fellow. . . . They at least earned
good salaries and were—yes, she compelled herself to face it
—were gentlemen; while he could not earn a penny" (203–
4). Ruth's confusion of values thus defines the world that
Martin increasingly rejects—the world in which a "professor" is defined by the accoutrements of class rather than the
attainment of knowledge.

Ruth herself is one of the novel's most successful characterizations. London's scathing yet not wholly pitiless dissection of her gentility is essential to the success of the

novel and has not been sufficiently praised.[14] Though necessarily a type, she is no caricature. Hardly the vapid, insipid
creature that some readers have found her, she is not unin-
telligent, nor does she lack a certain force of will, an inclina-
tion (up to a point) to assert herself in mild yet effective defiance of parental and social opposition. Yet her attraction
to Martin and her determination to marry him is based
purely on unexamined and uncomprehended emotion, not
at all on a critical scrutiny of the society and values to
which Martin has momentarily drawn her into opposition.
Those values, deeply rooted and complacently accepted, re-
impose their sway at last, making her final act of pretended
rebellion—her offer of herself in "free love" (396)—a trav-
esty of mature independence, for while making her bold leap
she has surreptitiously brought her brother along as a safety
net.

Ruth's name, surely, was chosen with some care, for Martin pointedly repeats it over and over, finding it "a talisman,
a magic word to conjure with" (33). London must have had
in mind the familiar biblical passage in which Ruth says to
her mother-in-law, Naomi, "whither thou goest, I will go;
and where thou lodgest, I will lodge: thy people shall be my
people, and thy God my God" (Ruth 1:16). In *The Iron Heel*,
Avis had echoed these words when pledging her devotion to
Ernest and her willingness to abandon her own class (108).
In *Martin Eden* the echo is ironic: unlike the biblical prototype, Ruth Morse will not, finally, commit herself unreserv-
edly to a new mode of life. Up to a point (to shift the biblical
parallel), she plays Eve to Martin's Adam, offering him (he
thinks) a forbidden knowledge that is the sum of all beauty
and truth. In his disillusionment, he sadly recognizes that
the only knowledge she can provide is the kind that eluded
him earlier at the library: the key to the "visiting-card conduct" of "polite society."

Martin Eden, then, represents London's first attempt at a
novel of manners since the early failure in *A Daughter of the
Snows*, and the great superiority of the later book is a measure of the advancement of his art in the intervening seven

years. Yet for all his success in portraying the minor persons
and places that are the stock-in-trade of the realist's art, he
does not share the realist's frequent penchant for massive
documentation of the external world. With the rare exception of the laundry episode, he does not include lengthy
genre scenes such as Norris's opening depiction of the buzz
of activity on Polk Street in *McTeague* or the accounts of
the wheat harvest and rabbit roundup in *The Octopus*.[15] Nor
does he share Wharton's fascination with the decoration of
interiors or Dreiser's inexhaustible interest in the para-
phernalia of middle-class success. Instead, his descriptions
are briefer and more functional, more directly related to the
inner life of the protagonist. For it is the unfolding consciousness of Martin Eden that is at the center of the novel
and makes the final choice of title an apt one. And most of
all, Martin's consciousness is that of an artist.

Before he ever writes a line, Martin responds to the world
with extraordinary imagination, and this innate artistic sensibility governs the first phase of his creative life. The second phase results from his increasing interest in ideas and
his wider reading, which drives him to formulate a new artistic credo. While this development is taking place, London
also probes Martin's artistic motivation, especially the conflict between his devotion to pure art and his need to survive
in the workaday world. A final phase then involves Martin's
total disillusionment with art and his decision to write no
more. The reasons for that development and its effective-
ness as an ending have been widely debated and will require
careful examination.

As a novel of the education of an artist, *Martin Eden* has
its closest affinities with Hardy's *Jude the Obscure* (1895),
which he read and praised in 1900, and with Lawrence's
Sons and Lovers (1913), which he hailed in fulsome terms
soon after it was published.[16] In each of these novels, a
young man strives to burst the prison of working-class
status in order to attain an ideal realm of beauty and truth,
and each novel dramatizes the conflict between such ideals

and the demands of sexual passion. In some ways even closer to *Martin Eden* is Melville's *Pierre* (1852), which London probably had not read but which deals with a young artist driven to suicide by much the same internal conflict that destroys Martin.

From the beginning, Martin is "keenly sensitive" to beauty. So intense is his craving that London resorts to metaphors of hunger and thirst. As Martin enters the Morses' house, his eyes "drank in the beauty" of the interior (2); and seeing a book of poetry on the table, he is like "a starving man at sight of food" (3). Music affects him "like strong drink" (22), and when he first reads Spencer he becomes "drunken with comprehension" (108). Similarly, as hunger and thirst signal the craving for beauty, the physical sense of taste is associated with Martin's acquisition of more discriminating esthetic standards. Eating, he discovers at the Morses', is not merely a "utilitarian function" but also "aesthetic" and "intellectual" (16); and he soon applies this new realization to his friend Jim in a fine comic scene at the Higginbothams'. As Jim rambles on about last night's binge, Martin is "oppressed by the utter squalidness" of his banalities at the same time that he rebels at the taste of the "cold, half-cooked oatmeal mush" (41). His existence, he finds, does not "taste good in his mouth" (43). Later, London uses the same phrase for Martin's revolt from the drudgery of the laundry (152); and like Norris's McTeague, he loses his taste for steam beer, discovering at the Bricklayers' picnic that his former mode of life is now "distasteful": "as the steam beer had tasted raw, so their companionship seemed raw to him" (363). Socially, Martin never loses his allegiance to his own class; esthetically, he can't go home again.

But while his craving for beauty is rooted in the sense of taste, his esthetic perceptions are more often visual: it is Martin's *eyes* that drink in the beauty of the Morse home; it is the *sight* of books that makes him feel like a starving man. When he picks up one of the books and is struck by the poetry of Swinburne, he exclaims that this poet truly "had eyes'' and had certainly ''seen color and flashing light'' (3–4). At the Morses' dinner table, as he tells of an adventure at sea, he is ''lost in the joy of creating, in making life as he knew it appear before his listeners' eyes.'' In thus developing Martin's unconscious artistic credo, London seems to have recalled Conrad's celebrated dictum, in the preface to *The Nigger of the Narcissus,* that the duty of the artist is above all to make us see,[17] for Martin ''saw with wide eyes, and he could tell what he saw. . . . He communicated his power of vision, till they saw with his eyes what he had seen. He selected from the vast mass of detail with an artist's touch, drawing pictures of life that glowed and burned with light and color'' (20). Two years later, working on his ambitious sea novel, ''Overdue,'' Martin remarks proudly to himself that there is ''only one man who could touch it . . . and that's Conrad'' (318).

Throughout the novel, but especially in the early chapters, London pays minute attention to Martin's visual perceptions, describing how they originate in his mind and achieve formal embodiment. The psychological process is the familiar one of association; and even before Martin becomes a conscious artist, he exhibits merely a more intense version of a process common to all: ''He was extraordinarily receptive and responsive, while his imagination, pitched high, was ever at work establishing relations of likeness and difference.'' When Arthur Morse addresses him as ''Mr. Eden,'' the unexpected courtesy triggers a chain of recollections: ''His mind seemed to turn, on the instant, into a vast camera obscura, and he saw arrayed around his consciousness endless pictures from his life, of stokeholes and forecastles, camps and beaches, jails and boozing-kens, fever-hospitals and slum streets, wherein the thread of association was the fashion in which he had been addressed in those various situations'' (4). Much later, after Martin has developed this natural talent into a source of conscious artistry, the underlying process of association is still spontaneous:

Martin's trick of visioning was active as ever. His brain was a most accessible storehouse of remembered fact and fancy, and its contents seemed ever ordered and spread for his inspection. Whatever occurred in the instant present, Martin's mind immediately presented associated antithesis or similitude which ordinarily expressed themselves to him in vision. It was sheerly automatic. . . . Just as Ruth's face, in a momentary jealousy, had called before his eyes a forgotten moonlight gale, and as Professor Caldwell made him see again the Northeast Trade herding the white billows across the purple sea, so, from moment to moment, not disconcerting but rather identifying and classifying, new memory-visions rose before him, or spread under his eyelids, or were thrown upon the screen of his consciousness. (238)

This process, fundamental to the poetic imagination, also underlies one of the major innovations of the modern novel, the stream-of-consciousness. In technical brilliance, London does not approach a Joyce, a Proust, or a Faulkner; but in his concern with the reservoir of memory and the principle of association, he does anticipate their experiments.

Once the well of memory has yielded its pictures, Martin's mind assembles them in the manner of a montage or collage, projecting them on the "screen" of his imagination before translating them into words. London's metaphors for this process vary. At one point Martin's mind is a "camera obscura" (4), at another a "kaleidoscope" (13). Sometimes the effect is of a "portrait gallery" (5) or a "series of pictures" (28), at others a "palimpsest" of superimposed images (154). Always, however, the process is fundamentally the same: he sees "arrayed around his consciousness endless pictures from his life" (4), and he sees them in terms of "associated antithesis or similitude" (238). When for the first time he sees Ruth's mother, "a thousand pictures" of similar elegant ladies "began flashing before his eyes" (13), and the dinner table "became a background across which moved a succession of forecastle pictures" (14). The technique is almost cinematic. As he stares at the "befouled background" of the water-stained wall in his room, Ruth's face "shimmered before him, suffusing the foul wall with a golden radiance" (33); but soon the image on this screen dissolves into the face of the East End tenement girl Margey (37). Examples could be multiplied indefinitely, for Martin's nervous imagination is constantly at work assembling the images of his world, projecting his experience, like a continuous slide-show, on the walls of his mind.

One further extension of these framed images, both literally and figuratively, is the mirror. At times the mirror seems, like the screen, merely another metaphorical canvas on which Martin's mind paints the images of the outer world. Yet closer inspection reveals it to be not only the traditional mirror of mimetic art, the passive reflector of the outer world, but also a mirror of the mind, a window into the self. It is the purely fanciful, idealized "vision" of drifting with Ruth through a "world without end of sunlit spaces and starry voids" that convinces him of the "pitiful inadequacy of speech" and stirs in him "the desire to paint these visions that flashed unsummoned on the mirror of his mind" (89). The same inwardness appears in a later use of the metaphorical mirror, when Martin's vision is deadened by the toil of the laundry: "A black screen was drawn across his mirror of inner vision, and fancy lay in a darkened sickroom where entered no ray of light" (152).

At other times, however, Martin gazes at himself in a real mirror. There is, to be sure, a certain narcissistic compulsion in London's continual representation, in this novel and elsewhere, of faces and bodies indistinguishable from his own.[18] But here the mirror effectively signals some crucial points in Martin's psychological development. When Martin returns to his room after his first visit to the Morses, he looks in his mirror because "for the first time [he] was becoming conscious of himself":

He passed a towel over [the mirror] and looked again, long and carefully. It was the first time he had ever really seen himself. His eyes were made for seeing, but up to that moment they had been filled with the ever changing panorama of the world, at which he had been too busy gazing, ever to gaze at himself. He saw the head and face of a young fellow of twenty, but, being unused to such appraisement, he did not know how to value it. Above a square-domed forehead he saw a mop of brown hair, nut-brown, with a wave to it and hints of curls that were a delight to any woman, making hands tingle to stroke it and fingers tingle to pass caresses through it. But he passed it by as without merit, in Her eyes, and dwelt long and thoughtfully on the high, square forehead,—striving to penetrate it and learn the quality of its content. What kind of a brain lay behind there? was his insistent interrogation. What was it capable of? How far would it take him? Would it take him to her? (34).

Though Martin may seem to gaze all too lovingly at his square-domed forehead and nut-brown hair, the main thrust of the passage is inward. Just as he must wipe the superficial dirt from the mirror to see his face, he must "penetrate" his outer features to see the quality of his mind—a mind packed with impressions of the outer world but unacquainted with its own inner landscapes.

His next use of his mirror comes when he encounters Lizzie Connelly while he is accompanied by Ruth. The juxtaposition of the two young women dramatizes the cultural limbo he inhabits, for he has risen above Lizzie without reaching full equality with Ruth:

Who are you, Martin Eden? he demanded of himself in the looking-glass, that night when he got back to his room. He gazed at himself long and curiously. Who are you? What are you? Where do you belong? You belong by rights to girls like Lizzie Connolly. You belong with the legions of toil, with all that is low, and vulgar, and unbeautiful. You belong with the oxen and the drudges, in dirty surroundings among smells and stenches. There are the stale vegetables now. Those potatoes are rotting. Smell them, damn you, smell them. And yet you dare to open the books, to listen to beautiful music, to learn to love beautiful paintings, to speak good English, to think thoughts that none of your own kind thinks, to tear yourself away from the oxen and the Lizzie Connellys and to love a pale spirit of a woman who is a million miles beyond you and who lives in the stars! (104–5)

Once again Martin makes his social discriminations in esthetic terms, contrasting the "unbeautiful" smells and stenches with the "beautiful" music and painting. Yet what is at stake here is Martin's very identity. He no longer knows who he is or where he belongs. His awakened self-consciousness has torn his roots from his own class without firmly replanting them in the genteel world of the upper middle class, and he has thus been prepared for the later disintegration of his self and the loss of his will to live. His encounter with Spencer causes yet another reexamination. " 'You fool!' he cried at his image in the looking-glass. 'You wanted to write . . . and you had nothing in you to write about' " (110). Ten days later, at the nadir of his disillusionment, surrounded by a pile of returned manuscripts, he gazes again into the mirror, calling up the vision of his younger self and the fights with Cheese-Face. The memory gives him courage to renew his assault on the magazines.

The mirror, then, has three functions: it reflects mimetically the images of the outer world; it is a magic looking-glass on which arise spontaneously the fantasy-images out of Martin's mind; and it is the medium of self-examination, the reflector of Martin's inner life. It is, in a sense, both a mirror and a lamp, for Martin's mind is both observant (recording the outer world) and expressive (projecting the inner). Hence the images that flash onto the screen of his mind frequently imply a contrast between a beautiful illusion and some less enticing reality. As a conscious artist, he strives toward a compromise between the two; but unconsciously, emotionally, he is mortally wounded by the relentless destruction of the illusions that have sustained his will to live.

Martin's introduction to the conflict between the real and ideal comes, significantly, through a work of art: the oil painting in the Morses' home. From a distance the storm-tossed schooner is a thing of beauty. But its beauty is an illusion—a "trick," as Martin too negatively phrases it—for as he comes close to the painting, the "beauty faded out of the canvas" and he finds himself staring merely at "what seemed a careless daub of paint." Because he "did not know painting," he feels "indignation that so much beauty should be sacrificed to make a trick" (3). Later in the evening, his own mind recreates the same "trick," turning the arid abstractions of mathematics, and the "whole field of knowledge which they betokened," into "so much landscape," into "vistas of green foliage and forest glades, all softly luminous or shot through with flashing lights. In the distance, detail was veiled and blurred by a purple haze." Because the distance and haze blind him to the real "detail," he imagines that behind this purple haze lies "the glamour of the unknown, the lure of romance" (20).

For Martin, this intoxicating "lure of romance" is inseparable from the image of Ruth, for "straightway from the back of his consciousness rushed the thought, *conquering, to win to her, that lily-pale spirit sitting beside him.*" At this point Ruth seems to him not a real woman but a "glimmering vision" (20), an image—almost literally an icon—of transcendent beauty and truth, a figure out of books yet endowed with the qualities of plastic art:

Here was intellectual life, he thought, and here was beauty, warm and wonderful as he had never dreamed it could be. He forgot himself and stared at her with hungry eyes. Here was something to live for, to win to, to fight for —ay, and die for. The books were true. There were such women in the world. She was one of them. She lent wings to his imagination, and great, luminous canvases spread themselves before him, whereon loomed vague, gigantic figures of love and romance, and of heroic deeds for woman's sake—for a pale woman, a flower of gold. And through the swaying, palpitant vision, as through a fairy mirage, he stared at the real woman, sitting there and talking of literature and art. (8–9)

The irony of the last line is that he does *not* see the "real woman" through the "fairy mirage." What he sees is what Poe reveals in "To Helen": a woman whose beauty is transmuted by the mind into the "statue-like" and Psyche-like figure who inhabits the "Holy Land" of imagination. So en-

tirely does Martin's mind create this ideal figure that he actually describes her as the essence of created form, the divine word made flesh. Her "beautiful spirit" is no more
beautiful "than the flesh that gave it expression and form."
Yet her body is "more than the garb of her spirit. It was an
emanation of her spirit, a pure and gracious crystallization
of her divine essence" (25). Though Martin insists that the
love of a woman transcends even the love of art, it is of the
greatest importance to see that in his mind the woman he
loves *is* art, *is* beauty. He is scarcely without sexual desire,
but that desire is intensified, and, yes, purified, by being inextricably bound up with his Platonic longing for ideal
beauty. Thus London has in mind more than the stock Vic-
torian notion of a wayward man reformed by a good woman
when he tells us that the "very thought" of Ruth "ennobled
and purified" Martin (33), drawing out the streak of the "ascetic" (35) that complements his sensuousness. Small wonder that when his ideal image of Ruth fails, his devotion to
art soon follows.

One further evidence of Ruth's emblematic nature is the
recurrence of the metaphors of hunger and thirst. In one
sense hunger carries its usual association with sexual desire,
but here it suggests that sexual desire is but a part of the
larger craving for beauty. Martin "drink[s] in the pale
beauty of her face" (8) and seems "suddenly hungry" when
he notices that her laughter sounds like "tinkling silver
bells" (9). Soon afterward, stimulated by Ruth's piano playing, he is driven into a Dionysian frenzy of imaginative intoxication. Her music "was like strong drink, firing him to
audacities of feeling,—a drug that laid hold of his imagination and went cloud-soaring through the sky. It banished
sordid fact, flooded his mind with beauty, loosed romance
and to its heels added wings." But just as he "caught the
swing" of the rhythms, they "vanished away in a chaotic
scramble of sounds that was meaningless to him, and that
dropped his imagination, an inert weight, back to earth"
(22).

Martin's reaction to Ruth's music effectively illustrates

his imaginative conflict: his aspiration toward divine harmonies constantly runs afoul of earthbound dissonances—the "chaotic scramble" of "meaningless" sounds or, alternatively, a succession of "meaningless pictures" (188). The realist in him rebels against two kinds of nonrealistic attitudes. At times he adopts the antiromantic posture of Howells, sharing that critic's aversion to the melodramatic heightening of emotions and passions. After his dream of the fight with Cheese-Face, he mocks his own elevated emotions as a "bit of hysteria and melodrama" (138); and when he and Ruth attend the opera, he loves the music but protests against the "unrealities" of the acting, acknowledging that he is a "hopeless realist" (205).

A second source of his realism lies in his rejection of the genteel fastidiousness of the Morses and their class. In his early innocence, he defers to their presumably superior standards, blushing with embarrassment at the realization that "such sordid things as stabbing affrays were evidently not fit subjects for conversation with a lady" (7). But as he gradually acquires confidence, he sees that it is Ruth who is innocent of real life. She is blind to the sexual basis of her fascination with Martin because "her only experiences in such matters were of the books, where the facts of ordinary day were translated by fancy into a fairy realm of unreality" (68). When Martin writes an adventure story for boys, he reverses Ruth's priorities, preferring fact to fancy: "While his imagination was fanciful, even fantastic at times, he had a basic love of reality that compelled him to write about the things he knew" (79). But those "things" usually strike Ruth as "nasty" (124); and it is Martin's realization of the narrow limits of her taste, as well as the discovery that she is capable of sexual desire, that leads to the scene in which the cherry stain on her lips transforms her from an ineffable goddess into a palpable human being.

Martin's love of reality, however, does not prevent him from espousing a fundamentally romantic-expressive esthetic, which repeatedly presents the creative act as free, spontaneous, ecstatic, and ineffable. From the beginning he is impelled to burst the bonds of cautious, conventional language. Attempting to heed the Morses' standards of linguistic decorum, "he was oppressed by the consciousness that this carefulness of diction was . . . preventing him from expressing what he had in him," and his "love of freedom chafed against the restriction in much the same way his neck chafed against the starched fetter of a collar" (17). The creative spirit is "restive and urgent," so powerful that he becomes little more than a passive medium: "He was swiftly mastered by the concept or sensation in him that struggled in birth-throes to receive expression and form, and then he forgot himself and where he was, and the old words —the tools of speech he knew—slipped out" (18). In the familiar metaphor of generation and birth, Martin is the passive female, on whom the creative spirit begets the offspring that struggle in "birth-throes" toward "expression and form"; and he later thinks of his stories as his "children" (139). The creative spirit is associated with such elemental forces as flood and fire (20), and his helplessness before them causes him to resemble the traditional romantic symbol of the wind-harp: "He was a harp; all life that he had known and that was his consciousness was the strings; and the flood of music was a wind that poured against those strings and set them vibrating with memories and dreams." The whole process is "magic" (23).

Though this ecstatic "joy of creating" (20) is sometimes associated with his idealization of Ruth, it would be a mistake not to take it seriously, for although he later qualifies it, he never abandons it—not, at least, until he has given up writing altogether. When he begins to write verse, he seeks the "intangible and evasive something that he caught in all great poetry . . . the elusive spirit of poetry itself that he sensed and sought after but could not capture," though he was sometimes rewarded by catching "shreds of it and weaving them into phrases that echoed in his brain with haunting notes or drifted across his vision in misty wafture of unseen beauty. . . . He ached with desire to express and could but gibber prosaically as everybody gibbered" (92).

Discovering the "joy of creation that is supposed to belong to the gods," he experiences the transfiguration through which mundane realities dissolve into the higher reality of mind: "All the life about him—the odors of stale vegetables and soapsuds, the slatternly form of his sister, and the jeering face of Mr. Higginbotham—was a dream. The real world was in his mind, and the stories he wrote were so many pieces of reality out of his mind" (93). London's attitude toward such ecstasy, like his attitude toward Martin's worship of Ruth, is not without some gentle irony. Martin's delusion is the madness of insight—what Melville called the "sane madness of vital truth."[19]

Ultimately Martin seeks a compromise between his love of earthbound reality and his exalted romanticism. Though he adopts the Howellsian criterion of fidelity to real life as the basis for rejecting the melodramatic extremes of the opera, he will not go to the opposite extreme (also implicitly Howellsian) of embracing the merely commonplace. He is repelled by the vast body of magazine fiction with "no breath of life in it." Like Norris, he wants a more strenuous realism:

Life was so strange and wonderful, filled with an immensity of problems, of dreams, and of heroic toils, and yet these [magazine] stories dealt only with the commonplaces of life. He felt the stress and strain of life, its fevers and sweats and wild insurgences— surely this was the stuff to write about! He wanted to glorify the leaders of forlorn hopes, the mad lovers, the giants that fought under stress and strain, amid terror and tragedy, making life crackle with the strength of their endeavor. And yet the magazine short stories seemed intent on glorifying the Mr. Butlers, the sordid dollar-chasers, and the commonplace little love affairs of commonplace little men and women. (117)

Rejecting a tepid bourgeois realism, he struggles toward the red-blooded realism that can encompass life's "foulness as well as its fairness, its greatness in spite of the slime. . . . moral grandeur rising out of cesspools of iniquity" (125).[20]

Martin's special version of realism reflects his encounter

with scientific philosophy, especially that of Herbert Spencer, which drives him "from pitch to pitch of intellectual living" (108). Whereas he had previously "just accepted" beauty, he now feels that the "grass is more beautiful . . . now that I know why it is grass, and all the hidden chemistry of sun and rain and earth that makes it become grass" (120, 121). Later, though he admires Professor Caldwell's brilliance, he accuses him of "lack[ing] biology" (239); and his essay on the mysticism of the Maeterlinck school is "an attack from the citadel of positive science upon the wonder-dreamers, but an attack nevertheless that retained much of beauty and wonder of the sort compatible with ascertained fact" (246). The same combination governs his conception of his novel "Overdue," which would be a "rattling" tale of "adventure and romance" that would also deal with "real characters, in a real world, under real conditions" (317). It would be "true of its particular characters and its particular events" while at the same time telling, "thanks to Herbert Spencer," the "great vital things" that are true of "all time, and all sea, and all life" (318).

His encounter with Spencer also moves him to modify his earlier vision of the creative act as the spontaneous overflow of powerful feelings and to acknowledge the necessity of conscious craftsmanship. He can no longer "work blindly, in the dark, ignorant of what he was producing and trusting to chance and the star of his genius that the effect produced should be right and fine." Now he begins a story or poem with its form "already alive in his brain, with the end in sight and the means of realizing that end in his conscious possession." But he has not abandoned the earlier experience of creative ecstasy and wonder, for he still "appreciated the chance effects . . . that came lightly and easily into his brain. . . . Before such he bowed down and marvelled, knowing that they were beyond the deliberate creation of any man." He knows "from his Spencer" that he will never lose the fundamental sense of the "mystery of beauty" (197). By such steps as these he arrives at his mature artistic credo: he seeks "artistry" combined with "strength,"

"realism" imbued with the "fancies and beauties of imagination," an "impassioned realism" combining the "school
of god" and the "school of clod" (231, 232).

Implicit, I hope, in everything I have said about Martin's
development as a writer is the certainty that he is not a hack
but a true artist—one such as Emerson had in mind when he
distinguished those of mere "poetical talents, or of industry
and skill in metre," from the "true poet."[21] Yet there is still
a strong tendency on the part of some readers to define Martin's struggle for success as a quest for money and social
advancement, and to view him as having betrayed his artistic ideals.[22] London himself, it must be admitted, contributed to the confusion by asserting that if Martin had been a
socialist he would not have died,[23] driving some readers to
the fallacious conclusion that if Martin was not a socialist
he must have been a money-grubbing social climber. But
the issue of socialism is a red herring that has little or nothing to do with what really happens in the novel. Martin
himself says, "My desire to write is the most vital thing in
me" (273), and his statement should be taken quite literally. His creative energy is his vitalizing force: when it
burns out, he dies.

To put it this way does oversimplify—though I believe it
does not distort—Martin's complex motivation. Earlier I
tried to show that his social discriminations are characteristically more esthetic than economic, and that his idolizing
of Ruth is but the externalization of his larger craving for
beauty. His irresistible desire to shape his thoughts into
words is evident from the beginning, and his decision to
write stems directly from his South Sea voyage, on which
his imagination is fired by both his reading of Shakespeare
and his vision of the "exquisite beauty" of the world. Under
these influences, "the creative spirit in him flamed up . . .
and urged that he recreate this beauty for a wider audience
than Ruth" (76). Later, he is "oppressed by a sense of failure" when his writing is rejected—not because he will earn
no money, not even because his work fails to impress Ruth,

but because he himself comes momentarily to believe that "beauty and wonder had departed from him" (153).

Some have faulted Martin for abandoning serious art for magazine hack work, but his own attitude toward that writing is consistently contemptuous. To him it is merely "a means to an end": he intends to make enough money to eat and live, and eventually to marry Ruth; and to provide himself with the time to study and eventually to write the serious works he knows he is capable of. He does admittedly begin to sound like a confirmed hack when he asserts that the "income of a successful author makes Mr. Butler look cheap" and that a best seller "will earn anywhere between fifty and a hundred thousand dollars." But his words should be understood as part of his effort to convince Ruth that he must at all costs stick to writing rather than follow Mr. Butler into business, which he regards as "dull, and stupid, and mercenary, and tricky" (190). Though he acknowledges that the hack work, too, is "just so much dull and sordid plodding," he insists that at least it "keeps me in touch with things literary and gives me time to try bigger things" (189). It is better, he believes, than "going to sea again" or resorting to manual labor (187), which, as his laundry experience has shown him, leaves him no time or energy for any kind of writing at all. Better "hack-work and income first," he says—"masterpieces afterward" (189).

These are not mere rationalizations or empty expressions of good intentions. When a magazine promises him forty dollars for a cheap thriller, his first thought is that he is now free to abandon hack writing: "He would devote himself to work, good work, and he would pour out the best that was in him" (221).[24] Again he pins his faith on his "later work," striving to be "something more than a mere writer of magazine fiction" (231). When he discovers that a magazine is bowdlerizing his "Sea Lyrics," he writes "immediately," despite his desperate need for the money, "begging the editor to cease publishing the lyrics and to return them to him" (254). Later he rejects Ruth's suggestion that he become a reporter on the grounds that it would "spoil my style"

(265). Ruth asks the inevitable question: why wouldn't his style as easily be spoiled by hack work? But no, Martin insists, "the cases are different." The magazine fiction can be "ground out . . . at the end of a long day of application to style," while reporting is "all hack from morning till night . . . without thought of any style but reportorial style, and that certainly is not literature." Even so, he says, "every word" of his hack work is "a violation of myself, of my self-respect, of my respect for beauty" (266).

Even Martin's often-noted desire to rise to a higher social class evaporates in the light of his stronger desire to attain a classless realm of intellect and art. He wishes to rise to Ruth's class only so long as he believes that hers is a world of genuine culture. Nothing is more disappointing to him than the gradual realization that Ruth condemns his writing chiefly because he cannot "sell his wares" (204). She is incapable of valuing either him or his writing by any other standard than that of the marketplace, and that standard Martin contemptuously rejects—even after the magazines fill his pockets with dollars in an orgy of indiscriminate enthusiasm, gobbling up his worst as eagerly as his best. He comes to see *all* classes as prisoners of the same corrupting system, "his sister and her betrothed, all the members of his own class and the members of Ruth's class, directing their narrow little lives by narrow little formulas" (263). On Ruth's last visit to his room, he condemns the philistine "vulgarity" (394) of her and all her class, realizing that it was "an idealized Ruth he had loved. . . . The real bourgeois Ruth . . . he had never loved" (395).

For a time, as his belief in Ruth disintegrates, he keeps up his will to write through sheer momentum and through the hope that he can carry her to the heights with him. But as that hope flags, he is buoyed by up the appearance of Russ Brissenden, the decadent poet who serves as his artistic alter ego, sharing his contempt for the magazines and inspiring him with an example of Dionysian creative energy. Needless to say, Brissenden supplies what the Morses lack: the "flaming uncontrol of genius," the "living language" of a true poet (279). Like Martin, Brissenden is a combination of the ascetic and the voluptuary, yet he has gone beyond Martin in his fierce hunger for experience, his burnt-out life foreshadowing the direction of Martin's future. As many critics have observed, his socialistic inclinations—one cannot call them convictions—are feeble and meaningless, and their introduction is a lapse of judgment on London's part explicable only as wishful thinking, a vain hope that he could provide the novel with a socialist message. Brissenden cares for only two things, life and art; and he is rapidly losing his desire for the former. A wounded deer, he makes one last imaginative leap in his "Ephemera" and then dies. Martin, stung by the coincidence of Brissenden's suicide and (again the metaphor of "taste") the "nauseating" (345) vulgarity with which his poem is published, is driven another long step toward his own death, for at this point he ceases to write.[25]

For these reasons and others, there seems little justice in the view that Martin's suicide is insufficiently prepared for and inadequately motivated. Strong as was his inner compulsion to write, he had invested too much of that compulsion in two idealized figures, Ruth (a false ideal) and Brissenden (a true but fragile one). Disillusioned by the discovery that Ruth's vaunted culture is dessicated and meaningless, and that all of Brissenden's genius cannot sustain his will to live, Martin for the first time turns to ideals that are not associated with writing. At the Bricklayers' picnic, Lizzie Connolly provides him momentarily with a symbol of the natural beauty and vitality he has lost, but he recognizes that in his long pilgrimage toward intellect and art he has "exiled himself" (363) from her world. A more promising symbol is the golden world of the South Seas. Soon after Brissenden's death, Martin takes comfort from a vision of himself paddling a canoe in a lagoon beyond Tahiti in the "sweet land" of Papara. But the vision fades into the "disorder" of his "squalid" room: "He knew there was singing among the trees and that the maidens were dancing in the moonlight, but he could not see them. He could see only the littered writing-table, the empty space where the typewriter had stood, and the unwashed window-pane" (346, 347). Earlier the befouled wall of his room and his unwashed mirror had been magically cleared by the vision of Ruth and of his own face, eager for the challenges of life. Now the pane remains dark, his vision clouded by the failure of his illusions. At last he recognizes that even the South Seas are a chimera, which "charmed him no more than did bourgeois civilization" (404).

This final disillusionment is foreshadowed in his increasing desire for the relief of sleep, rest, oblivion. He is oppressed by the "grayness of life" (269) and by his recurrent "loneliness" (303), feelings that eventually give way to stronger notes of alienation, exile, and existential nausea. His reiterated protest against the world's failure to value him for "work performed," which Charles Child Walcutt has dismissed as a sophomoric whine, actually signals a deep inner distress.[26] On the more obvious level, it points to his disgust with a world that values art only after its price has been bid up by the marketplace. More disturbingly, it indicates a dangerous division within his own self, and a consequent loss of identity: "He drove along the path of relentless logic to the conclusion that he was nobody, nothing. Mart Eden, the hoodlum, and Mart Eden, the sailor, had been real, had been he; but Martin Eden, the famous writer, did not exist. Martin Eden, the famous writer, was a vapor that had arisen in the mob-mind and by the mob-mind had been thrust into the corporeal being of Mart Eden, the hoodlum and sailor" (386). Martin, it is true, has always felt these two selves within him, but only toward the end does his "real" identity threaten to be absorbed by the fictitious creation of the "mob-mind." He protests that he is "unable to associate his identity with those portraits" of himself in the magazines; he is not "that colossal appetite that all the mob was bent upon feeding" (386). It requires only a small twist of these words—*appetite, mob, feeding*—to catch the implication that Martin is playing an unwilling part in some terrifying ritual, in which the scapegoat figure of his public self is being symbolically devoured before his eyes.

The logic of the ending, then, is finally the logic of myth. Subtly invoked throughout the novel but more frequently toward the end are the myth of the dying god discussed by Frazer in *The Golden Bough* (1890; 1900) and the Dionysian prototype of the tragic hero described by Nietzsche in *The Birth of Tragedy* (1872; 1886). The rise and fall of the tragic hero-god is associated with the sun and hence with sexual energy and artistic creativity, and his death is a figurative return to the mother preceded by overtones of ritual sacrifice. For both Frazer's dying god and Nietzsche's Dionysus, the central event is the ritualistic dismemberment of the god by his society, which is solidified by its participation in the murder of the scapegoat and the communal feasting, actual or symbolic, on his body and blood.

Nietzsche's Dionysus is the artist as inspired seer, enchanted, ecstatic, intoxicated with creative energy that expresses itself in the frenzied music of the dithyramb. In his "paroxysms of intoxication the artistic power of all nature reveals itself to the highest gratification of the primordial unity." But Nietzsche goes on to describe the way this "rapture of the Dionysian state" annihilates the "ordinary bounds and limits of existence," creating a "chasm of oblivion" between the "worlds of everyday reality and of Dionysian reality." Nietzsche's description of the results of this clash is highly pertinent to the disillusionment of Martin Eden. When the "everyday reality reenters consciousness, it is experienced as such, with nausea: an ascetic, will-negating mood is the fruit of these states." As with Hamlet, "knowledge kills action; action requires the veils of illusion." In this state of spiritual nausea and paralysis, "no comfort avails any more. . . . Conscious of the truth he has once seen, man now sees everywhere only the horror or absurdity of existence." For the true Dionysian hero, it is at this point that "*art* approaches as a saving sorceress, expert at healing.''[27] Yet this source of renewal is precisely what Martin Eden cannot recover.

Martin's own moments of ecstatic inspiration, as I suggested earlier, are associated with Dionysian imagery of intoxication and music. The ultimate embodiment of such a state, however, is Brissenden's dithyrambic "Ephemera"—a "fantastic, amazing, unearthly thing." It is a "mad orgy of imagination, wassailing in the skull of a dying man who half sobbed under his breath and was quick with the wild flutter of fading heart-beats." The poem, Martin says, has "gone to my head. I am drunken with it" (304, 305). Yet the fate of Brissenden's poem, his surrogate self, is also the Dionysian one of dismemberment at the hands of the mob; and as such it is explicitly linked to the fate reserved for Martin. He is "the fad of the hour," the titanic "adventurer who had stormed Parnassus while the gods nodded. The hundreds of thousands read him and acclaimed him with the same brute non-understanding with which they had flung themselves on Brissenden's 'Ephemera' and torn it to pieces—a wolf-rabble that fawned on him instead of fanging him" (374).

Yet Martin will be fanged soon enough. Though he shrinks from his public self, insisting that he is "not that sun-myth that the mob was worshipping and sacrificing dinners to" (386), his very denial implies a terrified recognition of the sacrificial role he is destined to play. Throughout the novel, in fact, London has subtly implied the background of the seasonal cycle and hinted at Martin's identification with the energy of the sun. In one sense Martin is identified with the cycle of organic life, for his musings on the grass foreshadow the pattern of his own existence: the grass, he says, "has achieved its reason for existence. . . . It quickened with ambition under the dreary downpour of last winter, fought the violent early spring, flowered, and lured the insects and the bees, scattered its seeds, squared itself with its duty and the world, and—" (120). Yet just as, like the grass, he is quickened with ambition, he is also metaphorically sunlike, for "there was something cosmic in him. . . . The blaze of tropic suns was in his face" (69). As he reads one of his stories to Ruth, "she was warmed . . . not by the story, but by him," by the "excess of strength that seemed to pour from his body and on and over her" (126). Ruth, in contrast, is as "remote and inaccessible as a star" (37). In a moment of jealousy her laughter is "metallic," the light in her eyes "cold," reminding Martin of "a gale at night, with a clear sky and under a full moon, the huge seas glinting coldly in the moonlight" (229).

But what awaits the dying sun-god, like the tragic Dionysus, is the ritual of dismemberment. A full prefiguration of that fate occurs during Martin's dream of the childhood fight with Cheese-Face, a ritualistic ordeal that recalls Buck's fight with Spitz in *The Call of the Wild*. In his memory he sees "the ring of boys, howling like barbarians as he went down at last, writhing in the throes of nausea, the blood streaming from his nose and the tears from his bruised eyes" (130, 131). He survives this initial battle to fight again amid the "blood-lust" of the "crowd of brutes" (136), and he barely triumphs over his antagonist before sinking into "blackness and oblivion." At this point he is jolted out of his dream "like one from the dead" (137). Passing through this ritual of death and rebirth, he "arise[s] from the mud" to "thrust [his] shoulders among the stars." The memory of the ordeal renews his courage, and he vows to "lick the editors if it takes twice eleven years to do it in" (138).

But even as he does at last conquer the editors, he is moving toward the dismemberment that precedes his final passage into the western sea. He recalls the fate of Kipling, how the "world-mob, having read him and acclaimed him and not understood him in the least, had, abruptly, a few months later, flung itself upon him and torn him to pieces." Deluding himself with the belief that he will "fool the mob" and escape Kipling's fate, he determines to "be away, in the South Seas . . . catching sharks and bonitas" (402). Yet ironically, he has forecast his final dismemberment. He will not catch sharks and bonitas; it is they who will catch him. As he swims away from the *Mariposa*, a "bonita struck at his white body," and he finds that it had "taken a piece out" (410). As in the myths, the dismemberment signals the dispersal of the body to the elements, the penultimate turn of the cycle of life (Martin's death takes place in the winter) prior to regeneration in the spring.[28] In *Martin Eden*, however, no such regeneration occurs. Though the bonita seems to hint at the ongoing process of natural life, what Martin seeks and finds is surcease and oblivion.

Literally and figuratively, Martin is always a homeless orphan. His parents are dead, and he has "never found his permanent abiding-place," never really "taken root" (239). He moves from place to place, from his dingy rented room at the Higginbothams' to the claustrophobic cell at Maria Silva's and finally to even more impersonal quarters in the Hotel Metropole and the tiny stateroom on the *Mariposa*. As he realizes at the Bricklayers' picnic, he has "found no new home" and has no old one to return to (363). Small wonder that his increasing longing for rest and peace is presented as a longing for a return to the enfolding presence of the mother sea. He is "haunted by Longfellow's lines":

> The sea is still and deep;
> All things within its bosom sleep;
> A single step and all is o'er,
> A plunge, a bubble, and no more. (271)

When he is in such moods, even Ruth becomes not cold and distant but maternally nourishing and consoling. "I am more hungry for you," he declares, "than for food, or clothing, or recognition. I have a dream of laying my head on your breast and sleeping an aeon or so" (272). After at last making his reservation on the *Mariposa*, he goes to sleep "as gently as a child" (399), and he lowers himself out of the porthole into the "milky wash" of the sea (409).

Martin's suicide is thus no sudden whim. Prefigured in his earlier meditation on the lines from Longfellow, his death-wish emerges in full force in the stanza from Swinburne's "The Garden of Proserpine" which he reads on board the *Mariposa:*

> From too much love of living,
>   From hope and fear set free,
> We thank with brief thanksgiving
>   Whatever gods may be
> That no life lives forever;
> That dead men rise up never;
>   That even the weariest river
>   Winds somewhere safe to sea.

What moves Martin here is not an intuition of rebirth or even naturalistic dispersal but the consoling thought that "dead men rise up never." This thought remains "the one beneficent thing in the universe," a refuge from the "aching weariness" of life, a promise simply of "everlasting sleep" (409). Though Martin's passage through the porthole seems almost too obviously an image of rebirth, perhaps it is a mistake to see it as such. Martin is explicitly not reentering the world but leaving it. The porthole is the orifice of the womb, the door of the world, but Martin is passing through it backwards, returning to the dark womb of the maternal sea.[29]

But if Martin's suicide is the result of a long quest for peace, it is also an active rejection of the version of peace offered by the South Seas. When London sketched the novel in his notes, he worked out the ending thus:

Suicide
>   Maybe shot
>   "   poison
>   "   drowns himself ~~at sea~~
>   "   sails for Hawaii, & goes overboard
>   quietly some night
>   His thoughts of the old, care-free days—
>   But he could not go back to them.[30]

One of London's first thoughts, to have Martin poison himself, reflects the ending of the earlier "PLOT FOR PLAY." By the time he began making his notes for the novel, he naturally began to think of having Martin drown himself on the way to Hawaii, where the Londons were then residing. By February of 1908, however, when he actually wrote the final chapter, intervening events had caused the ending to crystalize in a somewhat different fashion.

The chief event involved one of London's reasons for making the *Snark* voyage in the first place: his boyhood infatuation with Melville's *Typee* (1846) and his consequent determination someday to visit the Marquesas. Hence Melville was much on his mind during the fall of 1907 as the writing of *Martin Eden* proceeded and the *Snark* made the two-month traverse to the Marquesas from Hawaii. He had brought with him on the voyage copies not only of *Typee* but also of *Omoo* (1847), *Moby-Dick*, and probably *White-Jacket* (1850);[31] and unsurprisingly, echoes of Melville turn up in *Martin Eden*. At one point Martin recalls a time when he jumped ship in the Hawaiian Islands, made his way over a rugged mountain ridge, and stumbled into an outlaw leper colony, where he remained captive for three months until a beautiful native girl helped him escape (227–28). London himself had climbed such a ridge near the leper colony on Molokai, but the more romantic details of the adventure parallel Melville's account of his captivity among the cannibals and his adventures with the beautiful Fayaway in *Typee*, which London had reread approximately two weeks before writing this passage.[32] A few pages later the chain of association surfaces once more when London gives the name Melville to a minor character attending a party at the Morses' (234).

Thus expectations were high when London anchored the *Snark* in the bay at Nukahiva on December 10 and prepared to retrace Melville's path over the ridge and down into the Typee Valley. But on reaching the valley, he was dismayed to discover that Melville's "garden" had become a "wilderness," an "abode of death," its few remaining inhabitants ravaged by disease. His disillusionment, recorded on the spot in a travel sketch called "Typee," also entered into the conclusion of *Martin Eden*.[33] Toward the end, Martin dreams not of a misty generality but of a specific place: "He knew a valley and a bay in the Marquesas that he could buy for a thousand Chili dollars. . . . It was filled with tropical fruits, wild chickens, and wild pigs, with an occasional herd of wild cattle, while high up among the peaks were herds of wild goats harried by packs of wild dogs. The whole place was wild. Not a human lived in it" (355). On the surface, what Martin describes is a tropical paradise, but on closer inspection it becomes only another landscape of alienation and defeat. Like the Typee that London had encountered, it is not a garden but a wilderness where, in an ominous echo of the imagery of dismemberment, the goats are hunted down by packs of wild dogs. And the land is devoid of human life; he would be utterly alone. Thus Martin anticipates the failure of his last ideal, thinking wearily that when he reaches Tahiti he will "have to order his trade-goods, to find a passage on a schooner to the Marquesas, to do a thousand and one things that were awful to contemplate." What he is heading for, he knows, is not the valley of a South Seas paradise but the "Valley of the Shadow" (408).

The last event, in which Martin summons a final act of will—the will to die—is one of the finest passages London ever wrote. Characteristically, however, when an interviewer remarked that the description of Martin's sensations while drowning was "highly imaginative," London disclaimed the tribute: "Not at all. I've been nearly drowned myself twice. I've taken anesthetics twice. The description of Martin Eden's sensations when he was dying is simply an account of my own sensations when I took an anesthetic modified by what my experience taught me of the feelings that come with drowning. There's no imagination necessary to do such a piece of writing. All that's necessary is experience and observation."[34] Though such belittling of his imagination was in part a familiar London pose, there is undoubtedly some truth to this account of how he created the drowning scene. Certainly, too, the inspiration for the precise method of the suicide—slipping out a porthole of the *Mariposa*—came to him only after he himself had embarked

on the same vessel shortly before the novel was completed.
But as he imagined Martin's long dive into the sea, he may
have had help from an unacknowledged resource: Melville's
climactic description of the fall from the yardarm in *White-
Jacket*. This passage, much praised by Melville critics, is a
crucial one because the protagonist's life, both physically
and psychologically, hangs in the balance. During his
plunge, White-Jacket has a strong premonition of death, until at the nadir of his descent he is brushed by "some inert,
coiled fish of the sea," at which point "the thrill of being
alive again tingled in [his] nerves, and the strong shunning
of death shocked [him] through." As he rises to the surface
and rips away his jacket, he is symbolically reborn.

Several of the images in *Martin Eden* recall those in Melville's episode. White-Jacket sees his ship in the darkness
"gliding by like a black world," whereas the *Mariposa*
"rushed past [Martin] like a dark wall" (410). White-Jacket
hears "a hum in [his] head, as if a hornet were there"; Martin hears "a buzzing in his head" (411). Beneath the sea,
White-Jacket finds himself amid a "soft, seething, foamy
lull. . . . Purple and pathless was the deep calm now around
me, flecked by summer lightnings in an azure afar."[35] Similarly, Martin "seemed floating languidly in a sea of dreamy
vision. Colors and radiances surrounded him," and in his
mind he sees a "flashing, bright white light" (411). Yet
what is important here is not so much these incidental parallels as the way London inverts Melville's meaning. White-
Jacket dives deep to emerge reborn, whereas Martin Eden
dives to his death. Both protagonists are jolted by the sudden touch of a fish, but they are jolted into opposite actions.
The "coiled fish" shocks White-Jacket with the "thrill of
being alive," moving him toward a "strong shunning of
death." But when a bonita strikes Martin Eden, it "reminded him of why he was there" (410). During his last
dive, he hopes the bonitas will not strike, for they "might
snap the tension of his will" to die. At the critical moment,
the bonitas refrain from touching him; and "grateful for this
last kindness of life" (411), Martin dives down to stay.

There is thus a rightness to this last act which London carefully prepares for and brilliantly realizes. Admittedly, compared with the first half, the pace of the last half of the book frequently slackens, and the prose throughout is woefully uneven. Charmian once observed that Jack "practically never writes of experiences while he is in the thick of them" but waits and "gains perspective and atmosphere through time."[36] That perspective is achieved in the early and middle chapters, when Martin is struggling to win Ruth and master his art. In the later chapters, as Martin's plight comes closer to that of the Jack London of 1907, the esthetic distance decreases and the artistic flaws multiply. At the gathering of amateur philosophers (chapter 36), at the Morses' dinner table (chapter 37), and at the socialist meeting hall (chapter 38), Martin surpasses even Ernest Everhard in his intellectual arrogance and sophomoric rant. In London's hands, an idea was rarely a surgical blade, nearly always a blunt instrument.

Yet such weaknesses, typical of most of London's full-length fictions, are amply compensated in this one. London himself declared that *Martin Eden* was his best novel,[37] and I believe it is that and more: it is the central document of his life as an artist. Having re-created in Martin the intensity of his own early artistic ambition, he then unsparingly portrays the spiritual desolation that follows when such ambition is lost. But the loss was Martin's, not London's. By purging his despair—by making Martin his scapegoat—London enabled his own creative impulse to survive. On February 24, 1908, Charmian recorded in her diary that Jack had finished the novel with Martin's suicide but that he was not depressed. No wonder he was not. Though in his life he continued to suffer pains beyond cure, in his art he knew he had done well. And though the ghost of his darker, nihilistic self would continue to haunt him to the end, he was on the threshold of a new affirmation, the return to the land, which would be tested in his next three major novels, beginning with *Burning Daylight*.

8

Three Frontiers
Burning Daylight

When London began *Burning Daylight*, he was headed for home. A few months earlier, in the winter of 1909, he had been forced to abandon the *Snark* voyage when constant exposure to the tropical sun caused his hands to swell fearfully and his skin to peel off in layers. After recuperating in an Australian hospital, he auctioned off the *Snark* for a fraction of its original cost and took passage on a Scottish freighter heading east. He began the new novel on the fifth of June, in Quito, Ecuador, where he and Charmian spent a month before returning to California. Though originally projected as a potboiling narrative of the adventures of a Klondike mining baron, it ultimately grew into a semiautobiographical account of a young man from the provinces who, like Martin Eden, reaches the pinnacle of success and then walks away from his achievement. Martin, more deeply disillusioned, had found his peace in sea; Elam Harnish, nicknamed Burning Daylight, finds love and bucolic tranquility in the Valley of the Moon. Thus both novels mark London's imagined valedictory to a decade in the punishing light of public controversy, but *Burning Daylight* goes beyond *Martin Eden* to portray the relief and hope with which London turned to his ranch for salvation.

Although London did not begin this novel until 1909, it had been in his mind ever since his Klondike winter of 1897–98. Years later he recalled that during his encampment at the mouth of the Stewart River, he had struck up an acquaintance with a miner named Elam Harnish: "We traveled trail together a great deal that winter. The name always stuck by me, and later on I used it for my hero in BURNING DAYLIGHT. I do not know where Elam Harnish came from originally, but I do know, prior to his departure for the Klondike, that he had lived for some years in eastern Oregon; and among other things he had been interested in hydraulic mining."[1] Soon after his return from the Northland, London had recorded the following item under the heading "CHARACTERS": "Elam—burning daylight; see my smoke; hitting the high places; in spite of hell and high water; lean-jowled dog to a bone; laid over in Missouri to rest the cattle." Further on, he noted "how Charley Meyers and Elam sold hydraulic plant to French Syndicate."[2] What struck London about Harnish was his Western vitality, his ability to pull off a big business deal in high style, and, not least, his colorful frontier colloquialisms. Such a character seemed a natural for a Klondike novel, as London recognized in another note made at about the same time: " 'Burning Daylight'—Elam Harnish as central figure typifying title."[3]

But though the protagonist retained the name and some of the traits of the original Elam Harnish, London grafted onto him a few of the exploits of another Klondike hero, Frank Dinsmore, whom he had sketched in "The Gold Hunters of the North" (1903) as a formidable miner and frontiersman. Born in Maine, Dinsmore had prospected for gold in the Black Hills and the Coeur d'Alene before going north; and among his feats were lifting thirteen fifty-pound flour sacks and dancing all night after a seven-hundred-mile trip.[4] In 1909, when London began expanding his notes for the novel, he described his protagonist as a "young man, a la Frank Densmore [sic], in Klondike, [who] strikes it rich. He is a strong, severe harsh young man, with a vein of grim humor running through him. He has the integrities. In the battle of the strong and in the hardest part of the battle-field, namely, Alaska, he has survived." In a further note, London developed his conception of the opening scene: "In the morning, after dancing all night, 2000 miles on end, at the bar, takes his oath and prefaces it by telling his story, a la Frank Densmore: How he first entered the land, in the spring, over Chilcoot and how he came out in the Fall, starving, in ragged overalls and with a quart of beans."[5]

By the time he made these notes on the two Klondike prototypes, London had made one other decision: his novel would not be confined to the Northland. After amassing a fortune in gold mines, Burning Daylight would come "down to civilization," play "the business game," fall in love, and finally abandon his business and retreat with his bride to a "little mountain-ranch." But once Daylight had left the Klondike, his career could no longer be based on the exploits of Harnish and Dinsmore. For Daylight the financier, London needed new models, and, as Wayne W. Westbrook has shown, he found one of them in James R. Keene, who made millions in stock speculation in San Francisco before heading for Wall Street in 1877. There he encountered more formidable opponents in Jim Fisk and Jay Gould (the models for John Dowsett and Nathaniel Letton), who fleeced him of his millions in a stock scheme almost identical to the one to which Daylight succumbs in the novel. Keene reportedly confronted Gould with a pistol in the offices of Russell Sage, but the outcome for Keene was less satisfactory than it was for Daylight: when he left, he was still without his money. Back in San Francisco, according to Westbrook, Keene had engineered the collapse of the Bank of California, which resulted in the suicide of its president, much as Daylight wrecks the California & Altamont Trust Company, whose president then commits suicide in prison.[6]

The model for Daylight's later real estate ventures was the career of another San Francisco financial wizard, George Sterling's uncle and erstwhile employer, F. C. Havens, who had made a fortune in land developments on the eastern shore of the Bay. According to Cloudesley Johns, Havens launched his Realty Syndicate before the turn of the century when his "fertile imagination" was stimulated by the beauty of the Berkeley Hills and he began to sense a potentiality for residential housing. Undeterred by the lack of ready access to San Francisco, Havens negotiated with the Southern Pacific Railroad for an extension of the elevated railroad lines and an increase in ferryboat service from San Francisco to the Oakland Mole. Eventually Havens circumvented the Southern Pacific altogether by building a new mole, constructing new railroad lines, and setting up an independent ferry service. The Southern Pacific tried to "capture or wreck the enterprise, but the Realty Syndicate thrived and Havens became rich."[7] London appropriated virtually all of Havens's exploits for Burning Daylight, and he may have found still more material in other notorious contemporary business maneuvers as yet undetected.[8]

But if Elam Harnish the financier is based chiefly on Keene and Havens, he also owes much to his creator, Jack London, a literary entrepreneur who prided himself on his handling of editors and his ability to command top dollar for his wares. In 1911 he wrote crustily to one editor that "this writer who is a business man has never been up against such slack business dealings in his life,"[9] and his fictional version of Daylight's six-gun showdown with the New York tycoons may contain psychological traces of his own visit to the office of the Overland Monthly in 1899, when he collected the five dollars owed him for a story by threatening the editors with force. Elam also, no doubt, reflects something of London's penchant for risky business ventures and his burgeoning role as a land-baron—planter of thousands of eucalyptus trees and, eventually, builder of barns and silos, pig palace and redwood mansion.

According to his notes, London intended to end the novel by sending Elam and Dede Mason to a ranch on the Merced River in the Sierras, but he later decided to make the ending more closely autobiographical by placing the ranch at Glen

Ellen and putting Elam through a period of emotional strain, heavy drinking, and physical deterioration that reflects the ordeal the Londons underwent in the fall of 1909. In September and October, Charmian suffered through a harrowing emotional breakdown. Burdened by the multiple pressures of ranch life, continual rounds of visitors, chronic insomnia, and the physical symptoms of her as yet undiscovered pregnancy, she found herself crying uncontrollably and withdrawing to her room, unable to face their guests. Jack, in turn, exhausted by the whole ordeal, escaped on a month-long cruise, and Charmian spent a week recuperating in a sanitarium in nearby Altruria. In late December, a final stroke of misfortune came when a cart overturned and smashed Jack's ankle. But with the new year, as Jack's ankle and Charmian's emotions mended—and as they shared their joy in the prospect of a child—the novel moved toward the optimistic ending it achieved when the final pages were written in early February.[10]

Thus, in his metamorphosis from frontier hero to financial magnate to rural homesteader, Elam Harnish reflects some of London's perennial tribulations as well as fulfilling three of his most cherished fantasies: his early dream of a big strike in the Klondike, his later success as a literary entrepreneur, and his final vision of a return to the land. Unsurprisingly, some critics have found such metamorphoses improbable, the materials too heterogeneous, and the novel another instance of London's tendency to begin well but allow the narrative to fall apart somewhere in the middle. Such a view is easy to understand, for *Burning Daylight* undeniably has its weaknesses, most of which occur in Part Two, after Elam leaves the Klondike for San Francisco and meets Dede Mason. At this point, so goes the prevailing view, a convincing novel of action gives way to a sentimental love story, just as *The Sea-Wolf* is thought to be ruined by the introduction of Maud Brewster.[11] Yet for all its lapses of style and sentiment, a case can be made for the continuity of the action. Seen in the light of some traditional patterns of comedy, the plot retains a fundamental coherence not very different from that in *Martin Eden.*

Like *Martin Eden, Burning Daylight* portrays the ascent and apotheosis of the hero; but unlike the earlier novel, it carries the protagonist beyond his symbolic death to the point of rebirth, adhering more closely to the radical comic pattern of the fertility rite. The mythic pattern is an ancient one, yet in a domesticated version it lends itself especially well to the metamorphic nature of the American frontier hero. Most critics of this novel have noticed that the frontier tradition lies behind Elam's character while he is in the Klondike and even after he descends on San Francisco. The entry of Dede Mason, however, does not mark London's abandonment of the frontier theme; on the contrary, the love story derives almost as much from the frontier tradition as do Elam's adventures in the North. The fundamental plot is that of the domestication of the hero, the taming of the marriage-shy bachelor by a woman of spirit, imagination, and guile. This is the comic protagonist epitomized by the reluctant Benedick in *Much Ado about Nothing.* Translated into American comic folklore, he becomes the stalwart frontiersman, ever at ease with a man-comrade or a charging bear but at the sight of a woman, alarmed into flight or reduced to stammering paralysis. Sometimes the hero eludes his female pursuers; but once a woman has captured him, he enjoys his captivity even as he protests against it, enduring sheepishly the guffaws of his former comrades.

Gordon Mills, in his provocative comparison of Elam Harnish and Cooper's Leatherstocking, touches on this point when he notices that both Leatherstocking and Elam are afraid of women.[12] But by dwelling on the more serious implications of the contrast between rusticity and refinement, Mills misses the way Leatherstocking's fear of women points toward Elam by way of Southwest humor and the dime novel, and more proximately by way of Bret Harte's bashful miners and Norris's comic misogynist Annixter in *The Octopus.*[13] The finest distillation of this variety of frontier comedy occurs in Stephen Crane's "The Bride Comes to Yellow Sky," in which the erstwhile bachelor-lawman Jack Potter, returning from San Antonio with a bride, feels obliged to sneak back into town like a felon. He confesses his treachery to his former nemesis, Scratchy Wilson, who ruefully acknowledges that marriage has incapacitated Potter for frontier heroics. The comic domestication of Crane's Potter or Norris's Annixter does not differ fundamentally from the domestication of London's Elam Harnish, though London's feebler comic art has obscured the kinship.

But while Elam descends partly from the rowdy heroes of frontier humor and the Western pulp novel, he also belongs in the tradition of the business magnate inaugurated by Howells's Silas Lapham and continued in such figures as Norris's Magnus Derrick in *The Octopus* or Curtis Jadwin in *The Pit* (1903). Ward Bennett of *A Man's Woman*, though strictly speaking an explorer rather than a businessman, is in some ways even closer to Elam Harnish, for Bennett, too, survives his Arctic adventures to return to civilization and woo an independent-minded career woman. All of these novels involve a crisis that casts the masculine world of rugged independence and hard cash against the claims of conscience, genteel propriety, and marital love. The result of such a conflict can be the tragic destruction of a Magnus Derrick; the eventual marriage of the two worlds, as in *The Rise of Silas Lapham*; or the hero's abandonment of business for domestic life, as in *The Pit*. The businessman is thus another version of the frontier hero, who must finally decide whether to make his peace with the standards of gentility institutionalized in the world of women and the rite of marriage.

Elam Harnish is not the first such frontier tycoon to inhabit London's fiction. He is preceded by Jacob Welse of *A Daughter of the Snows*, who has much the same pioneering background and, like Elam, has established himself as the leading Klondike entrepreneur. Nor is this London's first display of interest in frontier humor and local color. Such an interest appeared in his earliest stories, written for the Oakland *High School Aegis* in 1895. In one of them, "A Night's Swim in Yeddo Bay," a grizzled old sea-dog named Long Charley regales a crowd at a San Francisco saloon with a comically exaggerated tale of a swimming exploit of his earlier years. Two others, both narrated in dialect by "'Frisco Kid" in the manner of the Southwest humorists, deal with the Kid's adventures on the road. Such other early stories as "Bald-Face" and "A Hyperborean Brew" follow these first efforts, similarly employing a theatrical narrative frame like that of "A Night's Swim in Yeddo Bay" or Western dialect like that of 'Frisco Kid; and both of them involve the improbable heroics or wild exaggerations typical of humorous frontier fiction. Others of London's Klondike stories also draw on this boisterous atmosphere with its saloons and brawls, outlandish bunco schemes and all-night card games.[14]

Burning Daylight opens in just such an atmosphere, and the vividness of the early chapters illustrates how even the most conventional formulas of popular fiction can be charged with fresh energy. The theatricality of the opening incident, in which the languid Circle City saloon is brought electrically to life when Daylight pushes through the door, has been a standard in Western fiction for a century; and in Daylight himself, we find all the ingredients of the Western comic hero. This humorous dimension of the hero stems from the quality of excess: everything about Burning Daylight is outsize. Though he has been described as a Horatio Alger type,[15] in reality no one could be further from Alger's earnest, industrious strivers. For London's true Alger character, Mr. Butler in *Martin Eden*, a no-limit poker game would be unthinkable, and Elam Harnish is quintessentially the frontier gambler, for whom "honest work for sure but meagre returns did not count. A man played big."[16] It is this gambler's nonchalance that distinguishes Daylight from the more sinister, sadistic Wolf Larsen, for while Daylight's character has "harshness," it also has "sweetness" and "laughter." Such qualities "saved him from a nature that was essentially savage and that otherwise would have been cruel and bitter" (7, 8).

Frontier humor is fundamentally a matter of language; and though London does not rival the greatest of the Western humorists, he does show an awareness of the tradition and an ability to exploit it effectively. Here is Daylight beginning the poker game with the whoops and brags of an authentic ring-tailed roarer: "Get down to the ground, you-all, Malemutes, huskies, and Siwash purps! Get down and dig in! Tighten up them traces! Put your weight into the harness and bust the breast-bands! Whoop-la! Yow! We're off and bound for Helen Breakfast! And I tell you-all clear and plain there's goin' to be stiff grades and fast goin' tonight before we win to that same lady. And somebody's goin' to bump . . . hard" (13). Instead of being a southwestern species, half horse and half alligator, Daylight proclaims himself a northern cousin, "the mangy old he-wolf," exhorting the crowd to "listen to me howl" (4).

Elam's theatrical entrances and roaring rhetoric are plainly aimed at an audience. When he returns from the sixty-day mail-run, his entrance into the Tivoli is "spectacular, melodramatic; and he knew it" (58). The same is true of his once-natural but increasingly exaggerated Western drawl, which is sprinkled with *you-all* and *nary* and *dawg* almost to the point of self-parody (" 'I tell you-all,' Daylight answered, 'Wilkins, Carmack's strike's so big that we-all can't see it all' " [103]). Yet, at its best, his talk has the authentic flavor of the Western vernacular, as when he justifies himself for buying up seemingly worthless claims: "supposing you-all knew it was going to rain soup," he asks. "What'd you-all do? Buy spoons, of course. Well, I'm sure buying spoons. She's going to rain soup up there on the Klondike, and them that has forks won't be catching none of it" (103). By the time he is embroiled in business conspiracies in San Francisco and New York, his Western mannerisms have become a conscious mask: "Discovering the delight the newspapers took in his vernacular, in his 'you-alls,' and 'sures,' and 'surge-ups,' he even exaggerated these peculiarities of speech, exploiting the phrases he had heard other frontiersmen use, and inventing occasionally a new one of his own'' (140). His final interview with the three swindling financiers thus becomes a humorous burlesque of the fabled showdowns in Deadwood or Tombstone. As he enters their office, the ''free, swinging movements of the trail-traveller were unconsciously exaggerated in that stride of his,'' and the ''geniality in his lazy Western drawl reassured them'' (146). When he pulls his Colt's .44, the scene is saved from melodrama by the humor of his frontier invective: ''Take that chair over there, you gangrene-livered skunk. Jump! By God! or I'll make you leak till folks'll think your father was a water hydrant and your mother a sprinkling-cart'' (151).[17]

Yet for all the humor, Daylight is endowed with genuinely heroic traits. Among the oldest of the ''original pioneers,'' he crossed the Chilkoot twelve years earlier, at the age of eighteen, with five companions, four of whom died. He has ''grown up with the land'' and is accounted an ''elder hero,'' for ''in point of time he was before them. In point of deed he was beyond them'' (5). As the novel opens, he is about to celebrate his thirtieth birthday, and the festivities at the Tivoli consequently have the stylized qualities of an established frontier ritual. First are the ritualistic feats of strength: arm-wrestling, lifting of flour sacks, and finally Daylight's challenging of all comers to be wrestled onto their backs in the snow. One by one they are ''baptized'' (26), while others seek to escape Elam's awesome efficiency by kneeling ''in mock humility, scooping snow upon their heads and claiming the rite accomplished'' (27). The entire night of boisterous carousing is, in fact, a ritual of masculine camaraderie in which the drinking and poker-playing are carried out according to a code of minute proprieties and taboos,[18] while the climactic feats of strength become a rite of preparation for the ordeal of the trail. Yet this birthday rite is transitional in another way as well. After a twelve-year apprenticeship as a footloose adventurer, Elam is ready, on the eve of the gold rush, for a more ambitious phase of his life.

Up to this moment, he has retained a primitive frontier innocence, which can encompass violence but not dishonesty or cruelty. Though he is an "elder hero" who, according to one miner, "never was no kid" (29), Daylight also seems eternally boyish. To him women are "toys" to be played with in moments of relaxation from the "bigger game" of life (10), and he prefers adolescent comradeship to domestic bondage. The saloon girl called the Virgin, though a "nice bit of a woman, healthy and strapping and good to look upon," nevertheless exhibits "all a woman's desire to rope him with her apron-strings and tie him hand and foot for the branding" (11). He considers love "more terrible than frost or famine" and "as contagious as smallpox. . . . It was like delirium tremens, only worse" (113).

His innocence, indeed, is that of the land itself, of the Northland before the gold rush—a paradise before the Fall when "there were no rascals and no tin-horn gamblers. Games were conducted honestly, and . . . a man's word was as good as his gold in the blower" (12). Daylight both expresses that standard in his own character and presides over it as the land's acknowledged lawgiver, being "above the Law" and yet doing the right "in finer and higher ways than other men" (60). There is more than a hint here of the Nietzschean ethic, and Elam later becomes more explicitly a "superman" (160). Yet in the North, he retains the frontier innocence of an American Adam. The wilderness renders him an ascetic, almost priestly figure: on his return from the ordeal of the trail his parka "hooded him like a monk" (57).

It is on the long trail, in fact, far from the world of women, that he finds the apotheosis of masculine companionship. He and his Indian dog-driver, Kama, "the pick of his barbaric race" (22), make a perfect team, coordinating their work so efficiently that scarcely a word need pass between them. As a white man and dark-skinned companion, the two are part of the tradition that includes Leatherstocking and Chingachgook, Ishmael and Queequeg, Huck and Jim. Daylight and Kama thus provide one more illustration of Leslie Fiedler's no-longer-so-notorious theory that the typical American hero, in his flight from women and adulthood, takes refuge in an adolescent world of innocent homoerotic companionship.[19]

And like Leatherstocking in the forest, Ishmael at sea, or Huck on the river, Elam Harnish finds in the wilderness the spiritual values that have sustained his youth and will return to sustain him in the end. Yet those values do not belong to the wilderness itself, for this "dead world" of "silence and immobility" (38) will be not his solace but his antagonist, requiring that he find within himself the qualities necessary for survival. Accordingly, the prose harks back to the best of London's early Klondike period. Here are the two men finishing their meal and preparing for their first night:

Once, with a muttered imprecation, Kama leaped away, a stick of firewood in hand, and clubbed apart a tangle of fighting dogs. Daylight, between mouthfuls, fed chunks of ice into the tin pot, where it thawed into water. The meal finished, Kama replenished the fire, cut more wood for the morning, and returned to the spruce bough bed and his harness-mending. Daylight cut up generous chunks of bacon and dropped them in the pot of bubbling beans. The moccasins of both men were wet, and this in spite of the intense cold; so when there was no further need for them to leave the oasis of spruce boughs, they took off their moccasins and hung them on short sticks to dry before the fire, turning them about from time to time. When the beans were finally cooked, Daylight ran part of them into a bag of flour-sacking a foot and a half long and three inches in diameter. This he then laid on the snow to freeze. The remainder of the beans were left in the pot for breakfast.

It was past nine o'clock, and they were ready for bed. The squabbling and bickering among the dogs had long since died down, and the weary animals were curled in the snow, each with his feet and nose bunched together and covered by his wolf's brush of a tail. Kama spread his sleeping-furs and lighted his pipe. Daylight rolled a brown-paper cigarette, and the second conversation of the evening took place. (41)

Without self-conscious homilies or lyrical flourishes, London renders, with perfect concreteness and precision, the look and feel—almost the smell—of wilderness experience.

But even more than his legendary mail-run, what distinguishes Elam from the ordinary pocket-miner is what distinguishes Martin Eden from Mr. Butler: imagination, creative vision. Elam is a "free lance" (156); and like Martin's, his romantic fancy is tempered by realism. He "had vision," yet "his mind was orderly, his imagination practical, and he never dreamed idly" (68). At the barren conjunction of the Klondike and Yukon rivers, he stands "gazing out over the lonely flat and visioning with constructive imagination the scene if the stampede did come," picturing in his mind a town of 40,000 men (47). When his vision is fulfilled by the rise of Dawson, his lust for power becomes a form of Nietzschean creative energy: "In a way, the part he played was creative. He was doing something. . . . Gold, even on the scales, was, after all, an abstraction. It represented things and the power to do. But the sawmills were the things themselves, concrete and tangible. . . . They were dreams come true, hard and indubitable realizations of fairy gossamers" (107–8). The Jack London who said he would rather win a water fight than write the great American novel acknowledges here that creative energy can take many forms, and that the struggle of the unlettered Elam Harnish to realize his "fairy gossamers" does not differ fundamentally from Martin Eden's yearning toward ideal beauty.

The final phase of the Northland apprenticeship occurs during the ill-fated expedition up the Stewart River, where Daylight experiences the symbolic death and rebirth that precedes his rise to power. In the heady aftermath of his record mail-run, he feels invincible, immortal: "Deep in his life-processes Life itself sang the siren song of its own majesty, ever a-whisper and urgent, counselling him that he could achieve more than other men, win out where they failed, ride to success where they perished" (61). It is the last illusion of his youth, the "old, old lie of Life fooling itself, believing itself immortal and indestructible" (62). But in the camp on the Stewart, as he nears death from starvation, for the first time "Life faltered and forgot to lie." Contrasting his own mortality with the eternal cycle of nature, "he seemed to see back through the past to a time when neither white man nor Indian was in the land. . . . And he saw also into an illimitable future, when the last generations of men were gone from off the face of Alaska, when he, too, would be gone, and he saw, ever remaining, that river, freezing and fresheting, and running on and on" (81). What he is confronting is the White Logic that London, in *John Barleycorn*, would find at the bottom of a whiskey bottle: "Only the dead things remained, the things that were not flesh and nerves and sensitiveness, the sand and muck and gravel." Life was but "a scurvy game," an "everlasting funeral procession" (81–82).

As his strength ebbs and he resigns himself to death, the words recall the ending of *Martin Eden*. Dying is "easy," he discovers, "easier than he had ever imagined; and, now that it was near, the thought of it made him glad" (82). But at that critical moment a "new vision" comes to him of the "feverish city of his dream—the gold metropolis of the North" (82); and summoning his last strength for one self-consuming yet revitalizing act, he strives "with the soul of him as well as with the body, consuming himself, body and spirit, in the effort" (83). He launches his boat into the Stewart and passes through a dreamlike period of sleeping and waking until he is rescued and eventually recovers to begin a new life as a Klondike mining baron and San Francisco financier.

Most of the account of Elam's business career in California represents a falling-off in narrative power, perhaps in part because London lacked intimate knowledge of financial careers like those of Keene and Havens. Though he could record the externals of Havens's real estate machinations, he could derive the inner psychology of such a man only from his own more limited experience. Possibly it was the avocational nature of that experience that lends to Elam's financial ventures a quality of play. The Jack London who spent his adult life making up for the boyhood he believed he had missed is present in the boyish *Burning Daylight*, whose prolonged Klondike adolescence, though tempered by the financial jungle, continues until he takes a conclusive step toward maturity with Dede Mason. Both in the Klondike and in California, Elam's career is a "game"—a recurrent metaphor that suggests not only the naturalistic world of chance but also the air of unreality, of childlike make-believe, in the account of his wheeling and dealing. Elam himself describes his career as "playing business" (327), and after his abandonment of the game, Dede speaks of him as a "great big boy . . . breaking the thirty-million toy with which [he] had grown tired of playing" (333). Compared with the authenticity of the business dealings of a Silas Lapham or a Frank Cowperwood, Elam's seem a pale imitation.

The more serious dimension of Elam's business career is his gradual abandonment of hale-fellow Klondike camaraderie for the ruthless ethic of the city. In the North, comradeship was not a game of pursuit but a sharing of risks. The "business essence" of this spirit was that "each did his best. . . . Some men were stronger than others—true; but so long as each man did his best it was fair exchange, the business spirit was observed, and the square deal obtained" (11). The result was a makeshift frontier version of Marxian egalitarianism: from each according to his ability, to each according to his need. But as his wealth and power increased, Daylight departed from this egalitarian spirit, joining the Mine-owners' Association and "effectually curb[ing] the growing insubordination of the wage-earners"; for this was "a new era, and Daylight, the wealthy mine-owner, was loyal to his class affiliations." Though he paid high wages and favored the old-timers, his benevolence was no more than a residual nostalgia: "In his heart he could not forget the old days, while with his head he played the economic game according to the latest and most practical methods" (110). Out of the rationalizations of Spencerian social Darwinism and the Nietzschean will to power, Daylight developed the ethic of self-interest that he carried with him to San Francisco.

At first a part of his frontier innocence clings to him. He naively believes that the city financiers will "play fair" (127); and when he encounters the wily magnate John Dowsett, he is taken in by Dowsett's smooth manner, "honest blue eyes," and descent from "prime old American stock" (129). He is thus ripe for the plucking he receives in New York, when Dowsett combines with two other financial sharpers to bilk him of his fortune. From then on, Elam is prepared to play the new game on its own terms. Though he remains "square" in his financial dealings, he now plays "remorselessly," becoming a "veritable pirate of the financial main" (155). Society, he thinks, is organized into a "vast bunco game" operated at the expense of the "hereditary inefficients" and the "fools." Businessmen are "schemers" who get between a worker and his product and charge "all the traffic can bear" (157, 158). From an elevator boy who moonlights as a proletarian radical, he learns how the railroads juggle their rates to squeeze the ranchers,[20] and he also learns the cynical wisdom of P. T. Barnum, that "a sucker was born every minute" (159).

In his attitude toward the "great stupid mass of the people," however, Daylight remains of two minds. The Nietzschean and Spencerian side of him believes that such people do not count, for life, after all, is "a savage proposition at best" (161). Yet he has no heart for "swindling the workers"; such an act would not be a "sporting proposition." Instead, "like Robin Hood of old" (162), he robs the rich and gives to the poor. Nevertheless, his charity remains a matter of whim, and the mixture of impulsive generosity and ruthless self-seeking is not very convincing characterization. London seems to intend it as a natural outgrowth of Elam's Klondike openhandedness, tempered now by the realities of the business ethic, and in another sense it may represent an effort to retain the reader's sympathy for a man who is rapidly degenerating. But in trying to make Daylight

both a hero and an object lesson, he succeeds only in blur-
ring the previously sharp outlines of his character. In *Martin
Eden*, he escaped that problem because Martin never became the object lesson London believed he had created.
Burning Daylight, however, begins to sound not only like a
cautionary tale about the moral perils of capitalism but even
like a temperance novel.

At this point, drinking heavily, losing both his muscle
tone and his moral fibre, Daylight is ripe for rescue; and a
rescuer soon appears in the form of his stenographer, Dede
Mason. At first he is reluctant to approach her, for in addition to possessing the "innate chivalry of the frontiersman," which forbids him to take advantage of a subordinate, he also continues to fear the "spectre of the apron-
string" (172). But their initially tentative courtship soon becomes a power struggle in which it is Daylight, not Dede,
who stoops to conquer. She finally consents to marry him,
but only on her own terms, which stipulate a radical altera-
tion of his life and character.

The courtship is treated with considerable humor, part of
it deriving from a comedy of manners like that of *Martin
Eden*, though here the humor is broader and more clearly at
the expense of the protagonist. When Daylight first came to
San Francisco, even before meeting Dede he had grasped the
necessity of improving his English and learning to "eat and
dress and generally comport himself after the manner of civilized man." Nevertheless, he had "remained himself," the
Western barbarian who never hesitated to "stride rough-
shod over any soft-faced convention if it got in his way"
(125). But the gentility of Dede is another matter. At first he
accepts her as merely a "female creature and a bit of office
furnishing" (167), but when she penetrates his consciousness by silently correcting a *will* to a *shall* in one of his business letters, London portrays his befuddlement and suspicion with an uncharacteristically fine comic touch. Elam's
blunders as a suitor keep Dede torn between indignation and
laughter, and she, in turn, is one of London's few attractive

heroines, her streak of independence and unconventionality balanced by a sense of proportion and humor. As a "new woman," she is far more convincing than Frona Welse in *A Daughter of the Snows*.

Temperamentally, the two lovers resemble the horses they ride during their courtship. Dede, like her mare Mab, is spirited but well behaved, while Elam's stallion Bob is dangerously skittish. But Dede vows she can handle Bob, and when Elam reluctantly consents to her riding the stallion, to his amazement she controls him with an expert hand. Afterwards, Dede herself makes the right connection by declaring, "I'm sure I wasn't frightened of Bob, or you" (232).[21] Yet Daylight persists in believing that such a woman is made to be dominated by a man: "God, she was the wife for a man! . . . And to think of her hammering all week at a typewriter. That was no place for her. She should be a man's wife, taking it easy, with silks and satins and diamonds (his frontier notion of what befitted a wife beloved), and dogs, and horses, and such things" (229). Much of the remainder of the novel portrays Dede's effort to disabuse Elam of this "frontier notion" of a woman's place and capacity, for his "love of fair play" insures that "somewhere within him was a higher appraisement of love than mere possession" (243). He soon learns to regard Dede not as a "toy" but as a "comrade and playfellow and joyfellow" (247). If there lingers here a hint of the boyishness he will never outgrow, there is also a willingness to see women in a more fully human light.

It is Dede's unwillingness to be considered merely a "brief diversion" (294) from an obsession with business that strengthens her resistance to Elam's humorously importunate courtship. By now Elam has abandoned his frontier suspicion that "women gave little and wanted all" (11). To his amused consternation, he finds himself submitting to Dede's subtle power: "Here I am, used to having my will with man and beast and anything. And here I am sitting in this chair, as weak and helpless as a little lamb. You sure take the starch out of me" (279). He even goes so far as to assure her that as his wife she would be "independent" (282). Yet Dede, with her working-woman's view of men, takes an unconventionally realistic attitude toward married love: "I am not romantic.. . . . It might be better for me if I were. Then I could make a fool of myself and be unhappy for the rest of my life. But my abominable common sense prevents" (291). She then confirms her unconventionality by frankly confessing her love, acknowledging that she is behaving "in what many men would think was an unwomanly manner" (291). Not until Daylight agrees to abandon his business—to give up his exclusively masculine preserve and power—do they reach the kind of accommodation that makes their marriage possible. Dede, in turn, surrenders much of her own independence to devote herself to their life together.

Thus, throughout the courtship, London strives to counter sentiment with humor and to deal realistically with the accommodations required in a modern marriage. Yet beyond this power struggle, Elam and Dede are enacting a final rite of passage. Just as the earlier rituals marked Elam's passage from frontier innocence to a life as a Klondike mining baron, a new series of rituals will seal his transition from the destructive world of finance to a fruitful life on the land. The ritual has two phases, the first concerning Elam alone, the second centered on his marriage to Dede. Both are fertility rites permeated by the imagery of the solar and seasonal cycles.

Figuratively, Elam is another sun-god, who is dismembered, immersed in cleansing waters, and then reborn. His legendary dominance is sunlike from the beginning; his name, after all, is Burning Daylight. Yet at the zenith of his success in the Klondike, he moves to the city and gradually degenerates in body and mind. Like Martin Eden, he is "torn to shreds" by the newspapers (181). At that point, "jaded with all things business" (182), he rides out into the country, feeling like an all-night poker-player emerging to "taste the freshness of the morn" (183). He soon finds himself in a redwood grove, a "cathedral nave of lofty trees," at the center of which is a single California lily. Overcome by a "vague religious feeling" (184), he compares the whole experience to a "cleansing bath," while his sensations are of "purification and uplift" as his "city-rotted body and brain" surrender to the "potent charm of nature" (188).

This alignment of his life with the cycle of nature is ritualistically confirmed through his marriage to Dede—not in the marriage ceremony itself but in the horseback ride they take when the ceremony is over. In this episode London intertwines with some skill the language of spiritual and sexual ecstasy. First the two horses, Mab and Bob, are reunited; and the ensuing ride, with its traditional erotic connotations, is embued with imagery of penetration. Elam feels "drunken as with wine" and finds himself ascending to the "topmost pinnacle of life." The woman and the land become almost indistinguishable embodiments of the fertility he is embracing, for even as he rejoices in the "virginal possession of a mate," he watches the "joy mount in her face" as she gazes on the "sweet, fresh land" with its "rolling stretches of ripe grain" (336). As they cross the boundary of their own land, jumping "the ruined remnants of the stake-and-rider fence," Dede is in "an unending ecstasy." They proceed into a "deep cañon" and up a "slippery horse trail" until they come to a clearing full of ripe grain, which Dede picks and nibbles between her teeth, all the while uttering "cries and ejaculations of surprise and delight" (337). They force their way higher and higher along the "rough horse trail," making their way through a "sea of foliage," the forest roof only here and there opening "rifts that permitted shattered shafts of sunlight to penetrate" (337). At the summit, Dede "stopped her horse and sighed with the beauty of it all," envisioning their symbolically sexual ascent as a final ritual of immersion. "It is as if we are swimmers," she says, "rising out of a deep pool of green tranquility. Up above is the sky and the sun, but this *is* a pool, and we are fathoms deep" (338). From such a height (or depth) of ecstasy, they descend into the valley, noticing as they go a quail with its young, nests of birds and animals, until they arrive at last at their own farmhouse.

The final picture of the lovers in their cozy cottage is not without sentimentality; and the prospect of the arm-wrestling frontiersman's taking up the violin, along with the poetry of Kipling and Henley, is nothing if not startling. Yet London distinguishes carefully between "city-bred" romantics, who "fled to the soil" only to go through a process of "savage disillusionment," and Elam and Dede, who had been "born on the soil" and "knew its naked simplicities and rawer ways." They had "merely come home again," and "what might appear sordid and squalid to the fastidiously reared, was to them eminently wholesome and natural" (340). The sentimental primitivism, in short, is leavened by a strong measure of agrarian practicality, which receives "the sanction of [Elam's] reason" (341).

The sentimentality is also tempered by a humane modification of stereotypical notions of the "masculine" and "feminine," a resolution prepared for by the struggles of courtship. Though the two retain a part of the traditional conception of man's and woman's work, their lives and labor are "woven into a fabric of mutual interest and consideration. He was as deeply interested in her cooking and her music as she was in his agricultural adventures in the vegetable garden" (350). The "masculine" tendencies Dede exhibited on horseback are now well met by Elam's burgeoning cultural interests, which he would earlier have considered too feminine. They thus approach the kind of balance that Humphrey Van Weyden and Maud Brewster had achieved in *The Sea-Wolf.*

Appropriately, then, this novel of the taming of a frontiersman ends not with a vision of new frontiers but with a return to the civilizing, if rustic, conventions of domestic life. Elam resumes his boyhood practices of arm-wrestling and horse-breaking, and he and Dede plan a ride to their childhood homes. Yet this process if not so much a regression as a recognition of the limits of independence, an acceptance of family bonds. By celebrating his birthday "in the old-fashioned frontier way'' (346), and by reburying the gold he accidentally uncovers, Elam enacts his final rituals of acceptance and rejection, making his compromises, settling for the gains and losses that accompany adult life. *Burning Daylight* is not a great novel, certainly not London's best. But it does possess considerable charm, a fundamental coherence of design, and at the end a new maturity of outlook. It thus points the way toward the two novels in which London examines more closely the psychology of marital love.

9

• Urban Discontents
The Valley of the Moon

In mid-winter of 1910, as the composition of *Burning Daylight* drew to a close, the Londons' spirits were reviving. Charmian's emotional breakdown and Jack's ankle injury had receded into the past, and in January they began to purchase building stones for Wolf House, the stone and redwood mansion they were planning to build on their ranch. As they eagerly anticipated the birth of their child, they had good reason to be more optimistic about their prospects than they had been for many months. In his novella *The Scarlet Plague*, written during their three-week visit to Carmel in late winter, London gave dramatic evidence of his disillusionment with the corrosive life of the city, ending the narrative with a lyrical celebration of the cycle of life.

These hopes, however, were to remain unfulfilled, for the next year was to be a time of severe disappointments and of creative energies dissipated in miscellaneous hack work. The play *Theft*, written in the spring, was turned down by the actress for whom it was intended, and it never found a producer. Through the summer London worked intermittently on a novel to be called *The Assassination Bureau, Ltd.*, but it bogged down and was left uncompleted. The most crushing disappointment came on June 21, when the long-awaited baby, a daughter named Joy, died after only thirty-eight hours of life. The following day London was maneuvered into a brawl at an Oakland bar, and when the police court failed to exonerate him as fully as he wished, he took his revenge on the judge in a mean-spirited story called "The Benefit of the Doubt." At about the same time, his friend Joseph Noel persuaded him to invest $4000 in a new lithograph process called the Millergraph, an ill-advised venture that not only lost him his money but eventually precipitated a bitter quarrel with Noel that did considerable damage to his reputation. Charmian's convalescence, moreover, had been long and precarious; and it was not until the fall, when they purchased a new yacht, the *Roamer*, and began the first of a series of annual cruises on the upper Bay and the Sacramento and San Joaquin rivers, that the fragments of their world began falling back into place.

As the cruise continued through October and November, London recovered his creative rhythm as he worked on *The Abysmal Brute*, which follows *Burning Daylight* and *The Scarlet Plague* in depicting a searing experience of urban life and a consequent retreat to the revitalizing airs of the country. The cruise ended while this novel was in progress, and when he returned to the ranch on November 14, he would have soon found in his mail the November 12 issue of the *Saturday Evening Post* containing his story "The Benefit of the Doubt." In the same issue was another narrative, Le Roy Armstrong's "The Man Who Came Back: Two Twentieth Century Pilgrims and Where They Landed," which he read and clipped out, penciling in the top margin, "*Novel Motif*." What he had found was the germ—indeed the entire structure and many details—of *The Valley of the Moon*.[1]

"The Man Who Came Back" is the story of how a Chicago typesetter struggles with an urban working-class life until his wife at last persuades him to leave the city in search of a better environment in the West. Before his marriage he enjoyed regular work at good pay and laughed at the doomsaying labor-organizers. But after his marriage to Mary and

the death of their baby, hard times set in and he slides into
debt, quitting his job in a moment of anger after a session of
drinking and poker-playing. "I loafed two months straight,"
he says, "and got steadily madder at the great big Something
that was against me and against all workingmen." After further jobs lead only to further layoffs, he comes to recognize
that there are "too many of my kind here in Chicago." At
this point, Mary has an idea: "Isn't there vacant land somewhere—land for settlers?" Her grandparents, she remembers, had walked from Baltimore to Indiana. Why couldn't
she and her husband find a special valley of their own in the
West? They head toward Colorado on the train, and then begin a 1000-mile trek over the Rockies, stopping here and
there to earn money, spending nights with farmers, occasionally catching a ride on a wagon. When at last they find
their valley, they start farming and eventually have a new
baby. The narrative draws to a close with the husband's expression of delight that he finally owns his own land and
works for himself.

For the time being, London filed this clipping away while
he worked on the Smoke Bellew and David Grief stories for
Cosmopolitan and the *Saturday Evening Post*. By the spring
of 1911, however, he was already thinking ahead to the new
novel. On May 30, with his usual combination of salesman-
ship and honest enthusiasm, he sent nearly identical plot
outlines to George Brett and to Roland Phillips of *Cosmopolitan*. The motif, he proclaimed to Brett, would be *"back
to the land"*; and though "for once" his story would not offend "bourgeois morality and bourgeois business ethics," it
would nevertheless be something of which he would "absolutely and passionately believe every word." The plot would
develop thus:

I take a man and a woman, young, who belong to the working-class
in a large city. Both are wage-workers, the man is unskilled—a
driver of a brewery wagon, or something of that sort. The first third
of the book is to be devoted to their city environment, their meeting, their love-affair, and the trials and tribulations of such a mar-

riage in the working-class. Comes hard times. The woman gets the vision. She is the guiding force. They start wandering penniless over the country of California. Of course, they have all sorts of adventures, and their wandering becomes a magnificent, heroic, detailed pilgrimage. After many hints and snatches of vision, always looking for the spot, they do find the real, one and only spot, and settle down to successful small-scale farming.

The novel, he insisted, would begin and end as a love story, its central thread being "the thing that will make their love live to the end."[2]

Though he shifted the opening scenes from Chicago to Oakland, at this point London adhered closely to his source in the Armstrong story. Nevertheless, the plot remained to be filled out, and a few days later he and Charmian embarked on a three-month wagon journey into northern California and southern Oregon, which he hoped would provide materials for the "detailed pilgrimage" he had envisioned for Saxon and Billy Roberts. Eventually he also incorporated observations from his Carmel visit of 1910 and his spring cruise on the *Roamer*. In the novel, for example, George Sterling figures prominently at Carmel as the poet Mark Hall; and Jimmy Hopper, another Carmel friend, appears as Jim Hazard. The Londons themselves make a cameo appearance as Jack and Clara Hastings, and in a younger incarnation Jack is the venturesome boy with the sailboat who convinces Saxon that Oakland is just a place to start from.

After his return from the wagon journey, London studied the history of westward migration and began clipping articles on the experiences of city-dwellers who had moved to the country. At the top of a September 9 *Collier's* article by Mary Rankin Cranston, "My Beginning as a Farmer," he penciled "San Jose woman," underscoring the author's opening description of herself as a former "business woman, a librarian, in New York City." He went on to mark several passages describing how the woman had bought a small farm, eventually paid off her mortgage, developed her orchard, and stocked the farm with chickens, ducks, and cows. With the novel in mind, London expanded on these hints by noting in the margin: "married. husband died. small life insurance."[3] A further hint for the San Jose woman (Mrs. Mortimer in the novel) came from a *Saturday Evening Post* article by Forrest Crissey telling of an enterprising man who had settled next to a small town in Michigan and developed a thriving produce business by surrounding his vegetable garden with flowers.[4]

Crissey, in fact, contributed a series of articles to the *Post* in the fall of 1911 under the heading of "Lessons from Our Alien Farmers," and London found plenty of material in such installments as "Pointers in Profits from the Thrifty Portuguese" and "John Chinaman as a Crop-Coaxer."[5] In the margins of the latter clipping he tried out scraps of dialogue for Billy and Saxon, and the details of Chinese farming methods were incorporated into the advice given Billy by Gunston, the man he meets on the train to San Francisco. During the same months another series of back-to-the-land articles appeared in *Country Life in America*. London clipped and annotated several of these, along with an article from *Technical World Magazine* in which he marked passages on the wearing out of farmland by successions of tenants and its rejuvenation by manuring and crop rotation.[6]

All of these materials, however, were intended for the final third of the novel. When London began making notes for the early scenes, he was forced to reach further back in his memory. The name of his protagonist had come to him during a visit to Los Angeles the previous January, when he met a woman named Saxon Brown.[7] Charmian, however, as the main model for Saxon, supplied Jack with considerable information about her own early life and family background. But since she had grown up in relatively genteel circumstances, London had to dig into his own past for the details of working-class life.

Billy Roberts, the teamster and former prizefighter, like Martin Eden the sailor and former cowboy, is an exaggerated version of London's own teenage years as an Oakland waterfront roughneck, fleshed out with details from the life of the disillusioned Chicago laborer in "The Man Who Came Back." But London's experiences as a laundry work-beast, already used in *Martin Eden*, were now transferred to Saxon, and further details of her life seem to have been resurrected from an early set of notes for a "San Francisco Slum Study," which London had planned as a novel of "natural selection under capitalism" but had never written. Its protagonist was to be a young woman whose family had descended on the social scale and who would make futile efforts to retain her respectability and chastity in an atmosphere of importunate young men and willing girls. Scenes were to be set on Sunday picnics and buggy rides, in cheap restaurants and dance saloons; and the heroine's gradual abandonment of her genteel standards was to have been hastened by a "religious element in the struggle." First would come the "God and heaven idea," followed by the influence of "the talk of some materialist and atheist she somewhere knows." As she wavered in her views, she would make "crude and incomplete and very childish generalizations of the subject." Expanding the religious idea, London imagined a boat steerer named Harry, who would tell an "atheistical story" that "affects her deeply." As a result, "she sees many unjust and terrible things in the slums which she cannot accredit to God, and which she cannot otherwise explain—except, they just so happened, and she was intelligent enough to see thus far, to see that just happening negated God." Finally, this young woman would be affected by her acquaintance with "some strong vicious girl. . . . Dominant and vicious, but good naturedly and naturally vicious." The story would move eventually to "the man she does give in to," from which point London planned to "work up the tragedy."[8]

Much of the social life of this young woman and her friends—especially the religious conflict—suggests the life of Saxon and her friend Mary during the early chapters of *The Valley of the Moon*. The contrast between Saxon's escape and Mary's descent to prostitution very likely emerges from these notes, which in turn reflect London's recollections of his own early social life in West Oakland. Another memory from those early years helped to shape the characterization of Saxon's kindly but ineffectual brother, Tom, and his slatternly, unstable wife, Sarah. In her hysteria and shabby-genteel snobbery, Sarah embodies the worst of London's recollections of his mother, while Tom is modeled loosely on her long-suffering husband, John London.[9] The labor strife depicted in Book Two, as Sam S. Baskett has shown, was based mainly on the Bay Area labor unrest of 1901, though for dramatic effect London concentrated and exaggerated the violence of the participants and the severity of the sentences meted out to the strikers.[10]

With this much of his material in hand by late November, London set to work, and on December 7 Charmian observed that the novel was progressing well. Two weeks later, however, he decided to go to New York to look after his Millergraph business and also to try to book passage on a schooner for a voyage around Cape Horn. On January 2, 1912, he and Charmian arrived at Pennsylvania Station and settled into an uptown apartment for what was to become the worst two months of their marriage. For a few days progress on the novel continued; but before long London had abandoned both his novel and his wife in favor of his business affairs or his drinking binges with Noel and other companions. Cold, miserable, and desperate, Charmian got around as best she could on her own until plans for the voyage finally crystalized and she was able to get Jack to Baltimore and on board the *Dirigo*. As the sea atmosphere worked its magic, London stopped drinking and resumed writing, his routine restored by the regularity of nautical life and the absence of urban temptations.

Ever since he had read the Armstrong narrative in the *Post*, London had intended for the wife, Saxon, to instigate the move from the city. As in that source narrative, financial troubles and the loss of a child provided motive enough for the flight of Saxon and Billy Roberts. But now the bitter weeks of the New York estrangement suggested a new way of filling out the novel's crucial middle section. As they sailed south toward the Cape and were gradually reconciled, the Londons began an active collaboration, Charmian furnishing Jack with notes on her domestic life, her pregnancy and childbirth, her severe headaches and emotional breakdowns, and finally her resentment of the lonely, desperate weeks in New York. Later she contributed notes on the *Roamer* cruise and the northern wagon trip, and at one point she worked up a description of the life of Ninetta and Edward Payne, which, she proudly noted, Jack incorporated "almost word for word" into the sketch of the Hales.[11] When the five-month voyage ended, London had finished his book and repaired his damaged marriage. He could thus affirm with some feeling what Billy and Saxon discover on the eve of their departure from Oakland: that love, like any other crop, will "grow and blossom" only in the "proper soil."[12]

This novel thus derives not only from the vogue of "back to the land" stories but also from deep stresses in London's creative and marital life. In early 1911, as he cranked out one potboiler after another, he fretted about his "going out of vogue" and his "natural and inevitable deterioration as a writer."[13] His discouragement over his continuing childlessness, moreover, no doubt contributed to the tensions that came close to destroying his marriage during the miserable winter in New York. Surely it was his and Charmian's preoccupation with barrenness and fertility that led him to make a significant departure from his source in Armstrong's "The Man Who Came Back," in which the narrator and central figure is the husband. In *The Valley of the Moon*, prominent as Billy Roberts is, London subordinates him to Saxon, from whose point of view the action is presented. At first, in fact, London intended to have Saxon narrate the story herself. Though he quickly abandoned that device in favor of third-person narration, the focus remains on Saxon throughout the best portions of the novel, books One and Two.[14]

This narrative method and its interpretive consequences have not been clearly recognized. London's earlier attempt to create a female protagonist—Avis Everhard in *The Iron Heel*—was a failure. *The Valley*, too, is a highly uneven novel, but here that unevenness has nothing to do with the centrality of the woman. On the contrary, unlike Avis, Saxon is characterized with penetration and sensitivity. Important misinterpretations have arisen from the failure of critics to recognize that Saxon's is the normative point of view, which serves as a corrective to Billy's emotional gyrations and egotistical bluster.[15] Indeed, Book Three is weaker than its predecessors largely because at that point Saxon is relegated to the background.

Before that falling-off, London skillfully etches the scenes of working-class life, such as the opening episode in the laundry, which contrasts carefree youth with the gritty realities of a lifetime of sweatshop labor. Mary and Saxon's girlish chatter about "gentlemen friends" and a "heavenly" danceband is suddenly interrupted by an elderly woman, pregnant with her eighth child, whose back—"loose, bulging, and misshapen"—begins a "convulsive heaving." Screaming, "Gawd! O Gawd!," she flings "wild glances, like those of an entrapped animal, up and down the big whitewashed room that panted with heat and that was thickly humid with the steam that sizzled from the damp cloth under the irons of the many ironers." After making a partial recovery, the woman collapses on the floor, her "long shriek rising in the pent room to the acrid smell of scorching cloth." Lying on her back, "drumming her heels on the floor," she shrieks "persistently and monotonously, like a mechanical siren," until two other women drag her into an adjoining room and her screams are drowned out by the "vast, muffled roar of machinery" (3, 4).

This is the nightmare of the social pit, the specter that had haunted London ever since his own term in the Erie County Penitentiary during his tramping days of 1894, his stint as a laundry work-beast in 1897, and his sojourn in the East End of London in 1902. The scene has the lurid coloring of Stephen Crane's early Bowery fiction, and the mercilessly forced pace of the work resembles the steam-laundry scene in *The Long Day* (1905), the story of a young girl's struggle to survive in working-class New York which London had reviewed for the San Francisco *Examiner*.[16] Though the screams of the stricken woman have been drowned out, the smell of the scorched cloth lingers "ominously" in the air (4), and Saxon and Mary nervously attempt to assure themselves that no such fate lies in wait for them.

At the end of the workday, Saxon returns to a home that promises no relief from the fierce discord of the laundry. Like the Higginbothams' house in *Martin Eden*, the dingy dwelling of her brother and sister-in-law offers Saxon only a choice of nightmares. Greeted by the "screeching reproach" of the front gate, she negotiates the narrow walk and missing doorstep, then enters the kitchen with its sparse furnishings, stained plaster, and stove "worn through and repaired with a five-gallon oil-can hammered flat and double." The dinner awaiting her consists of a plate of "cold beans, thick with grease," which she rejects in favor of a slice of buttered bread and a cup of "cold tea that had been steeped so long that it was like acid in her mouth." Throughout the meal, she must endure the carping of her sister-in-law, Sarah, "middle-aged, lop-breasted, hair-tousled, her face lined with care and fat petulance" (6), whose incessant voice Saxon cannot escape even in the privacy of her bedroom.

In her hypocrisy, self-pity, and violent hysteria, Sarah recalls Crane's Mary Johnson, who harangues Maggie for daring to grasp at the hope of escape offered by Pete, much as Sarah raves about the disgrace of Saxon's keeping company with a prizefighter. Next she terrifies her young child with visions of "the mother that bore you" confined to a padded cell, "with the lunatics screechin' an' screamin' all around, an' the quick-lime eatin' into the dead bodies of them that's beaten to death by the cruel wardens" (69). When Tom comes mildly to Saxon's defense, Sarah turns on him a stream of accusations and aggressive self-pity: "An' what have you ever did for me? That's what I want to know—me, that's cooked for you, an' washed your stinkin' clothes, and fixed your socks, an' sat up nights with your brats when they was ailin'" (70). Tom pleads with her to be calm, but he succeeds only in precipitating her complete emotional disintegration: "In response, slowly, with utmost deliberation, as if the destiny of empires rested on the certitude of her act, she turned the saucer of coffee upside down on the table. She lifted her right hand, slowly, hugely, and in the same slow, huge way landed the open palm with a sounding slap on Tom's astounded cheek. Immediately thereafter she raised her voice in the shrill, hoarse, monotonous madness of hysteria, sat down on the floor, and rocked back and forth in the throes of an abysmal grief." Though Saxon feels "incensed, violated," she consoles Sarah by stroking her forehead with "slow, soothing movements" (71), working desperately to restore a measure of peace before Billy arrives.

Lurid as this scene is, London keeps it from melodramatic excess. Sarah remains a horrifying yet plausible figure, the counterpart of the screaming woman at the laundry. Both women, London makes clear, have been ground down in the relentless mill of urban squalor, their lives unrelieved by the slightest gleam of hope. Tom, it is true, manages to maintain an unassuming, ineffectual saintliness. Yet his is the easier life. It is the women, London implies, whose lives are the dreariest, whose burden of childbearing and domestic toil is frequently doubled by the necessity of labor in a stifling laundry or factory.

Equally effective are the crowd scenes: the games and brawls at the Bricklayers' picnic in the early chapters, and later the battle between the strikers and the scabs and police. The latter scene is particularly stunning, the violence exploding suddenly into the tranquil neighborhood of white picket fences, where children are playing in the street and housewives idling in doorways and windows. It is the children, in fact, who begin the battle by stoning the scabs, and from that moment Saxon is transfixed by the "rapid horror before her eyes that flashed along like a moving picture film gone mad'' (189). The nightmare is epitomized for her by a grotesque fat man, the leader of the scabs, whose ''head had become wedged at the neck between the tops of the pickets of her fence. His body hung down outside, the knees not quite touching the ground. His hat had fallen off, and the sun was making an astounding high light on his bald spot. The cigar, too, was gone. She saw he was looking at her. One hand, between the pickets, seemed waving at her, and almost he seemed to wink at her jocosely, though she knew it to be the contortion of deadly pain'' (188). Helplessly she watches as Bert is shot and as Chester Johnson, with whom she had danced before her marriage to Billy, backs a scab onto the fence and pounds his face with a revolver butt. When Chester is in turn shot by the fat man, Saxon finds ''the bodies of three men hung on her picket fence'' like laundry on a line (190).

With incredible swiftness, the eruption passes before her and is gone; and ''moving as in a dream,'' she comes down her front steps, her eye taking in images of dislocation surrealistically magnified and yet strangely trivial: ''The round-bellied leader still leered at her and fluttered one hand,'' and ''the gate was off its hinges, which seemed strange, for she had been watching all the time and had not seen it happen'' (190). In its suddenness and decisive carnage, and in its destructive effect on a young marriage, the scene recalls the climactic battle between the ranchers and the marshall's posse in Norris's *The Octopus*.[17]

Yet such naturalistic set-pieces are important primarily as stages in Saxon's experience. Though only the final journey in Book Three is explicitly a ''pilgrimage'' (444), the entire novel depicts Saxon's quest for her portion of happiness. The road to that happiness lies through the vicissitudes of marriage, which here is not permanent bliss but a process of painful growth and change. Much as Oakland itself is ''just a place to start from,'' the little Pine Street cottage,[18] with its neat geranium beds and picket fence, suggests the naive conventionality of Saxon's vision of an eternal honeymoon —a vision shattered when the battling strikers and scabs knock the front gate off its hinges, trample the flowers, and strew the fence with corpses. Her seemingly invulnerable domestic life has been shockingly violated, and the nature of the violation is confirmed by the death of her premature child and the disintegration of her marriage.

This quest for marital happiness is also a quest for the fulfillment of certain ideas and values. Most prominent of these is the struggle to recover the westering impulse which London associated with the Anglo-American spirit. Equally important, Saxon is searching for an acceptable form of religious belief. By some not-too-convincing process of cultural osmosis, she has absorbed the nineteenth-century crisis of faith, sensing the decline of old certitudes and the need for new sources of religious inspiration. If the answers she finds are not always credible, London writes convincingly of her desperate need to find them.

This religious anxiety emerges early, when Saxon and Mary nervously discuss Bert Wanhope's atheism. Intrigued though finally dissatisfied by Bert's negations, they struggle to articulate their own conceptions of the deity. To Saxon, God is a "funny proposition" who reminds her of "that little, wrinkly Mexican that sells wire puzzles." Like the Mexican, God "passes a puzzle out to everybody, and they spend all their lives tryin' to work it out. They all get stuck. I can't work mine out. I don't know where to start" (13). The place to start will soon present itself in the form of Billy Roberts; and her life with him, which at first seems the solution, eventually becomes only another part of the problem. Her marriage will be the territory through which she must search for acceptable beliefs in a world devoid of the traditional assurances of meaning and purpose. Yet the religion of love will offer only one possibility. Another has already emerged in a religion of race—a belief in Anglo-Saxon adventurism and in her own forebears as its embodiment.

From the beginning London stresses the psychological and quasi-religious nature of Saxon's racial attitudes. Finding the orthodox God remote and puzzling, Saxon discovers credible surrogates in the heroic figure of her father, a captain of cavalry who had died before she could know him; and especially her mother, a poet and an equally heroic California pioneer who had crossed the plains in a covered wagon and died when Saxon was a child. In the daguerreotype of her mother, her "deeply religious" nature finds a "concrete" object of worship. Her mother "meant to her what God meant to others"; and the relics of her mother's life—the daguerreotype, the manuscript poems, and the chest of drawers that traveled across the plains—have become her "high altar and holy of holies" (47). The poems are sacred scriptures containing an elusive "clue" with which "all would be made clear" (48), and she handles all her mother's possessions "with the deep gravity and circumstance of a priest" (49).

This idealized "mother-myth" (47) obviously originates in an orphaned girl's longing for the dimming figure of her memories. But Saxon's myth-making is more than a hunger for lost security. It is an espousal of her mother's qualities of mind and character—the raw courage, the "grit" (50), of the true pioneer who shepherded the family across the plains and held them together when they reached California. What especially arises in Saxon's mind like an imagined tapestry is the great adventure of westering, "palpitating and real, shimmering in the sun-flashed dust of ten thousand hoofs, . . . across a continent, the great hegira of the land-hungry Anglo-Saxon," through which, like "a flying shuttle, weaving the golden dazzling thread of personality, moved the form of her little, indomitable mother" (50–51).

Many readers, viewing Saxon's emotions in the light of later manifestations of Germanic and Anglo-American racism, will find her adulation of the "land-hungry Anglo-Saxon" ominous. Saxon does not, indeed, entirely escape the taint of racism, nor does London himself. Notions of Anglo-Saxon supremacy were in their heyday, and London's fiction often reflected—and perhaps contributed to—their advance.[19] Yet the attitudes of these characters should at least be recognized as a perennial form of working-class paranoia, which is aggravated during periods of economic hardship when the competition for jobs is the most fierce. The same impulse appears in Bert and Billy's lament for their kind as "the last of the Mohegans" (155), an echo of Cooper's elegiac record of the passing of an earlier frontier in the Leatherstocking Tales. Saxon, too, engages in these *ubi sunt* meditations, "dreaming of the arcadian days of her people, when they had not lived in cities nor been vexed with labor unions and employers' associations" (178).

London carefully distinguishes, moreover, between Saxon's pride of ancestry and the more belligerent chauvinism of Billy and Bert. When Bert rants about the fate of the "old white stock" (155), Saxon holds herself aloof; nor does she chime in with Billy's tirade against socialism as the haven of "a lot of fat Germans an' greasy Russian Jews" (170). At times, indeed, she is unable to allow such racial posturing to go unreproved. When Billy, observing the dense concentration of Portuguese farms near San Leandro, grumbles that "the free-born American ain't got no room left in his own land," Saxon replies, "Then it's his own fault." Billy, in turn, insists that Americans could easily farm like the Portuguese if they wanted to, but that they "ain't much given to livin' like a pig offen leavin's." Saxon remains unimpressed: "Not in the country, maybe. . . . But I've seen an awful lot of Americans living like pigs in the cities" (303). Later, in the face of Saxon's open appreciation of the Portuguese, Billy blusters, "Oh, sure, they got a good thing. . . . But they needn't get chesty with *me*, I can tell you that much—just because they've jiggerooed us out of our land an' everything." Again Saxon quietly deflates him, pointing out that the Portuguese are "not showing any signs of chestiness" (315). To be sure, her rejection of Billy's statements seems at times the result more of gentility than of true conviction, and occasionally she joins Billy in his xenophobia, envisioning the true "Americans" crushed by hordes of more provident and industrious "foreigners." But her sense of proportion and decency more than once offsets the extremes of Billy's racism, and hers is the dominant point of view throughout the novel.

The main motive of Saxon's quest, then, is the desire to resume the heritage of her mother's pioneering. The means to that end will be her marriage to Billy Roberts, to whom she is immediately drawn partly because he comes from a similar background. Their marriage, beginning in naive honeymoon bliss, soon confronts a new and more threatening frontier, the urban world of industrial strife. Throughout these early and middle chapters, Saxon examines three other marriages, each of which offers a cautionary example of destructive marital behavior or a useful lesson in marital realities. By the time she and Billy leave Oakland, she is ready to exchange the urban frontier for a resumption of the pioneers' search for open land, where her ancestral heritage and her marriage to Billy can be fruitfully united.

Even as her courtship begins, Saxon has before her, in Sarah and Tom, an instance of a marriage fallen into hopeless chaos. After Sarah's hysteria has subsided, Tom's reflections offer Saxon a lesson she would do well to heed. Urging her to enjoy herself while she can, Tom observes ruefully that she will "get old, and all that means, fast enough." Then, almost as an afterthought, he muses: "Hell! Think of it! Sarah and I used to go buggy-riding once on a time. And I guess she had her three pair of shoes, too. Can you beat it?" (72). But Saxon, who has defended her right to three pairs of shoes and is about to go buggy-riding with Billy, draws no parallel between Tom's past and her own future: "Fresh from the shattering chaos of her sister-in-law's mind, Billy's tremendous calm was especially satisfying, and Saxon mentally laughed to scorn the terrible temper he had charged to himself" (73). The irony of her naive reflections will be apparent soon enough.

Though Saxon never sees in Tom and Sarah's troubles any forecast of her own future, she is more wary of the friction between Mary and Bert. From the beginning Bert is "very possessive with Mary, almost roughly so" (19), and as a result Mary remains edgy and defensive. Even before their marriage they struggle for power, Mary insisting that "I'll lead the man around by the nose that marries me" and Bert rejoining, "I'll be everlastingly jiggerooed if I put up for a wigwam I can't be boss of" (108). When the two couples dine together, Bert's scathing cynicism and Mary's "unconcealed hostility" cause Saxon to be "concerned over the outcome of their marriage" (155). On a later visit Billy becomes aware that he is "making comparisons": Bert and Mary's house has no "satisfying atmosphere" (175).

But although Billy and Saxon avoid open acrimony, they do engage in a quieter power struggle of their own. After denying that she would ever attempt to rule her husband, Saxon maneuvers Billy into accepting her idea of how their wedding ring should be inscribed. Mary is quick to point out that Saxon is "having her own way and leading [Billy] by the nose already" (109), and Saxon momentarily acknowledges the justice of the charge. The lesson is soon reinforced by Mercedes Higgins, who insists that "the greatest of the arts is the conquering of men" (143) and from whom Saxon learns the guile she will need to get Billy out of Oakland, salvage her foundering marriage, and gain a full partnership in their work.

Mercedes is a preposterous but fascinating character. Acting as Saxon's mentor throughout Book Two, she exerts a powerful influence on the younger woman's attitudes toward marriage and on her religious and social beliefs. That influence is predominantly negative, though nonetheless insidiously attractive. She speaks for the dark side of London's vision, grim, cynical, nihilistic, yet full of the Dionysian energies of life and love. She is a demon that must be exorcised before Saxon's (and London's) more optimistic spirit can reassert itself in the agrarian dream of Book Three.

In one sense Mercedes scarcely belongs in a realistic novel of industrial strife. She seems to have wandered out of some exotic romance, where as the fabled temptress, the Dark Lady of lurid nightmare, she promises both unspeakable delight and ultimate thralldom. Unsurprisingly, her neighbors

suspect her of witchcraft, an honor she does not wholly dis-
claim. With her face "withered as if scorched in great
heats" and her black, flashing eyes betokening some "un-
quenched inner conflagration," Mercedes is "anything but
ordinary" (133–34). Born of an Irish father and a Peruvian
mother, she is (in London's ethnic stereotypes) hot-blooded
on both sides; and she has lived in every part of the world,
including the Klondike and the South Seas. What she hopes
to convey to Saxon is the knowledge drawn from her experience of men. To hold a man, and subtly to dominate him, is
a power that Mercedes equates with the life force itself. The
secret of this power is concealment and variety; its enemy is
"the commonplace" (140). As she plays bewitching melo-
dies on her ukulele, she gives utterance to a "lava rush" of
emotion, "scorching and searing"—a "wild farrago" in
which Saxon catches "profounds inexpressible and unthinkable . . . connotations lawless and terrible" (144).

This dithyrambic outpouring establishes Mercedes as a
kind of superwoman, whose Dionysian passions underlie a
pagan religious sensibility and Nietzschean social views.
Her rage for life proceeds directly from her vision of death,
which appears in one of the most horrific images London
ever created: the gruesome specter of the salt vats, where
the corpses of paupers await dissection. Visions of maggoty
cadavers and grinning skulls had always lurked at the pe-
riphery of London's consciousness, but this particular *me-
mento mori* has a special force because it combines the vision of death with London's other nightmare image, the
social pit. The salt vats exist only for the poor—only for
those who lack the price of a proper burial. The vats are also
a special hell for women, a Gothic chamber of horrors in
which Mercedes has glimpsed "the things men may do with
your pretty flesh after you are dead" (165).

Her terror of the salt vats leads Mercedes to the religion of
living passion. When Saxon asks her whether she believes in
God, she answers, "Who knows?" (165); she fears only the
salt vats. It is she who elevates the washing of "dainties"
into a "true sacrament of beauty" (135), in which she acts

as the priestess of a cult of love, performing her ablutions as if she were conducting a high mass. The apparent absurdity of this ritual, with its disquieting undertone of masculine fetishes, should not be permitted to obscure its importance for Saxon, who has been searching for the totems and incantations with which to worship her husband as she once worshipped her mother. Before long, she is indeed striving with a "fervor almost religious" (148) to make Billy's life perfect.

But although Saxon accepts much of what Mercedes teaches, an important difference remains. Mercedes's creed is all ego, an ethic of self-fulfillment which occasionally calls for the sacrifice of others. She indulges her expensive tastes while denying similar luxuries to her husband; and when she promises to sell Saxon's fine needlework for a small commission, she cheats Saxon out of part of the price. Discovered in her subterfuge, Mercedes invokes the salt vats: "To escape the vats I would stop at nothing—steal the widow's mite, the orphan's crust, and pennies from a dead man's eyes" (165). This self-serving ethic eventually becomes a full-blown Nietzschean creed of power. When two scabs are beaten by a mob, she looks on without pity. "Most men are born stupid," she declares. "They are the slaves. A few are born clever. They are the masters" (179). She can understand and applaud dying splendidly "for women, or ideas, or bars of gold, or fabulous diamonds," but she scorns the industrial strife in which men fight for jobs "like dogs wrangling over bones" (180).

Saxon, however, cannot accept an anarchic world without purpose, without justice, with no goal but self-fulfillment. Though desperately anxious for her own portion of happiness, she conceives of it only as something shared. She can fulfill herself only through Billy. She is horrified by Mercedes's contemptuous dismissal of the working class as "cheap spawn" who "fester and multiply like maggots" (182). To accept such a position would be to hold valueless her own life and Billy's, and, worse, to deny the humanity of the baby she is carrying. But though Saxon cannot "bring herself to believe much of what she considered Mercedes' romancing'' (182), she recognizes a certain remorseless accuracy in the old woman's picture of society—a picture that will be indelibly printed on her brain by the industrial strife that tears her world apart. She will then be forced to take Mercedes's pessimism more seriously and to find a new way to answer it.

The best part of the novel is the series of chapters in Book Two tracing the disintegration of Saxon's marriage, beginning with the battle between the strikers and scabs and culminating in Saxon's nervous breakdown while Billy is in jail. When the conflict erupts, Billy naturally sides with the strikers. Saxon, however, sees the larger tragedy, in which men die and families are destroyed on both sides. Recalling Mercedes's cynicism, she wonders whether Billy, too, is merely ''a wild beast, a dog that would snarl over a bone.'' Life, she acknowledges, is ''a strange puzzle. Perhaps Mercedes Higgins was right in her cruel statement of the terms of existence'' (197).

The gradual estrangement of Billy and Saxon is almost wholly convincing, the more so because London presents it from Saxon's point of view. While Billy remains blind to the forces destroying their marriage, Saxon can see them with a painful clarity while remaining powerless to halt them. She is thus an increasingly divided person, one part of herself experiencing and suffering while the other half remains detached, a spectator of her own tragedy. She feels triply bereft, mourning the loss of her baby, the deaths or departures of her friends, and Billy's growing preoccupation with the strike. Billy, for his part, ''dimly sensed her suffering, without comprehending the scope and intensity of it. He was too man-practical, and, by his very sex, too remote from the intimate tragedy that was hers'' (202). As he grows sullen, she urges him to talk; but when he does so, telling with relish of the scabs he has beaten, she is secretly horrified and only feels further estranged from him. ''It never entered his head,'' she discovers, ''that he was not absolutely right'' (212).

As Billy becomes more and more embittered by their narrowing circumstances and the public's hostility, his taste for violence grows. So does his taste for liquor. To Saxon he is "a stranger" from whom she is "beginning to shrink." Though not yet actively cruel to her, he is "rarely kind." His gentleness has become "mechanical," his caresses "habitual." In place of the boyishly engaging Billy of their courtship and early married life, the strike has brought out this "other and grisly self" (217, 218), and Saxon's love soon gives way to the "pity that is parent to contempt" (225). When Billy, maddened by the death sentences meted out to his fellow teamsters, earns a thirty-day jail sentence for assaulting their lodger, Saxon reaches the nadir of her married life.

Saxon's emotional breakdown is vividly portrayed, its bodily symptoms reflecting her psychic desolation. Her moments of delirium provide little escape from her present trouble, "with its parch in the throat, its ache in the breast, and its gnawing, vacant goneness" (245). The morning after Billy's imprisonment, she wakens with a "strange numbness . . . a feeling of constriction about her head as if it were bound by a heavy band of iron." She suffers from wayward impulses and inexplicable losses of memory, and at the same time experiences a "strange feeling of loss of self, of being a stranger to herself" (246).

But Saxon's personal distress also signals a crisis of the outer society—of both its economic system and its religious faith. Saxon's description of her feeling of "goneness," of "loss of self," of being "a stranger to herself," is the language not only of psychopathology but, more important, of spiritual alienation. She discovers the reason for this feeling as she wanders by the Oakland Estuary, where the "spaciousness" of the rock wall signals a world more "natural" and "rational" than the industrial inferno of the city: "Here, hopelessly man-made as the great wall was, nothing seemed artificial. There were no men there, no laws nor conflicts of men. The tide flowed and ebbed; the sun rose and set; regularly each afternoon the brave west wind came romping in through the Golden Gate, darkening the water, cresting tiny wavelets, making the sailboats fly. Everything ran with frictionless order. Everything was free" (252). What Saxon glimpses here is not so much the romantic vision of splendidly savage nature as the earlier Enlightenment conception of the world as a great "frictionless" machine, in which all motion is governed by immutable laws. The romantic notion that everything is wild and free gives way to the impression that everything is orderly and rational. The tide ebbs and flows, the sun rises and sets; and even the west wind, that capricious favorite of romantic poets, comes "regularly" into the bay to command the sailboats to obey its unwavering laws of force.

What Saxon is offered, in short, is a choice of machines: the grindingly destructive machine of industrial society or the harmonious beauty of the machine of nature. The breakdown of social justice is soon made painfully vivid:

One flood tide she found the water covered with muskmelons. They bobbed and bumped along up the estuary in countless thousands. Where they stranded against the rocks she was able to get them. But each and every melon—and she patiently tried scores of them—had been spoiled by a sharp gash that let in the salt water. She could not understand. She asked an old Portuguese woman gathering driftwood.

"They do it, the people who have too much," the old woman explained. . . . "It is to keep up the price. They throw them overboard in San Francisco."

"But why don't they give them away to the poor people?" Saxon asked.

"They must keep up the price."

"But the poor people cannot buy them anyway," Saxon objected. "It would not hurt the price."

The old woman shrugged her shoulders.

"I do not know. It is their way. They chop each melon so that the poor people cannot fish them out and eat anyway. They do the same with the oranges, with the apples." (252–53)

Saxon is stunned. She cannot understand "a world that did such things—a world in which some men possessed so much food that they threw it away, paying men for their labor of spoiling it before they threw it away" (253). But to recognize the insanity of such a society is to call into question the benevolence of God. Remembering Mercedes's tales of almost incredible social injustice, she can only conclude that God does not exist at all, for "God could not make a botch" (255). As she sinks into this "morass of pessimism," she concludes, like "hosts of more learned thinkers before her," that the universe is "without concern for men" (255).

But Saxon cannot accept this bleak view for long. Life may be a trap, but she is determined to escape it—to grasp her "small meed of happiness" before succumbing to the "black grave" or the "salt vats" (256). Her brother tries to convert her to socialism, but she dismisses his solution as "a dream"; she wants her fulfillment "real" and "now" (257, 258). She has long since recognized that Billy's disintegration was but a symptom of the larger social disease, not a sin for which he could be held responsible. Saxon, too, refuses to believe she is either sinful or stupid. After the inspiriting sojourn with the young sailor revives her courage, she wakes the next morning feeling "her old self" and begins "putting the neglected house in order" (270).

Up to this point, London has written a coherent and often affecting novel of a young woman's struggle for happiness in a world that seems to conspire against her. Unfortunately, his didactic impulse soon leads him astray. When Saxon's search for the bluebird of happiness goes on the road, the narrative becomes little more than a combination of agricultural pamphlet and California travelogue—and not even an interesting travelogue, at that. Places are visited, but they are not really seen. London could have sacrificed the visit to Carmel, where it is patently absurd for the unlettered Billy and Saxon to be taken up by the crowd of bohemian esthetes. The northern wagon excursion, too, is tediously prolonged, little more than a bare itinerary. Even after the pair settle at last on the Sonoma ranch, the dream of bucolic happiness rapidly becomes something of a rat race. Billy's capitalistic ventures, reminiscent of Burning Daylight's financial scheming in Oakland and San Francisco, are obviously a source of pleasure to him; yet one cannot but wonder how soon his enterprise will succumb to the economic chaos he has struggled to escape.

For Saxon, however, the agrarian dream, shorn of its racism and with due allowance for its portion of sentimentality, offers an attractive if somewhat simplistic answer to the discontents that have plagued her life in the city.[20] Frederick Jackson Turner's famous thesis had already proclaimed the closing of the old frontier, as Saxon's brother seems aware: "That was the spirit of them times—free land, an' plenty of it. But when we reached the Pacific Ocean them times was ended. Big business begun; an' big business means big business men; an' every big business man means thousands of little men without any business at all except to work for the big ones. They're the losers, don't you see? . . . They can't yoke up their oxen an' pull on. There's no place to pull on" (294).[21] Nevertheless, always mindful of her mother's example, Saxon believes that the frontier survives. Only its form has changed. "Perhaps the hard times were past," she wonders. "Perhaps [the Oakland struggles] had constituted *her* plains, and she and Billy had won safely across and were even then climbing the Sierras ere they dropped down into the pleasant valley land" (297).

Thus, as in *Burning Daylight*, the lyrical description of the entrance into the Sonoma Valley suggests that though the land is no longer free, it still promises values that the will can make real. The ethic of nihilism and power, embodied earlier in Billy and Mercedes, has been defeated by the civilizing impulses of Saxon, whose healed marriage offers yet another instance of London's struggle to close the divisions in his own mind and life. In *The Little Lady of the Big House*, the civilized order represented by his marriage and his ranch would face a final and more severe test.

10

A Broken Clock
The Little Lady of the Big House

When the Londons completed their voyage around Cape
Horn in the summer of 1912, Charmian was again pregnant,
and their renewed hope for a child had already found its way
into the ending of *The Valley of the Moon*. On August 12,
however, only eight days after their return to Glen Ellen,
Charmian suffered a miscarriage. Jack, in his disappointment, turned all the more fervently to the development of
his ranch and the construction of Wolf House. But on the
night of August 22, 1913, shortly before they were to move
in, the new house was destroyed by fire. These two losses—
of the child and the house—struck at the very heart of London's attempt to establish the permanent ties of blood and
soil that his early life had denied him. As he later acknowledged to his wife, 1913 had become his "bad year," during
which his face had "changed forever."[1] From time to time
his old energy and enthusiasm revived; but his final attempt
at a serious novel, *The Little Lady of the Big House*—conceived in 1913 and written in 1914—was in part the expression of these disappointments. Yet such misfortunes form
only the backdrop. In the novel, no house burns, no pregnancy is aborted. What does happen is the destruction of the

marriage of Dick and Paula Forrest when an old friend of Dick's, Evan Graham, visits the couple's ranch, falls in love with Paula, and finds his love returned by her. Just as the central action of *The Valley* had reflected the New York estrangement of early 1912, the new plot springs directly from another marital crisis that occurred during the early months of 1913.

On the surface, the year began auspiciously enough. In January, while starting work on the Cape Horn novel that would eventually be titled *The Mutiny of the Elsinore*, Jack also announced that his "ranch schemes" were making him happier than he had even been before. "Mate is full of pig-projects," Charmian noted on February 1; and a day later it seemed to her that their "Honeymoon Days" had returned.[2] Still, beneath this renewed companionship lay isolated hints of friction. During the terrible New York period of the preceding year, Charmian had been thrown largely on her own resources; and even as they recovered their balance on the *Dirigo*, she had remained restive. After her miscarriage in August she was ill and depressed, and sometime toward the end of the year, she jotted on the rear flyleaf of her diary an idea which, had he known of it, Jack would undoubtedly have found disquieting: "Motif for story. Man, somewhat tired of her—lost child, &c.[—]goes traveling to Honolulu say on business. She *thinks*. Gets there first—sailing vessel. Does some hustling—receives him in holokus."[3] Here, conceived from Charmian's point of view, are the initial ingredients of *The Little Lady:* a childless marriage; a husband emotionally distant, preoccupied with business; a wife forced to think hard about the course of her marriage, and to act accordingly. The only ingredient still missing was a potential lover. Before long, as if on cue, an acceptable candidate appeared in the person of one Joseph Edgar Allan Elphinstone Dunn.

Allan Dunn (or J. Allan Dunn, as he sometimes signed himself) was four years older than Jack and thus actually closer to Charmian's age. British-born and Oxford-educated, he had been a newspaper reporter in England before coming

to America with the *Rocky Mountain News* in Denver and
later the *Salt Lake Herald*, serving as a correspondent from
the Spanish-American War in 1898. Subsequently he had
moved on to Hawaii, where he married and became a reporter for an independent syndicate that took him to California and the Orient.[4] By early 1907 he was in San Francisco with *Sunset* magazine, in which capacity he and his
wife became friendly with the Londons, whom he inter-
viewed for an article on the building of the *Snark*. Charmian's diary records three meetings, including a picture-
taking session on the boat and a dinner at Coppa's with several other notables a month before the Londons sailed.
There were no further encounters, of course, during the two
years of the *Snark* voyage, and if they saw anything more of
Dunn between 1909 and 1912, the meetings must have been
inconsequential. Meanwhile, Dunn had enlarged his reputation as the author of such guidebooks as *Yosemite Legends*
(1910) and *California for the Sportsman* (1911), and on January 10, 1913, he inscribed and sent to Jack a copy of his
latest volume, *Care-Free San Francisco*.[5] The upshot was an
invitation to visit the ranch.

When he arrived, on February 27, Charmian noted in her
diary: "Allan Dunn comes in evening, & we enjoy him as always. He has sweet ways—'dear,' and 'dear heart.'" A few
days later she recorded that while Jack was off somewhere
looking at his goats, "Allan & I ride to summit of Sonoma
Mt. & have a glorious time watching the fog clear & crowd
in again. Lovely, rainless weather. . . . Trees blossoming,
and flowers. Feel fine, & having a lovely experience." A day
later, on March 5: "Spend a glorious morning on horseback,
Allan & I going to S.P. [Southern Pacific Railroad] station to
see stallion & mare arrive from Napa—Neuadd Hillside, &
Cockerington Princess. . . . Afternoon, Mate & I, with Allan
& [Finn] Froelich, do old mining-camp trail, crossing over &
down back by Clark's. Pretty tired, but awfully happy. Go
out on old promontory in morning, with Allan." On March
6: "Allan & I fool around in forenoon, watching for stallion
to come back from exercise. Allan reads me his Kahuna [?]

story after lunch. Later, he paints at bridge. I walk over."
Two days later, "Mate, Allan & I fool around in sunshine
with goats and Neuadd Hillside, &c., lie about in grass, &c.
. . . Afternoon, ride new places, over behind lagoon. Belle
[Charmian's mare] & her son both getting gay—Hilo. He is a
handsome young stallion. We decide to let the pair let nature take its course!"

Nature was indeed taking its course, for Charmian was in
the initial throes of a love affair amid circumstances that
would later be re-created in *The Little Lady*. Though the affair apparently remained unconsummated, for the time being it posed a genuine threat to her marriage. On March 10,
Dunn returned to the city, Charmian driving him to the station by way of Wolf House, then hurrying home to offer Jack
what little comfort she could. The two had "one grand pow-
wow" during which Jack exclaimed: "I am the proudest
man in the world; I have found that I have a heart; and I have
nearly died."[6] This intensification of his love under the
goad of jealousy led Charmian, in turn, to say of Jack: "The
Dear Man. I love him so." Thus, drawn strongly to Dunn
yet moved by Jack's renewed attentions, Charmian rose to a
state of exalted confusion: "Feel very much of a battle
ground. But what men. I can't help pouting [puffing?] out
my chest. But I am heartbroken over the realization of
Mateman's suffering. Just the same—he has 'learned about
women' from me—& can appreciate some of *my* 'white
nights.'" On March 13 she recorded her disappointment at
not hearing from Dunn—he was "keeping 'sober' counsel
with himself," she guessed—but the next day brought a
"perfectly serious letter from A.D." which prompted her
and Jack to have some "wonderful talks on the subject."

On the day of these "wonderful talks," March 14, Jack
wrote to Roland Phillips of *Cosmopolitan* to announce that
he had a "splendid motif" for a new novel involving a sexual
triangle "in which no sexual adventure is actually achieved
or comes within a million miles of being achieved."[7] But
such confidence in the outcome of the affair, though ulti-

mately justified, was premature, for the many blank pages and occasional brief shorthand entries in Charmian's diary in late March and early April speak mutely of Dunn's return to the ranch and the renewal of their affair. On April 10 she records simply: "Great days—full of beauty of interest and situation [*sic*]. Blue eyed men." And on April 13: "Allan finishes redwood picture. Beats any redwood painting *I* ever saw." This is the last reference to Dunn's presence on the ranch. Thereafter she mentions him (as A.D.) only when she reads about him in the newspaper or, much later, hears of his relations with another woman. On May 24 she had written revealingly, "Terrible thing to be doubted when one is innocent," and by this time she must indeed have resolved her dilemma in favor of loyalty to her husband. Whatever lingering suspicions Jack may have harbored, his appendectomy in July—and more certainly the burning of Wolf House in August—drew them back together; and by the fall of 1913 the whole affair appears to have blown over.

This episode thus provided London with the chief model for Evan Graham and the essentials of his plot. Yet even before the advent of Allan Dunn, bits and pieces of Jack's and Charmian's experiences had prepared the way, and later events added further details. Prophetically, Jack had confessed to Charmian in Tahiti five years earlier how devastated he would be "if his horrible dream of [her] infidelity came true."[8] After their return to the ranch, various sources of friction arose between them and eventually entered the novel. Though in her better moods Charmian enjoyed company and the life of the ranch, when she was ill and depressed she resented Jack's attention to their numerous guests and his preoccupation with agricultural experiments. She regretted, too, the way his fondness for combining alcohol with vigorous argument sometimes led him into unthinking tactlessness. In 1911 she recorded that he had driven their friend Blanche Partington to tears with an onslaught of "logic," and a few months later she fretted that Jack and Blanche had had another of their "long & fruitless discussions." Yet there were moments when she could forgive him anything. Possibly she told him of the "sweet dream" she had one night in which the two of them were "dying, looking into each other's eyes to the last."[9] By the time London actually began the novel, on April 3, 1914, the Dunn episode was already a year behind them, and the two were sufficiently detached from it to share in the making of notes and the writing of descriptive passages. He had written only a few thousand words, however, when he received a call from *Collier's* to go to Mexico to report the American intervention at Vera Cruz. Though the writing was interrupted for two months, the Mexican excursion supplied the novel with two final ingredients.

The first of these was perhaps supplied only indirectly. The fact that *Collier's* was a Hearst publication may have reminded London, if he hadn't already thought of it, that a few years earlier he had written a slightly tongue-in-cheek article on how to run a successful newspaper by catering to a working-class audience. He had illustrated his point with an account of the rise of William Randolph Hearst:

Not so many years ago there was a Senator Hearst of California, who owned the *San Francisco Examiner.* It was not a very respectable sheet. He did not directly make money out of it. He used it to advance his business and political interests, in the same way that many millionaires and corporations use newspapers in the United States to-day.

Senator Hearst also had a son. About the time the *Examiner's* usefulness had come to an end, the son emerged from college. His father offered him several advantageous openings for a start in life, none of which satisfied the boy, who, instead, asked for and received the *Examiner.*

Young Hearst looked about him with a calculating eye. He had keen business foresight, and he saw that the largest audience in San Francisco (and incidentally in California and the whole United States), was not being catered to. . . . He saw a fortune waiting for the right man to pick it up. William Randolph Hearst was the right man, for it was he that picked that fortune up.

In addition to splendid business ability, he had nerve. There was nothing cheap or shoddy in the way he went after that fortune. He bought up the best brains in the market, and paid unheard of prices. He bought business managers, lawyers, editors, writers, cartoonists, and illustrators. It did not matter what pay they were receiving from other employers, he gave them more. He gave them twice as much. He gave them more than they even dreamed of asking for.[10]

In a number of details—a wealthy father's only son, who insists on following his own instincts instead of the guidance of elders and who lavishly buys up brainpower—Hearst suggests Dick Forrest, the son of Lucky Richard Forrest, though London grafted onto Hearst's career some of his own youthful adventures and his later agricultural dreams.[11]

More directly, the sojourn in Vera Cruz gave London a chance to fill out the character of Evan Graham. Coincidentally, the second model for Graham was another man named Dunn—this time not Allan but Robert Dunn, a distinguished foreign correspondent with whom Jack had been friendly in 1904 when they were both in Japan and Korea reporting the Russo-Japanese War. Now, ten years later, while Jack was off at Tampico, "Bobby" Dunn invited Charmian twice for dinner and dancing along with some of his military friends; and when Jack returned but was laid up with dysentery, Dunn again squired Charmian to an "elegant dinner" with another of Jack's old cohorts from Korean days, Richard Harding Davis. The coincidence of surnames, as well as these excursions with Charmian, was apparently sufficient to cause London to fuse the two Dunns in his mind as he worked out the background of Graham. In the novel, just before Graham's arrival at the ranch, Dick reminds Paula that they had dined with him two years ago in Santiago:

"Don't you remember that big blond fellow—you talked music with him for half an hour while Captain Joyce talked our heads off to prove that the United States should clean Mexico up and out with the mailed fist."

"Oh, to be sure," Paula vaguely recollected. "He'd met you somewhere before . . . South Africa, wasn't it? Or the Philippines?"

"That's the chap. South Africa, it was. . . . Next time we met was on the *Times* dispatch boat on the Yellow Sea. And we crossed trails a dozen times after that, without meeting, until that night in the Café Venus." (94)

The reference to the American intervention in Mexico links this conversation to the Londons' meeting with Dunn in Vera Cruz (here disguised as Santiago). Jack had never reached South Africa, where he had been headed in 1902 before being sidetracked into the East End of London, but the reference to the "*Times* dispatch boat on the Yellow Sea" touches on their common experience as reporters in Korea. Robert Dunn's attentions to Charmian were probably no more than polite (his portrait of her in his memoirs, in fact, was unflattering), but his New England background, Harvard education, and adventurous life must have cast him in Jack's mind as another man who, like Allan Dunn, offered qualities capable, under the right circumstances, of turning Charmian's head.[12] In the novel, Evan Graham is a "Yale man" of "old American stock" (95).

But although Graham is based chiefly on the two Dunns, earlier readers have not been entirely wrong in viewing him as a projection of another side of London's own character.[13] London describes Evan as Dick Forrest's "foil" (100), though the more precise term would be *alter ego* or *double*, for psychologically they are two sides of a single self, each embodying traits that are latent but undeveloped in the other. Though in the novel Dick and Evan are the same age, Evan actually represents London's younger self—a more romantic figure than the preoccupied rancher that Dick Forrest and Jack London had become in their early middle age. At thirty-seven, London was no longer the ebullient adventurer of the *Snark* voyage. In a moment of frustration during the "bad year" Jack had considered returning to the sea, and he sensed Charmian's disappointment when he abandoned the idea. Charmian, in turn, confessed that she "*was* disappointed—why not? Had he not always proved a calmer, happier soul in a sea-existence away from the warring frictions of the land?"[14] Thus in 1913 London had two rivals: the real Allan Dunn and the ghost of his younger self.

The Little Lady, then, is a story of middle age and loss. Despite its title, it is the story principally of Dick Forrest, a supreme rationalist and pragmatist whose tragic illusion is that life can be planned and controlled—that by an act of will he can create and preserve a marital Eden and an agricultural utopia. In some ways, it is true, Dick's life is London's wish-fulfilling fantasy: in the novel the Big House does not burn, and London's deteriorating health becomes Dick's amazing physical vigor. The narrative is weakened, moreover, by lapses of style and by the badly mismanaged ending. But at its best, *The Little Lady* deals realistically with serious problems of adult life. For behind Dick's discovery of the vulnerability of the whole fabric of his life lie London's grief over his childless marriage and ruined mansion, his lingering anxiety about his wife's fidelity, and a more urgent awareness of his own mortality.

Yet that sense of tragic disillusionment is missing from the letter he wrote to Roland Phillips during the anxious interlude between Allan Dunn's visits to the ranch. Under the circumstances, in fact, the letter is oddly exuberant:

Three characters only—a mighty trio in a mighty situation, in a magnificently beautiful environment. Each of the three is good; each of the three is big. It will be a winner.

It is all sex, from start to finish—in which no sexual adventure is actually achieved or comes within a million miles of being achieved, and in which, nevertheless, is all the guts of sex, coupled with strength. Oh, my three are not puling weaklings and moralists. They are cultured, modern, and at the same time profoundly primitive.

And when the tale is ended, the reader will take off his hat to each of the three of the trio: "By God! he was some man!" or "By God! she was some woman!"

As I go over this novel, I am almost led to believe that it is what I have been working toward all my writing life, and now I've got it in my two hands.

Except for my old-time punch, which will be in it from start to finish, it will not be believed that I could write it—it is so utterly fresh, so absolutely unlike anything I have ever done.

This new novel, he continued, would be "big stuff," yet it would "offend no one." It would be a "cleancut gem," a "jewel of artistry."[15]

For critics with the advantage of hindsight, this letter has provided ample evidence that London was losing his artistic judgment; and undeniably it does carry his stylistic mannerisms, along with his characteristic obsession with "guts" and "strength," almost to the point of self-parody. One should note in all fairness, however, that the letter describes a novel not yet written, and that it is primarily a sales-pitch aimed at persuading Phillips to accept the new book in lieu of a series of short stories for which London was already under contract. Furthermore, whatever its exaggerations and evasions, the letter seems genuine in its optimism. London had always depended for his plots on real experience or on printed sources, and now life had suddenly dropped in his lap the ingredients of a full-scale novel. The letter was written at the height of his emotional involvement in the events he describes, when the danger of losing Charmian had sharpened the edge of feelings dulled by years of habit. Whatever outcome life was prepared to write for the two of them, he held before him a situation that he could work out on his own artistic terms. And he does seem to have believed that the novel would be better than hack work. Instead of ringing changes on his old formulas, he saw himself as taking a real chance, making a new departure. His final emphasis thus falls not on prospective sales but on "artistry." Obviously he hoped the book would sell—but on the basis of fresh merit, not stale predictability.

The novel was conceived, moreover, before the burning of Wolf House, at a time when London was sublimating the disappointment of his childless marriage into his attempts to build his ranch into a showplace of California agriculture. *Burning Daylight* and *The Valley of the Moon* had ended on the ranch with high hopes and burgeoning projects; now *The Little Lady*, set in this "magnificently beautiful environment," would give him a chance to depict the ranch as he envisioned it in full-scale operation. Not even the fire, when it came, could entirely dampen his passion for "pig-projects" and a variety of other agricultural experiments; and in 1914 (soon after beginning *The Little Lady*) he wrote to his architect that new logs had been cut and hauled to the house site, where they were "seasoning in preparation for the rebuilding."[16] In short, this novel, despite its elegiac ending, is not quite the valedictory to his ranch and life that some critics have thought it.

London has also been faulted for using the hackneyed plot of the love triangle. Aside from the fact that he did not pick this plot out of thin air, the complaint is still trivial; one never hears it made about, say, *Anna Karenina* or *The Great Gatsby*. The question is not whether the plot is new but whether the novelist has endowed it with fresh narrative energy and psychological insight, and plainly London intended to make this triangle a "modern" one that would avoid sentimental and didactic clichés. The archetypal triangle, in any case, is the myth of the Fall; and in an early scene Dick casts himself and Paula as Indian versions of Adam and Eve, while Graham, who is haunted by the memory of a lost South Sea Island paradise, thinks to himself that Dick is "lucky—too lucky" (121). Thus, with his special fondness for *Paradise Lost*, London recognized that his plot had legitimate roots in the biblical fable of innocence, pride, envy, and fallibility.

London's desire to elevate his plot and characters to the level of the fabulous perhaps explains his invocation of an atmosphere of witchcraft and enchantment, demonism and madness—terms suggesting the degree to which persons who conceive of themselves as rational beings can succumb to a variety of imps of the perverse. A similar intention to elevate the action may lie behind the imagery of medieval romance. Paula's gown is "a sort of medieval thing" (109); the great room of the Big House resembles "a feast-hall of some medieval castle" (124); and the Seven Sages of the Madroño Grove are "pledged knights of the Little Lady" (340). Possibly London had in mind another legendary medieval triangle, that of Arthur, Lancelot, and Guinevere; but in any case the medieval imagery is introduced with a coy whimsicality that makes it merely silly, as if London were attempting to write a realistic novel of the present day and at the same time to endow it with the popular appeal of *When Knighthood Was in Flower.*

Another way in which London evades the charge that his plot is hackneyed is by having his characters self-consciously acknowledge their chagrin at having fallen into so conventional a "situation." Echoing London's beloved Ecclesiastes, Graham muses to himself that their affair is "nothing new under the sun" and that the "countless triangles of the countless generations had all been somehow solved" (255). Later, Paula thinks with an edge of bitterness: 'Graham had called the situation a triangle. Well, Dick could solve it. He could solve anything. Then why didn't he?" (310). Dick's strange forbearance as he watches the affair develop derives from his incurably scientific cast of mind. Until Evan and Paula's passionate kiss shatters his detachment, he continues to regard the potential lovers as if they were chemical reagents in a test tube. His theoretical frame of mind emerges most clearly in chapter 22, when he puts the case of a hypothetical triangle in order to convince Paula and Evan of his enlightened rationality—to reveal his awareness that man is "a most complicated animal" (272), whose heart cannot be prevented from straying. By playing the scientist, putting the two lovers to the test while refusing to intervene, he can convince himself fatalistically that the whole affair is a "game" in which each must play his allotted part to the end.

By shifting the point of view—from Dick to Evan, back to Dick, and intermittently to Paula—London involves his characters in an elaborate *pas de trois* in which the chief effect is an almost constant dramatic irony. At times all three characters are together, each speculating about what is in the mind of the others. In other scenes two characters pair off, while the third is left to observe them and wonder what they are up to. Dick, for example, senses the tension between Evan and Paula while remaining anxious and uncertain about how far it has carried them. Evan, in turn, remains jealous of the marital intimacy of Paula and Dick, while Paula tries privately to fathom how much Dick knows and what he intends to do about it. Near the end, after Dick becomes certain of Paula's attraction to Evan, London forsakes dramatic irony in favor of old-fashioned suspense, leaving the reader in the dark concerning her final choice between the two men, just as Dick, too, remains in doubt until he hears the fatal shot. The effect is to stress the uncertainty of human relations for three characters who have considered their lives under complete control.

The first eight chapters belong almost exclusively to Dick, serving to establish for us the world he has made and the past life out of which he has made it. For many pages the narrative proceeds according to Dick's morning schedule, thus dramatizing the overregimented life that contributes so much to his illusion of control. The opening passage is especially fine, with its ironic emphasis on Dick's complacency —his unquestioned sense of identity even in the surrounding darkness:

He awoke in the dark. His awakening was simple, easy, without movement save for the eyes that opened and made him aware of darkness. Unlike most, who must feel and grope and listen to, and contact with, the world about them, he knew himself on the moment of awakening, instantly identifying himself in time and place and personality. After the lapsed hours of sleep he took up, without effort, the interrupted tale of his days. He knew himself to be Dick Forrest, the master of broad acres, who had fallen asleep hours before after drowsily putting a match between the pages of "Road Town" and pressing off the electric reading lamp. (1)

In light of this beginning, there may also be conscious irony, rather than unintentional bathos, when we are told that "Forrest threw a glance as his wrist watch as he talked, but in that glance, without pause or fumble of focus, with swift certainty of correlation, he read the dial" (100). As he proudly tells Graham the moment the latter arrives, "We run the ranch like clockwork" (99).

The clock, in fact, is one of the novel's central symbols. It suggests Dick's illusion of efficiency and order, behind which lie impermanence and mortality. The ranch itself is a clocklike wheel. The Big House is "the hub of the ranch organization" (17),[17] and Dick's tour of the ranch forms a "circle about the Big House" (19). The wheel metaphor, by extension, applies both to Dick and to those who work under his command. Dick himself is "the center of a system" (35): "Each man was a specialist, yet Forrest was the proved master of their specialties" (36). His life and work are admirably yet oppressively systematic: "Everywhere about him, large fields and small were arranged in a system of accessibility and workability that would have warmed the heart of the most meticulous efficiency-expert" (16). His bedroom is a paradise of push-buttons, the whole ranch a fantasyland of gadgets, servants, and pleasures on command. As Graham discovers after his arrival, "If he wanted a horse, or if he wanted a swim or a motor car, or any ranch medium or utility he desired, . . . all he had to do was to call for it" (134). The endless round of games betokens a prolonged adolescence, in the light of which even a devotion to work and efficiency seems only a superior form of self-indulgence.

The flaws in Dick's system appear early. The ranch is a marvel of fecundity, and Dick never tires of his embarrassing rendition of the stallion's chant: "I am Eros. I stamp upon the hills. . . . The mares hear me, and startle, in quiet pastures; for they know me." Yet the Forrests are themselves barren.[18] Early in the novel, after Dick has offered one of the ranchhands gratuitous advice about how to handle his daughter, the man smiles behind Dick's back, wondering to himself, "But where's the kid of your own, Mr. Forrest?" (23). Only gradually do we become aware of the importance of the Forrests' childlessness and the sublimation of their procreative energy. In her apartment in the Big House resides Paula's unfinished sketch of a colt "madly whinneying for its mother" (97), and she has taken to breeding horses, finding in her carefully bred foal a substitute child, "my dream come true at last" (147). Her eyes glow "in the warmth of the sight of the abounding young life for which she was responsible" (150). Yet her unfulfilled desire for motherhood is mocked by the fountain in her apartment with its "life-sized babies wrought from pink marble. . . . So good was the color of the marble, so true had been the sculptor, that the illusion was of life. No cherubs these, but live warm human babies" (331). Children, Dick realizes, "had been her passion" (332). Without them she is driven to the decadent amusements of which the experiment with Evan Graham is the inevitable extension.

The "illusion of life" that Dick finds in Paula's marble babies suggests the corollary illusion that all is well with their marriage. From the time, years earlier, when Dick carefully postponed the sowing of his wild oats, he has believed that love and sex could be subjected to the rule of reason. Hence he fails to sense Paula's increasing dissatisfaction with his rigid routine and his obsession with the ranch. When she pays him his regular morning visit, before he turns his full attention to her, "his eyes lingered a full half minute longer on the totals of results of Professor Kenealy's hog inoculations on Simon Jones' farm at Washington, Iowa." And even as he abandons his statistics and kisses his wife, "with insistent right fore-finger [he] maintained his place in the pages of the pamphlet" (83). When after a time she catches him eyeing the clock once again, she gently mocks him as that "ultra-modern man, the last word of the two-legged, male human that finds Trojan adventures in sieges of statistics, and, armed with test tubes and hypodermics, engages in gladiatorial contests with weird microorganisms. Almost, at times, it seems you should wear glasses and be bald-headed" (86). When their tete-a-tete is interrupted by Dick's secretary and Paula makes her way out, Dick is "unaware that her voice was a trifle, just the merest trifle, subdued" (88).

The son of a San Francisco mining and railroad baron, Dick spent his youth as the "reared aristocrat" of a "Nob Hill palace" (47) but was sent to public grammar school to learn "two-legged, two-fisted democracy" (42). His years of wandering adventure and his self-designed education have made him a paragon of the "all around" (70). Yet when he marries Paula and establishes his ranch, his life settles into an increasingly narrow routine, in which democracy gives way to an agrarian economy that is not communitarian but feudal. Though his aim is to create a modern agricultural utopia based on the latest scientific principles, it is he who will preside over the estate as feudal overlord. His latest plan, already being executed, is the division of a 5000-acre plot into 20-acre holdings, each of which is to support one family engaged in intensive farming. The tenants, he says, "*must* farm, with individual responsibility, according to the scientific methods embodied in our instructions. The land is uniform. Every holding is like a pea in the pod to every other holding. The results of each holding will speak in no uncertain terms. The failure of any farmer, through laziness or stupidity, measured by the average result of the entire two hundred and fifty farmers, will not be tolerated. Out the failure must go, convicted by the average of his fellows."[19]

Dick insists that his plan is a "fair deal" for the farmer, who will be guaranteed a salary and any profit above the six percent that must be paid to the ranch. But Terrence McFane, one of the Seven Sages who often serve as foils to Dick, takes a less sanguine view of so dismal a grind. " 'Tis repulsive," he declares "the thought of the work, each on his twenty acres, toilin' and moilin', daylight till dark, and after dark—an' for what? . . . A full belly and shelter from the cold till one's body drops apart in the dark moldiness of the grave?" (129–30).

London also implies a criticism of Dick's obsession with gadgetry and scientific breeding. One afternoon Dick proudly takes Paula and Evan to see his new circular plowing contraption, in which a riderless tractor, once started, is pulled by a long cable in ever-narrowing concentric circles, thus plowing the field while the farmer sits on his front porch and reads the morning paper. But as Dick exults over his invention, Graham finds himself "divided between watching the circling tractor and casting glances at the picture Paula Forrest was on her mount" (190). Soon the tractor breaks down, and Dick remains in the field tinkering with his machinery, leaving Evan and Paula free to continue on without him.

Dick's experiments in animal breeding have encouraged in him a tendency to take a scientific view of people. He speaks of "five additions" to his farming colony much as if they were livestock. Paula responds that she thought the membership was full. " 'It was, and still it,' Dick beamed. 'But these are babies. And the least hopeful of the families had the rashness to have twins' " (286). Later, as Dick delivers a Solomonic solution to an adulterous triangle among the ranchhands' families, his voice takes on a "cold, hard, judicial note" (316); and he explains that his decision to fire one of the trio was made "not because you climbed over another man's fence—that's your business and his; but because you were guilty of causing a disturbance that is an impairment of ranch efficiency" (317). His conception of human behavior appears revealingly in his manner of driving a car: "He drove alone, and though he drove with speed he drove with safety. Accidents, for which he personally might be responsible, were things he did not tolerate. And they never occurred" (301). Yet Dick's well-planned life, like his machinery, is capable of breaking down. Indeed, even as he asserts his immunity to accidents, his world is disintegrating around him.

Part of the vulnerability of his system is traceable to the rigidity of his philosophy. "Dick hates mystery," Paula declares. "At once he is for ripping the husks and the heart from mystery, so that he will know the *how* and the *why*, when it will be no longer mystery but a generalization and a scientifically demonstrable fact" (235). For Dick, the "old, eternal test of truth" is still the pragmatic one: "*Will it work?*" (245). For Paula, however, Dick's pragmatic test offers no answer to her very real human dilemma. "Philosophy, like religion," Dick insists, "is what the man is"; but Paula, lacking such "surety of self," becomes aware of a "slipping and giving of convictions so long accepted that they had seemed part of her." Finding Dick's windy theorizing increasingly irritating, she declares that "too much philosophizing about life gets one worse than nowhere. A philosophic atmosphere is confusing—at least to a woman. One hears so much about everything, and against everything, that nothing is sure" (244). While she craves solid guides to moral conduct, Dick's relativism leaves her "compassless, rudderless, chartless on a sea of ideas" (245).

Paula's problem is indeed the lack of a "surety of self," a solid center around which her multifaceted personality can cohere. Graham admiringly describes her as "protean" (146), but it would be more accurate to regard her as fragmented. Being "too diversely talented" (221), she is everything and nothing. As Dick muses, "We've been married ten or a dozen years now, and, d'ye know, sometimes it seems to me I don't know her at all, and that nobody knows her, and that she doesn't know herself" (107). In this she is her father's daughter, for Philip Desten combined the dutiful rectitude of his "old New England stock" with the "streak of madness" that stemmed from a trace of French blood (218). Inheriting this troublesome combination of qualities, Paula retains both the need for moral absolutes and the strain of instability that finds an outlet in her "madcap escapades" (221) and her sensuous nature: her passion for music and painting and, implicitly, for sex. For a time after her marriage, she seemed to "find herself" through Dick (221); but as Dick drifts away from her, and as her continuing childlessness suggests both the literal and figurative barrenness of her life, her passions inevitably turn elsewhere for fulfillment.

Paula's flirtation with Graham is obviously a weapon against Dick's passivity, an attempt to jolt him out of his comfortable world of work and talk. "If Dick knew—since he knew, she framed it to herself—why did he not speak? . . . She both desired and feared that he might, until the fear faded and her earnest hope was that he would" (309–10). Dick, however, will not intervene, and Paula persists in her "ardent recklessness, trying not to feel the conscience-pricks of her divided allegiance, refusing to think too deeply." In her pride at attracting two such formidable lovers, there is "almost a touch of cruelty" (310), even while "deep down she was conscious of her own reckless-ness and madness" (311). In a sense she is conducting an ex-periment of her own, testing her undiscovered self against the possibilities of new experience. "I find I am a puzzle to myself," she acknowledges to Dick. "All my concepts have been toppled over by my conduct (367). As the end nears, Dick confesses to himself his understanding of her belated journey of self-discovery: " 'Poor little kid,' he murmured, 'having a hard time of it just waking up at this late day' " (374).

Evan Graham, too, at the age of forty, has a settled con-ception of himself, which is challenged by his infatuation with Paula. When the grand passion of his youth ended with the death of his Polynesian wife, he believed himself im-mune to further romantic entanglements, but he is jolted out of his complacency by his first view of Paula astride the stallion in the swimming tank. Later he marvels at the way her singing, "haunted with richness of sex" (169), is kept under control, and he begins to wonder whether she would be "equally mistress of her temperament in the deeper, pas-sional ways" (169–70). Graham's illusion is his belief that he can listen to Paula's siren-song, satisfying his curiosity while still avoiding the rocks of a deeper involvement. But as she continues to "witch-ride his man's imagination" (170), he discovers that "after the years he was just getting acquainted with himself. This was enchantment, madness.

He should tear himself away at once. He had known enchantments and madnesses before, and had torn himself away. Had he softened with the years? he questioned himself. Or was this a profounder madness than he had experienced?'' (214).

Thus, in this story of middle age, all three characters—Evan Graham as well as Dick and Paula—have settled into patterns of life which they believe immutable. By slow degrees, their conviction of permanence is challenged as each of them discovers (or rediscovers) a long-dormant capacity for emotion. Before the irrational facts of experience all theories collapse. They must become practical realists, dispensing with "priest and code" (254) and groping their way toward a solution that cannot but be painful to at least one of them. London was certainly mistaken when he proclaimed that the merit of this novel would lie in its "guts" and "strength." Its chief claim to a respectable place among his novels lies instead in its gradual—at times almost subtle—unfolding of the experience of self-discovery, and in its observant dramatization of the rationalizations, subterfuges, and occasional moments of honesty with which the three principal characters come to terms with the possibility of adulterous love.

Throughout the novel, London effectively orchestrates individual scenes to advance the action and to reveal character. Paula's ride on the stallion in the tank, for example, though somewhat overdrawn, is fundamentally well conceived, since it adumbrates the action of the entire novel. As both Dick and Evan watch Paula, Dick is calm, certain of her control, while Evan is profoundly disturbed by the nakedly erotic image she presents. In a later chapter, Dick and Paula's squirrel hunt offers a quieter but equally effective instance of London's ability to create a surface of physical action that distracts and protects the characters from the passions churning inside them.

Perhaps the most complex example of this creation of two levels of action occurs in chapter 22, in which the intellectual debate serves both to conceal and reveal the main characters' unspoken preoccupation with their private anguish. While Dick pursues a philosophical point, Paula, bored and frustrated by so many "words, words, words," turns to Evan for relief, complaining that what she needs is "to know what to do, what to do with myself, what to do with you, what to do with Dick" (259). Yet even as Dick senses that Evan and Paula are tuning him out, a "devil of speech" leads him to persist in his theorizing, to refuse to concede even a fraction of himself to his fears of betrayal:

> To look at Dick's face it would have been unguessed that he was aught but a carefree, happy arguer. Nor did Graham, nor did Paula, Dick's dozen-years' wife, dream that his casual careless glances were missing no movement of a hand, no change of position on a chair, no shade of expression on their faces.
>
> What's up? was Dick's secret interrogation. Paula's not herself. She's positively nervous, and all the discussion is responsible. And Graham's off color. His brain isn't working up to mark. He's thinking about something else, rather than about what he is saying. What is that something else?
>
> And the devil of speech behind which Dick hid his secret thoughts impelled him to urge the talk wider and wilder. (260)

As the debate proceeds with Shavian gusto, a controversy over the question "What is woman?" leads to the question of whether personality can be known, and finally to Dick's dangerous probing of the hypothetical triangle. The ideas here are important not in themselves but as props in an action that dramatizes the emotions lying beneath the surface of conventional life.

London has, then, a plot and, in Dick Forrest, a character that possess the potential for genuine tragedy. He falls short of such a result primarily because, as many readers have recognized, something goes wrong with the ending. The usual criticism is that Paula's interminable dying allows the novel to sink into sentimental bathos. Certainly the ending is weak in precisely this way, but the cause of that weakness lies a step further back. The suicide should have been not Paula's but Dick's.

In London's defense, it must be said that he planned the ending carefully, giving the suicide to Paula not (as some critics have suggested) because he secretly hated his wife and wished her dead, but because this ending struck both him and Charmian as morally and artistically right. When he sent the half-completed manuscript to his film agent, he wrote that he was "sorry to say" that at the end Paula would find that "the only way out is to kill herself."[20] In 1916 he wrote to his daughter Joan that Paula's suicide was "the only clean, decent way out,"[21] and he similarly assured a later correspondent that though he was sorry at being "compelled to kill Paula," he could "see no artistic compromise" and "preferred to have her be as generous as Dick and, in Dick's words, to beat him to it." He had done his best, he added, to "make Paula likable and missable."[22] Yet if he regretted the necessity of killing Paula, he also enjoyed tantalizing the readers of the serial version. "I dare to challenge you now," he wrote to one of them, "that you cannot determine in advance how the story is going to end." He was sure, though, that the reader would have no quarrel with the ending after reading the final chapter.[23]

Moreover, Charmian herself—always a sensitive barometer of her husband's moods—seems to have been entirely satisfied with the ending and may even have helped him determine it. The writing of this novel was in some measure a cathartic experience for both of them, a chance to lay the ghost of an affair that in late 1914 was already more than a year behind them. Midway through the penultimate chapter, Charmian penciled on the manuscript where Jack would see it the next day: "Good stuff, Dear Love, all of it. I cried over it—but oh! so happily for me." She cried again when he read her the ending, but here too the tears seem to contain no trace of resentment. A day later she reported that Jack had read over the finished novel and enjoyed it, and the next day they both experienced a "happy home-coming" at the ranch.[24] In 1915 he insisted that he was "damn proud" of this novel,[25] and for the rest of his life he continued to defend it against its many detractors.

Still, whatever the Londons thought of it, the ending does weaken a soundly conceived dramatic action. In shifting the suicide from Dick to Paula, London strives so hard to avoid predictability that he misses the interior logic of his plot. From beginning to end, this is Dick Forrest's story. His is the primary illusion of rationality and control, his the bitterness of discovering that the Big House is built of cards. The true climax occurs when Dick silently witnesses the passionate embrace of Evan and Paula, which confirms what he had suspected during the squirrel hunt—that "his world was crumbling about him" and "old landmarks were shifting their places" (297). He has been, he believes, "so safe, so sure of her," as sure as he was of "the diurnal rotation of the earth." But now the rotation of the earth was "a shaky proposition" (303). He notes that the "frictionless" machine of the Big House, like another clock, runs remorselessly on, but he begins to wonder "how long it would continue so to run on" (308). Dick's confident belief in an orderly cosmos and in rational human control gives way before the obdurate fact of human weakness and irrationality.

One of the strengths of the last chapters is London's depiction of the quiet stoicism with which Dick recognizes that the clock of his life is indeed breaking down. As he calmly sets his affairs in order, we sense before we are told it that he has decided to die:

On the way back from the sick mare, Dick paused once to listen to the restless stamp of Mountain Lad and his fellows in the stallion barn. In the quiet air, from somewhere up the hills, came the ringing of a single bell from some grazing animal. A cat's-paw of breeze fanned him with sudden balmy warmth. All the night was balmy with the faint and almost aromatic scent of ripening grain and drying grass. The stallion stamped again, and Dick, with a deep breath and realization that never had he more loved it all, looked up and circled the sky-line where the crests of the mountains blotted the field of stars.

"No, Cato," he mused aloud. "One cannot agree with you. Man does not depart from life as from an inn. He departs as from a dwelling, the one dwelling he will ever know. He departs . . . nowhere. It is good night. For him the Noseless One . . . and the dark." (358)[26]

The imaginary dialogue with Cato, another stoical suicide, is apt; and the ripening grain and drying grass poignantly evoke the cycle of natural life which Dick now sees, without self-pity, as a somber business of leave-takings as well as beginnings. His vision of the blotted field of stars prefigures his end, and his conception of death as a departure from a dwelling aptly suggests the collapse of the dreams of which the Big House was the central symbol. Such quietly objectifying images preserve this moment from the mawkishness that pervades the attenuated account of Paula's dying.

It is Dick's final sense of the irremediable natural world—paradoxically counterbalanced by his refusal, as an incurable rationalist, to cease trying to impose some artificial order on it—that dictates that the final act of self-destruction should have been his. Thus it is difficult to accept Earle Labor's view that the novel might have been rescued from its failure if London had "hewed to the theme of agronomy, of successfully uniting machine and garden through the loving application of scientific knowledge for purposes of redemption rather than exploitation."[27] To have done so would have been not to salvage this book but to write a wholly different one—one as dull, probably, as the last part of *The Valley of the Moon*. For all its imperfections, what London actually wrote is a more sober, more mature performance than any of his earlier novels, including his best ones. In earlier works London might have taken Dick's posturing seriously; here the whole point of the novel is Dick's discovery of its ultimate futility.

Epilogue

Although *The Little Lady of the Big House* was London's last important novel, it did not mark the end of his artistic growth. As James I. McClintock has shown, London's intense interest in Jungian psychology in 1916, the last year of his life, led to some of the most interesting and successful work of his career—a final ripening that appeared in such shorter tales as "The Red One" and the best of the Hawaiian stories collected in *On the Makaloa Mat* (1919).[1] Yet by focusing only on the short stories, McClintock is led to describe that final year as an unexpected period of "rebirth" preceded by years of "decline." Despite his excellent final chapter, therefore, his book has the effect of reinforcing the long-standing notion that after his early years London never again wrote well. Actually McClintock can call the period from 1906 to 1912 a "decline"[2] only in the sense that by then London was writing short stories merely to boil the pot. London had become, in fact, a novelist, husbanding his best energies for his major books: *The Iron Heel*, *Martin Eden*, *Burning Daylight*, and *The Valley of the Moon*.

The myth of the decline has also been fostered by such critics as Joan London and Philip Foner, both of whom found the power of his fiction waning in proportion to his loss of interest in socialism.[3] This view, however, constitutes an excessively rigid ideological litmus test, which ignores the fact that the fading of London's socialism was compensated by a variety of other interests that had an equally vitalizing effect on his art. Intellectually, he never abandoned his socialism, but when it failed to satisfy his imagination, he turned elsewhere for inspiration. Similarly, Andrew Sinclair in his recent biography has unsparingly detailed the physical deterioration that plagued London's final years, but Sinclair's brief glances at the fiction never succeed in showing that as the body failed, the art followed suit.

If these seem oversimplified descriptions of Jack London's career as a novelist, how might we more accurately view its contours? What were the principal influences on his novel writing, and what dimensions and significance did that writing assume?

In late November of 1898, on the eve of his first literary success, London poured out his pain and determination in a long letter to Mabel Applegarth, the model for Ruth Morse in *Martin Eden*. Resisting Mabel's call for his surrender to her conventional sense of duty, he vowed that "if I die I shall die hard, fighting to the last, and hell shall receive no fitter inmate than myself. But for good or ill, it shall be as it has been—alone."[4] There is a quality almost Byronic in this declaration—and not merely because it is something of a pose. Beneath the self-pity lies a bedrock of determination, of an insurgent will to power nearly demonic in its intensity. He must live according to his own lights or be damned; and it is this demonic will, combined with a brooding, uncompromising intelligence, that becomes the driving force of the major novels of London's early and middle years.

The lonely ego, thwarted and battered by a hostile world, emerges in its first full expression in *The Call of the Wild*, in which Buck struggles against both human oppressors and the various incarnations of the white wilderness. In *The Sea-Wolf*, the demonic ego is that of Wolf Larsen, the latter-day Lucifer whose caustic pessimism overmatches in dramatic intensity the superficially triumphant idealism of Humphrey and Maud. *White Fang* similarly portrays a lonely Ishmaelite, the implacable "enemy of his kind," whose "reign of hate" is ended only by a chance rescue and spiritual revolution. In *The Iron Heel*, Ernest Everhard becomes an unheeded prophet, ostracized, persecuted, and finally martyred by the society he dares to challenge; and *Martin Eden* traces something of the same fate in a brash young writer who assaults the bastions of genteel society and culture.

This theme of lonely struggle has one further dimension: it reflects not only London's personal feeling of isolation and conflict but also his struggle with powerful literary precursors, whose writings had helped him shape the character of his own career. As McClintock has shown in his discussion of the short stories, the first of these was Rudyard Kipling,[5] though in *A Daughter of the Snows* and *The Sea-Wolf* the Kipling influence was reduced to a usable device for launching a voyage of adventure, while *The Call of the Wild* in part constituted a rejection of the humanized animals of *The Jungle Book*. More important were the catalyzing intellects of Spencer and Nietzsche and, in *The Iron Heel*, the apocalyptic melodrama of Donnelly's *Caesar's Column*. Nietzsche especially remained a powerful intellectual presence, whose hold on his imagination London struggled all his life to break.[6]

Equally crucial in this period were the influences of Conrad and Melville. London's response to Conrad seems the less psychologically complicated, expressing itself as it did in open appreciation. The importance of Melville is more difficult to trace, especially the seminal influence of *Moby-Dick*. Paradoxically, London's very failure to mention this book during the early years of his career may reveal its critical importance to him.[7] As I tried to show in previous chapters, there is strong internal evidence of its effect on *The Call of the Wild*, *The Sea-Wolf*, and *White Fang*—an effect not only on plot and character but on the central symbols and indeed the entire imaginative vision. In *The Sea-Wolf*, most of all, London pitted his imagination against his pantheon of literary heroes, finding, like Melville before him, that in the work of Shakespeare and Milton lay the challenges to which no ambitious writer could fail to respond. When he later referred loftily to the "imaginative orgies" of *Moby-Dick*,[8] he gave evidence that he had emerged from under Melville's spell, defining his own literary personality along different lines. Indeed, in his later novels the importance of literary influences is diminished.

An antithetical influence on London's major novels was Charmian Kittredge, his second wife. Charmian has seldom been treated kindly by London's biographers,[9] and part of the blame must rest with her—especially with her own biography, *The Book of Jack London.* Garrulous, sentimental, self-promoting, and occasionally dishonest, it was intended as a worshipful monument to her husband, yet one of its chief effects is to give an unattractive impression of its author. Not surprisingly, in the intimate pages of her diaries a rather different woman emerges, a more appealing figure than the public persona she so carefully cultivated both during London's lifetime and after his death. Alternately tough and vulnerable, courageous and self-pitying, distraught and ecstatic, worshiping Jack and despairing of him, she remains through it all determined to serve his voracious needs while living her own life to the full. She may, like Zelda Fitzgerald, have sacrificed a part of herself to make this marriage, but it was a sacrifice made willingly by a woman whose energy and tenacity are beyond dispute. London, knowing if seldom admitting how much he asked of her, remained touchingly devoted. The marriage weathered dangers and stresses that would have destroyed a dozen others, and it became London's chief source of stability during the final eleven years of his life.

During these years, the importance of the marital tie emerged in all the major novels except *Martin Eden*, where its significance is indirectly measured by its absence. The endings of *The Sea-Wolf* and *White Fang* embodied the heightened emotions of the Londons' courtship, and *The Iron Heel*, written during the first year of the marriage, reflected the honeymoon atmosphere of romantic enchantment. But a year later, in *Martin Eden*, London returned to the memories of his lost love for Mabel Applegarth, which he combined with recollections of his "long sickness" after the failure of his first marriage. Martin represents what London might have become had there been no Charmian to come to his rescue, and Martin's death was an act of personal catharsis for his creator.

By destroying this fictional alter ego, London enabled his art to survive and in some ways even to flourish, for his last major novels—*Burning Daylight*, *The Valley of the Moon*, and *The Little Lady*—all testify to his belief that his only salvation lay in the love of a woman and the establishment of family bonds. His hope for a son, his development of his ranch, and his enthusiasm for Wolf House were manifestations of his intensifying desire to put down roots here and now, rather than await the Brotherhood of Man several centuries in the future. Yet these three late novels also contain an increasingly mature recognition of the difficulty of maintaining an intimate human relationship through seasons of distress. Hence the fading of the heroic conflicts of *The Sea-Wolf* or *The Iron Heel* and the attainment of the realist's more penetrating vision of the quiet drama of the inner life, the domestic scene, and the workaday world.

These two crucial influences, then—the lonely struggle of the proletarian artist and the domestic companionship with Charmian—provide the dialectic of London's career as a novelist. Another way to put the point is to say that London moves back and forth between the ironies of tragedy and the consoling affirmations of comedy. At the darkest level of his mind lies the modern sense of diminished human possibilities, toward which an occasional voice heroically raises itself in protest and in so doing invites destruction. Against the backdrop of the White Silence and the White Logic, such central characters as Wolf Larsen, Martin Eden, and Dick Forrest struggle to be heard and achieve success, only to find themselves staring into the pallid face of the Noseless One. Yet pitted against this streak of tragic irony is a comic vision of social order, a belief or hope that the principle of chaos can be evaded or transcended.

It is this double vision that links London with two of his

romantic predecessors, Poe and Melville. Against the night-mare world of Poe's Gothic tales must be measured his occasional glimpses of cosmic unity and supernal beauty. Melville similarly projects his darker impulses into Captain Ahab while permitting Ishmael to speak for his more benign intuitions of natural harmony and human companionship. Among writers of the next generation, this double vision is perhaps best exemplified by Mark Twain. Both he and London were disturbed by the conflict between their earlier reputations (Twain as humorist, London as brutal primitivist) and the stances of their later years (Twain as religious and social iconoclast, London as prophet of the return to the land). Indeed, the White Logic that London elaborated in *John Barleycorn* differs little from the nihilistic message of Twain's "Mysterious Stranger" manuscripts.

With the less apocalyptic tradition in American fiction—the one best represented by Hawthorne, Howells, James, and Wharton—London had little in common. He never mentions Hawthorne and seems to have had only slight interest in the other three. Though he himself wrote at times with great poetic power, he could not achieve these writers' consistent stylistic virtuosity, nor did he often strive for their subtler insight into the finely woven fabric of the social and moral life. Nevertheless, he knew and vividly recreated realms of experience that they could not even faintly imagine, and any attempt at comparison must recognize that his purposes were fundamentally different from theirs.

Among his closest contemporaries, his achievement requires no apology. In a novel like *The Valley of the Moon*, with its celebration of the land and the pioneers, he bears comparison with Willa Cather; but temperamentally the benignant Nebraskan and the mercurial Californian are wholly different. He has his clearest affinities not with the brilliant if mannered ironies of Stephen Crane or the massive documentary impulses of Dreiser but with the exuberant energies of Frank Norris. Yet what sets him apart from and perhaps above Norris is a stronger interest in fictional technique and a greater willingness to move beyond simplistic notions of atavistic instincts to an exploration of more complex human motives. Possibly if Norris had lived longer he would have written better; certainly *The Pit* shows signs of a new maturity. But if there remains something of the cultural primitive in both Norris and London, the latter had the advantage of a richer experience from which to draw the materials of his fiction. The point here is not so much to depreciate Norris as to suggest that London's strengths have been undervalued. The rubric of "naturalism," for so long a barrier to a clear vision of a number of writers, still has only a limited usefulness as a description of London's work, which contains far more subtlety and variety than its stereotyped popular reputation would lead one to believe. All readers of American literature are indebted to Charles Child Walcutt's demonstration of the complex roots of the naturalistic tradition in the earlier romantic period, and Earle Labor has added an important dimension to Walcutt's point by stressing the mythic and archetypal elements in London's fiction.

Undeniably, London's art and vision have glaring weaknesses. His longer novels tend to founder somewhere in the middle, perhaps because his initial enthusiasm for an idea was prone to diminish. His methodical work habits—his determination to finish everything he started—led him to persist even after inspiration flagged, and his refusal to revise is the cause of much undistinguished prose. At times, moreover, his narcissistic posturing can make him almost unreadable. He believed in experimenting, and the price of such ventures is the chance of a blunder. He descended so often to formulaic hack work that readers are in danger of overlooking the extent to which in his most serious work he strove to avoid repeating himself. He considered himself a thinker, a man of ideas; yet his ideas served chiefly as weapons, agents of conflict, a part of the struggle between man and world. His extraordinary openness to new knowledge was matched by his inability to detach himself from the fashionable ideas of the moment, for he had little of the true intellectual's capacity for the long view. Not until his last years did he begin to recognize fully the problematical nature of human motivation and of scientific and philosophical claims to truth.

This weakness for the ideologically fashionable partly explains, though it does not excuse, London's lamentable (and much lamented) racism. Our own vantage-point in a more tolerant era gives us the luxury of hindsight, and it is only fair to point out that London's racism was but one strand in a large tapestry of European and American imperialistic chauvinism, the results of which the present century has painfully witnessed. There is little to choose, one might suggest, between London's loud fulminations against the "yellow peril" and the genteel anti-Semitism of an Edith Wharton or a Henry Adams. Subtler minds than London's were infected with the racist virus, and London's racism was not necessarily more virulent merely because it was less mannerly. Nor were his racial views as dogmatic as many of his critics have made them seem. He had not merely a single racial attitude but many, some of them remarkably generous. Those who dismiss him as a racist often have not read much of his work, where the range of attitudes is easily demonstrable.

Yet whatever his failings, London has endured—both as a legendary figure in American popular culture and as a writer who continues to be widely if not always deeply read. He struck a universal note when he told a stirring tale of a dog who recovers his primordial heritage, and he created one of the central fables of the ambitious writer stricken by forces that have always confronted the artist who longs for a realm of pure imagination. If he had done nothing else, his career would have been justified. But he did much more, and though the remaining novels cannot match his best work, they contain many passages of insight and power. Far from having given up his efforts to think and write well, he persisted in his struggle to comprehend himself and his world. Life to him was movement; and the movement, though it sometimes faltered, never wholly ceased. As to whether at the end he deliberately took his own life, the evidence is

ambiguous, many facts lie beyond recall, and the precise nature of his intention will doubtless remain a mystery—may
indeed have been a mystery even to himself.[10] Thoughts of
suicide and a longing for oblivion, as even his wife acknowledged, were not unknown to him, and all his life he faced
unblinkingly the specter of personal annihilation. Yet like
Wolf Larsen, he clung the more desperately to the remnants
of life and the power of his imagination.

Years ago E. M. Forster divided novelists, provocatively if
oversimply, into "preachers" and "prophets," including in
the latter group only Dostoevsky, Melville, Lawrence, and
Emily Brönte. What characterizes the prophets, Forster said,
is a kind of "rapt bardic quality" combined with a "roughness of surface":

While they pass under our eyes they are full of dents and grooves
and lumps and spikes which draw from us little cries of approval
and disapproval. When they have past, the roughness is forgotten,
they become as smooth as the moon.
    Prophetic fiction . . . demands humility and the absence of the
sense of humour. It reaches back—though we must not conclude
from the example of Dostoevsky that it always reaches back to pity
and love. It is spasmodically realistic. And it gives us the sensation
of a song or of sound. It is unlike fantasy because its face is towards
unity, whereas fantasy glances about.[11]

I do not exactly wish to propose London for inclusion among
Forster's sacred few. Humility is hardly a cardinal London
virtue, nor can I claim that in restrospect his novels become
smooth as the moon. Yet with all due reservations, he is
still very much the *kind* of novelist Forster describes. His
best novels are prose poems like *The Call of the Wild*, or
passionate expressions of a longing to strip the last veil from
the mysteries of being, as in *The Sea-Wolf* and *Martin Eden*.

According to his wife, six days before he died London said
"something like the following" to an interviewer: "What is
the difference between anything that is strong and fine and
well arranged—be it words or stones or trees or ideas or what
not—and the same elements as they were in their unorga-

nized weakness? Man—the brain of man, the effort that man had put into man's supreme task—organizing! That is the work of man, work that is worth a man's doing—to take something second-rate and chaotic and to put himself into it until it becomes orderly and first-rate and fine."[12] London never abandoned his own version of the quest for order—in language or in life. The natural order might tend to chaos, the wilderness might be white and silent, but the brain of man would still go about its proper work.

Reference Matter

Notes

Chapter 1: An Impassioned Realism

1 *The Cruise of the Snark* (New York: Macmillan, 1911), p. 3.
The full context clarifies this notorious remark by showing that
London (hereafter abbreviated "JL") viewed both writing a
novel and winning a water fight as alternative kinds of creative
achievement: "The thing I like most of all is personal achievement—not achievement for the world's applause, but achievement for my own delight. It is the old 'I did it! I did it! With my
own hands I did it!' But personal achievement, with me, must
be concrete. I'd rather win a water-fight in the swimming pool,
or remain astride a horse that is trying to get out from under me,
than write the great American novel. Each man to his liking.
Some other fellow would prefer writing the great American
novel to winning the water-fight or mastering the horse."

2 JL to Cloudesley Johns, 24 October 1899, *Letters from Jack London*, ed. King Hendricks and Irving Shepard (New York: Odyssey, 1965), p. 62.

3 "American Fiction Lacking in Courage," New York *Sun*, 2
March 1912, clipping in Scrapbook 11, London Collection,
Henry E. Huntington Library, San Marino, Calif. (hereafter ab-
breviated "HEH").

4 Quoted in Joan London, *Jack London and His Times: An Unconventional Biography* (New York: Doubleday, 1939; rpt. Se-
attle: Univ. of Washington Press, 1968), p. 336. The original interview (with the socialist editor E. Haldeman-Julius) appeared
as "The Pessimism of Jack London," *Western Comrade*, 1
(1913), 90–92.

5 Charmian London, *The Book of Jack London* (New York: Century, 1921), II, 318. The mixture of motives in JL's view of his writing has been convincingly analyzed by Robert Belton Holland, "Jack London: His Thought and Art in Relation to His Time," Ph.D. diss. Univ. of Wisconsin 1950, pp. 1–64; Franklin Walker, *Jack London and the Klondike: The Genesis of an American Writer* (San Marino, Calif.: Huntington Library, 1966), pp. 209–12; Starling Price, "Jack London's America," Ph.D. diss. Univ. of Minnesota 1967, pp. 323–40; and Earle Labor, *Jack London* (New York: Twayne, 1974), pp. 82–89. My own comments here—and also in chapter 7, on *Martin Eden*—are intended only to give their point further support.

6 JL to Elwyn Hoffman, 6 January 1900, Hoffman Collection, HEH, Box 1.

7 See, for example, *Faulkner in the University: Class Conferences at the University of Virginia, 1957–1958*, ed. Frederick L. Gwynn and Joseph L. Blotner (Charlottesville: Univ. of Virginia Press, 1959), pp. 3, 65, and passim.

8 JL to Anna Strunsky, 3 February 1900, *Letters*, p. 88.

9 JL to Cloudesley Johns, 4 September 1905, HEH, JL 12203.

10 JL to Upton Sinclair, quoted in Philip S. Foner, *Jack London: American Rebel* (New York: Citadel, 1947), p. 110.

11 *The Letters of Herman Melville*, ed. Merrell R. Davis and William H. Gilman (New Haven: Yale Univ. Press, 1960), p. 128.

12 Quoted in Joseph Blotner, *Faulkner: A Biography* (New York: Random House, 1974), p. 758.

13 JL to Olga Nethersole, 9 February 1910, *Letters*, p. 299.

14 JL to Cloudesley Johns, 29 July 1899, *Letters*, p. 45.

15 JL to Editor of *Cosmopolitan Magazine*, 24 November 1906, *Letters*, pp. 224–25.

16 JL to Cloudesley Johns, 30 April 1899, *Letters*, p. 35. This object of editorial solicitude became something of a standing joke between JL and Johns. Though normally JL was willing to go along with editorial objections to profanity, on at least one occasion he balked. Upon returning the corrected proofs of *The Call of the Wild* to the Macmillan Company, he enclosed a list of pages containing oaths, expressing the hope that "some of the less vigorous one[s]" would be allowed to remain. Unwilling to delete them himself, he gave his editor "full permission to do whatever you please with all the oaths in the book—only,

if possible, I pray you leave me two or three" (JL to George P. Brett, 10 April 1903, photocopy in Merrill Library, Utah State Univ., Logan, Utah [hereafter "Merrill Library"].

17 JL to George P. Brett, 16 January 1907, HEH, JL 11085.

18 JL to Roland Phillips, 19 August 1913, HEH, JL 13150.

19 JL to E. A. Cross, 27 March 1914, HEH, JL 11511.

20 "The Question of a Name," *Writer*, 13 (1900), 177–80; rpt. *Jack London: No Mentor But Myself: A Collection of Articles, Essays, Reviews, and Letters on Writing and Writers*, ed. Dale L. Walker (Port Washington, N.Y.: Kennikat, 1979), pp. 20, 21.

21 "First Aid to Rising Authors," *Junior Munsey Magazine*, 9 (1900), 513–17; rpt. *Jack London: No Mentor But Myself*, p. 29.

22 JL to Cloudesley Johns, 16 June 1900, *Letters*, p. 108.

23 "Phenomena of Literary Evolution," *Bookman*, 12 (1900), 150. For further discussion of JL's prose style, see Susan Ward, "Toward a Simpler Style: Jack London's Stylistic Development," *Jack London Newsletter*, 11 (1978), 71–80.

24 "On the Writer's Philosophy of Life," *Editor*, 10 (1899), 125–29; rpt. *Jack London: No Mentor But Myself*, pp. 8, 9. JL's insistence on originality might at first glance seem belied by his self-acknowledged "lack of origination" (*Letters*, p. 54) and his heavy dependence on personal experience or printed sources —a dependence that occasionally led to charges of plagiarism. The latter question is especially thorny. For a writer of fiction, what distinguishes an act of plagiarism from a legitimate use of sources? Was Shakespeare plagiarizing from Holinshed's *Chronicles* in his history plays? Was Melville plagiarizing from Beale and Scoresby or the numerous other "fish documents" he pillaged when composing *Moby-Dick*? Perhaps the question to ask is whether the appropriation is an act of creative strength or a demonstration of weakness. Most novelists have read the work of predecessors, and none can escape absorbing and transforming the multifarious experiences of life, including those found in the writings of others. JL took a similar position, protesting that such borrowing was time-honored, inescapable, essentially creative, and that in any case the general motifs he had appropriated were in the public domain. For a good example of this defense, see his replies to Stanley Waterloo and B. W. Babcock, who in 1906 accused him of plagiarizing from Waterloo's *The Story of Ab* in *Before Adam* (*Letters*, pp. 213–15, 229–31).

25 "Again the Literary Aspirant," *Critic*, 41 (1902), 217–20; rpt. *Jack London: No·Mentor But Myself*, pp. 48, 52.

26 "The Terrible and Tragic in Fiction," *Critic*, 42 (1903), 539–43; rpt. ibid., pp. 61–64.

27 *The Call of the Wild* (New York: Macmillan, 1903), p. 91. Sam S. Baskett, in a paper written for the 1978 meeting of the Modern Language Association, "Calls of the Wild and Jack London's Esthetic Suppositions," has usefully focused on this passage as an expression of JL's artistic impulses.

28 *John Barleycorn* (New York: Century, 1913), p. 308.

29 For a helpful discussion of this topic, see Geoffrey Harpham, "Jack London and the Tradition of Superman Socialism," *American Studies*, 16 (1975), 23–33. Others who have stressed the problem of ideological conflict in JL's fiction are Sam S. Baskett, "Jack London's Fiction: Its Social Milieu," Ph.D. diss. Univ. of California, Berkeley, 1951; Robert B. Holland, "Jack London: His Thought and Art in Relation to His Time"; Gordon Mills, "Jack London's Quest for Salvation," *American Quarterly*, 7 (1955), 3–14; Roy W. Carlson, "Jack London's Heroes: A Study of Evolutionary Thought," Ph.D. diss. Univ. of New Mexico 1961; and Ronald Gower, "The Creative Conflict: Struggle and Escape in Jack London's Fiction," *Jack London Newsletter*, 4 (1971), 77–114.

30 JL to Anna Strunsky, 21 December 1899, *Letters*, pp. 76–77.

31 Quoted in C. London, *The Book of Jack London*, II, 78–80.

32 JL to Cloudesley Johns, 10 August 1899, *Letters*, pp. 50–51.

33 C. London, *The Book of Jack London*, II, 49.

34 JL to Ralph Kaspar, 25 June 1914, *Letters*, p. 425.

35 JL to Cloudesley Johns, 12 June 1899, HEH, JL 12101.

36 MS Notes, HEH, JL 812. For further comments on JL's struggle with spiritualism and the supernatural, see my essay "Jack London: Up from Spiritualism," in *The Haunted Dusk: American Supernatural Fiction, 1820–1920*, ed. Howard Kerr, John W. Crowley, and Charles L. Crow (Athens: Univ. of Georgia Press, 1983), pp. 193–207.

37 *Jack London: No Mentor But Myself*, p. 35. The review originally appeared in *Impressions*, 2 (1901), 45–47. Norris himself, it should be noted, advocated a strenuous Zolaesque naturalism that had much in common with romance fiction. For a more extensive analysis of JL's double-stranded theory of fiction, see chapters 2 and 3 of Robert B. Holland's dissertation, "Jack Lon-

don: His Thought and Art in Relation to His Time," pp. 65–177.

38 JL to Anna Strunsky, 20 December 1902, HEH, AW Box 3-A. This conception of fiction resembles the one advanced by Willa Cather in her 1922 essay "The Novel Démeublé," rpt. in *Not Under Forty* (New York: Knopf, 1936), pp. 43–51. Cather, like JL, rejects the "popular superstition" that realism consists of "the cataloguing of a great number of material objects" (p. 45).

39 JL to Editor of the *Bulletin,* 17 September 1898, *Letters,* p. 3.

40 "These Bones Shall Rise Again," in *Revolution and Other Essays* (New York: Macmillan, 1910), pp. 223–24. The essay was originally published in *The Reader,* 2 (1903), 27–32.

41 *Martin Eden* (New York: Macmillan, 1909), pp. 79, 232.

42 For a sociological and feminist perspective on this theme, see Clarice Stasz, "Androgyny in the Novels of Jack London," *Western American Literature,* 11 (1976), 121–33. Though awkwardly written, this article deserves credit for focusing on an important problem and contributing a number of valuable insights.

Chapter 2: Manners in the Northland

1 The best account of JL's early years can be found in the four chapters of Franklin Walker's uncompleted biography of JL (Walker Collection, HEH, HM 45284). Walker distilled the essence of those pages into the first chapter of *Jack London and the Klondike.*

2 JL to Cloudesley Johns, 15 March 1899, *Letters,* p. 22.

3 TS notebook (referred to hereafter as Post-Klondike Notebook), HEH, JL 1004.

4 JL to Cloudesley Johns, 23 July 1900, HEH, JL 12137.

5 JL to Cloudesley Johns, 18 August 1900, HEH, JL 12138.

6 JL to Cloudesley Johns, 9 September 1900, HEH, JL 12139.

7 JL to Elwyn Hoffman, 22 November 1900, Hoffman Collection, HEH, Box 1.

8 JL to Cloudesley Johns, 13 February 1901, HEH, JL 12149.

9 JL to Cloudesley Johns, 15 March 1901, HEH, JL 12150. On March 19 JL wrote to Ted Applegarth that the novel was finished (MS, Merrill Library).

10 *A Daughter of the Snows* (Philadelphia: J.B. Lippincott, 1902), p. 91. Page references appear hereafter in the text.

11 When Johns asked him whether he had written some of Strunsky's Dane Kempton letters, JL replied, "No, the Kempton letters were written entirely by Anna Strunsky, though the earmarks of each are to be found in the other's work—unconscious absorptions of style, I suppose" (2 July 1903, HEH, JL 12173). The "absorptions of style" were almost entirely one way, however.

12 The relationship between Vance and Frona contains one further anticipation of the intensifying friendship of JL and Anna Strunsky. At one point Frona asks, "Do you believe in a white friendship? . . . For I do hope that such a bond may hold us always. A bright, white friendship, a comradeship, as it were?" But Vance is skeptical: "I am afraid, after all, that your knowledge of man is very limited. Believe me, we are not made of such clay. . . . No, no; love cannot shackle itself with white friendships" (297). Ironically, only a few months later, on 26 December 1900, JL wrote to Strunsky of his delight in their "white beautiful friendship" (*Letters*, p. 119), only to discover later, as he fell in love with her, that Vance had been right all along. For further insight into the literary consequences of the JL-Strunsky relationship, see Robert Brainard Pearsall, "Elizabeth Barrett Meets Wolf Larsen," *Western American Literature*, 4 (1969), 3–13.

13 JL to Cloudesley Johns, 31 October 1899, *Letters*, p. 63.

14 Walker, *Jack London and the Klondike*, p. 110.

15 JL was familiar with both of these novels. His enthusiasm for Kipling is well documented, and he specifically mentions *Captains Courageous* in "First Aid to Rising Authors" (1900), rpt. in *Jack London: No Mentor But Myself*, p. 28. On 30 April 1899 he wrote to Cloudesley Johns, "Have you read [Norris's] *Moran of the Lady Letty*? It's well done" (*Letters*, p. 36).

16 Richard O'Connor, *Jack London: A Biography* (Boston: Little, Brown, 1964), p. 147.

17 Henry Nash Smith, *Virgin Land: The American West as Symbol and Myth* (Cambridge: Harvard Univ. Press, 1950; rpt. New York: Vintage, n.d.), pp. 126–35. See also William Wasserstrom, *Heiress of All the Ages: Sex and Sentiment in the Genteel Tradition* (Minneapolis: Univ. of Minnesota Press, 1959), pp. 40–45.

18 Wasserstrom, *Heiress of All the Ages*, pp. 68–83.

19 Charles Child Walcutt seems to me to have missed the point in

his otherwise helpful discussion of this novel in *American Literary Naturalism, A Divided Stream* (Minneapolis: Univ. of Minnesota Press, 1956), p. 99. Walcutt rejects the idea that the novel endorses "any sort of sexual freedom," noting that Frona remains "unwaveringly chaste" and that a "woman of questionable virtue [i.e., Lucile] is scarcely allowed to speak to the heroine." Surely the point is precisely the opposite: Frona does flout propriety and speak to Lucile in part because of curiosity about the latter's sexual experience. Although certainly the unmarried Frona is chaste, by the standards of the time she is openly eager for physical experience, including sexual experience within the sanctions of marriage.

20 Roy W. Carlson makes a similar point, noting that *A Daughter* is "a novel about sexual selection" in which Frona chooses a mate by "calculatingly watch[ing] them being tested in the hostile Arctic" ("Jack London's Heroes," p. 104).

21 As Walcutt has noticed (*American Literary Naturalism*, p. 100), there is also a Nietzschean note in Welse's credo. "Conventions are worthless for such as we," Welse insists. "They are for the swine who without them would wallow deeper. The weak must obey or be crushed; not so with the strong. The mass is nothing; the individual everything; and it is the individual, always, that rules the mass and gives the law" (184).

22 Clarice Stasz comments briefly on this theme in "Androgyny in the Novels of Jack London," pp. 122–23.

Chapter 3: Ghost Dog

1 JL to George P. Brett, 21 November 1902, *Letters*, p. 139.

2 JL to George P. Brett, 10 March 1903, *Letters*, p. 149.

3 This figure of $700 for the serial rights is the one reported by Charmian London in *The Book of Jack London*, I, 389; and it tallies roughly with the figure of three cents a word that JL reported to Brett in his letter of 10 March 1903 (*Letters*, p. 150). Irving Stone was thus apparently in error in recording that the *Post* paid $2000 (*Sailor on Horseback: The Biography of Jack London* [Boston: Houghton Mifflin, 1938], p. 175). The error recurs in Philip S. Foner, *Jack London: American Rebel*, p. 53, and in Dale L. Walker and James E. Sisson III, *The Fiction of Jack London: A Chronological Bibliography* (El Paso: Texas Western Press, 1972), p. 11.

4 JL to George P. Brett, 10 March 1903, 11 December 1902, *Letters*, pp. 150, 149, 146.

5 JL to George P. Brett, 12 February 1903, photocopy in Merrill Library. In the same letter, JL reported that *The Call* was the story he was working on when Brett visited him in Oakland. Since Brett's visit occurred during the first week in January (JL to Brett, 30 December 1902, photocopy in Merrill Library), composition must have continued for at least several more days.

6 JL to George P. Brett, 10 March and 25 March 1903, *Letters*, pp. 150, 151.

7 In a letter to Marshall Bond, 17 December 1903, JL wrote: "Yes, Buck was based upon your dog at Dawson and of course Judge Miller's place was Judge Bond's—even to the cement swimming tanks and the artesian well" (*Letters*, p. 154).

8 On 13 March 1903, JL wrote to Anna Strunsky that he had begun *The Call of the Wild* as a "companion to my other dog story 'Bâtard'" (HEH, AW Box 3-A).

9 "Bâtard," in *The Faith of Men and Other Stories* (New York: Macmillan, 1904), p. 230.

10 *The Call of the Wild* (New York: Macmillan, 1903), p. 221. Page references appear hereafter in the text.

11 Labor, *Jack London*, p. 71.

12 Walker, *Jack London and the Klondike*, pp. 241–42. Walker provides a detailed summary of JL's debt to Young.

13 JL to George P. Brett, 12 February 1903, photocopy in Merrill Library.

14 Alfred Kazin, Introd., *Moby-Dick* by Herman Melville (Boston: Houghton Mifflin, Riverside Edition, 1956), p. xi.

15 For a helpful gloss on JL's conception of animal psychology, see his essay "The Other Animals," first published in *Collier's*, 5 September 1908, and rpt. in *Revolution and Other Essays*. *The Call of the Wild* and *White Fang*, he said, constituted a "protest against the 'humanizing' of animals, of which it seemed to me several 'animal writers' had been profoundly guilty" (238). He went on to deny that there is an absolute gulf between human beings and animals; instead, he insists, there is a gradation of instincts and reason.

16 Walcutt, *American Literary Naturalism, A Divided Stream*. Walcutt's discussion of *The Call of the Wild* (pp. 103–7), is expanded on by Earl Wilcox in "Jack London's Naturalism: The

Example of *The Call of the Wild*," *Jack London Newsletter*, 2 (1969), 91–101. Earle Labor, on the other hand, suggests that Buck's history follows the traditional stages of the archetypal myth of the hero (*Jack London*, pp. 72–78), and Jon Pankake takes a similar approach, though with rather different and more tendentious conclusions, in "The Broken Myths of Jack London: Civilization, Nature, and the Self in the Major Works," Ph.D. diss. Univ. of Minnesota 1975, pp. 75–97.

17 Samuel Langhorne Clemens, *Adventures of Huckleberry Finn* (1885; facsimile rpt., San Francisco: Chandler, 1962), p. 159. Franklin Walker has noted that *The Call of the Wild* offers "a vicarious escape from industrialism, urbanism, and bureaucracy. Thus, though vastly different in mood and movement, it belongs on a shelf with *Walden* and *Huckleberry Finn*" (Foreword to *The Call of the Wild and Selected Stories* [New York: New American Library, 1960], p. xii). Gordon Mills also discusses the impulse to "escape from responsibility" that pervades JL's fiction, in "Jack London's Quest for Salvation," p. 4.

18 Jonathan H. Spinner rightly recognizes the importance of work, but in doing so he reduces the narrative to an allegory of the ills of industrialism ("A Syllabus for the 20th Century: Jack London's 'The Call of the Wild,'" *Jack London Newsletter*, 7 [1974], 73–78).

19 Ann S. Jennings, in "London's Code of the Northland," *Alaska Review*, 1 (1964), 43–48, comments on these symbolic oppositions, though I cannot altogether accept her association of cold with death, and light, fire, and warmth with life—at least not in *The Call of the Wild*, where the two symbols are more complex. What they do suggest is the conflicting impulses of Buck's life: his attraction to civilization and his increasing fascination with the demonic wilderness.

20 Andrew Flink analyzes the orphan theme rather mechanically and reductively in "'Call of the Wild'—Parental Metaphor," *Jack London Newsletter*, 7 (1974), 58–61.

21 *The Son of the Wolf: Tales of the Far North* (Boston: Houghton Mifflin, 1900), p. 7.

22 *Smoke Bellew* (New York: Century, 1912), p. 371.

23 Both Charles Child Walcutt (*American Literary Naturalism*, p. 105) and Earl Wilcox ("Jack London's Naturalism," p. 97) describe the emotions in this often-quoted passage as "materialistic." To me it would seem more accurate to identify them with

the ecstatic transport of the religious mystic and with the romantic conception of the inspired creative moment. For further exploration of this point, see my essay "Jack London: Up from Spiritualism," in *The Haunted Dusk*.

24 Maxwell Geismar, *Rebels and Ancestors: The American Novel, 1890–1915* (Boston: Houghton Mifflin, 1953), pp. 150–51.

25 Herman Melville, *Moby-Dick*, ed. Harrison Hayford and Hershel Parker (New York: Norton, 1967), p. 145. Irving Stone notes that during his boyhood JL read *Moby-Dick* "over and over again" (*Sailor on Horseback*, p. 41).

26 Lawrence Clayton notes that JL may have heard of such a ghost dog during his winter in the Klondike ("The Ghost Dog, A Motif in *The Call of the Wild*," *Jack London Newsletter*, 5 [1972], 158).

27 Melville, *Moby-Dick*, pp. 168–69.

28 Labor, *Jack London*, pp. 59–62.

29 Melville, *Moby-Dick*, p. 164.

30 Ibid., pp. 165–66.

31 David Mike Hamilton, in his unpublished study of the annotated books in JL's library, has discovered another possible source of JL's conception of the wolfpack, a passage that JL marked in his copy of John C. Fremont's *Memoirs of My Life* (1887): "Scores of wild dogs followed, looking like troops of wolves, and having, in fact, but very little of the dog in their composition."

Chapter 4: Lucifer on the Quarter-Deck

1 JL to George P. Brett, 21 November 1902, *Letters*, p. 139.

2 TS notes for "The Mercy of the Sea," HEH, JL 942.

3 JL to George P. Brett, 20 January 1903, photocopy in Merrill Library.

4 JL to George P. Brett, 12 February 1903, photocopy in Merrill Library.

5 JL to George P. Brett, 10 March 1903, *Letters*, p. 150.

6 JL to Cloudesley Johns, 5 May and 29 May 1903, HEH, JL 12170, 12172.

7 JL to George P. Brett, 24 July 1903, photocopy in Merrill Library.

8 JL to George P. Brett, c. 2 September 1903, *Letters*, p. 153.

9 An account of this period can be found in the TS of Johns's un-

published autobiography, "Who the Hell is Cloudesley Johns?," pp. 283–314, HEH, HM 42387.

10 JL to George P. Brett, 7 January 1904, photocopy in Merrill Library.

11 MS notes, HEH, JL 941. The name (though not the character) of the Cockney cook, Thomas Mugridge, came from an elderly man whom JL met in England in 1902 (see *The People of the Abyss* [New York: Macmillan, 1903], pp. 180–85).

12 The story of the Bricklayer's death was published posthumously under the title "That Dead Men Rise Up Never" in *The Human Drift* (New York: Macmillan, 1917).

13 JL recounts this episode in *John Barleycorn*, pp. 114–19. For an account of his initial experiences on the *Sophia Sutherland*, see C. London, *The Book of Jack London*, I, 110–17.

14 Franklin Walker, Afterword to *The Sea-Wolf and Selected Stories* (New York: New American Library, 1964), p. 343.

15 *The Sea-Wolf*, ed. Matthew J. Bruccoli (Boston: Houghton Mifflin, Riverside Edition, 1964), p. 3. This is the only one of JL's books that has been edited according to current standards of textual scholarship. Page references to it appear hereafter in the text. Bruccoli's introduction also remains among the best essays on *The Sea-Wolf*.

16 JL's enthusiastic reading of Conrad began early and continued for the rest of his life. On 4 June 1915 he wrote Conrad to congratulate him on the publication of *Victory*. "I had just begun to write when I read your first early work," he said. "I have merely madly appreciated you and communicated my appreciation to my friends through all these years" (*Letters*, p. 452). Nine months later he was more specific. Boasting that he had been one of Conrad's "first discoverers and boomers in the United States," he went on to ask: "Have you never read his NIGGER OF THE NARCISSUS? His LORD JIM? His NOSTROMO? His VICTORY? His—oh, well, at least ten more of his books that you do not mention in his bibliography?" (JL to Harry W. Frantz, 7 March 1916, HEH, JL 11731). Two or three months before beginning *The Sea-Wolf*, JL strongly urged Cloudesley Johns to read *Lord Jim* (TS of Johns's autobiography, p. 260, HEH, HM 42387).

17 For evidence of JL's reading of these two novels, see chapter 2, note 15. C. T. Peterson remarks on JL's use of the *Captains Courageous* formula in *The Cruise of the Dazzler* (see "The

Jack London Legend," *American Book Collector,* 8 [January 1958], 16–17]; and Franklin Walker has noticed that JL's Humphrey Van Weyden resembles the protagonists of *Captains Courageous* and *Moran* in his Afterword to *The Sea-Wolf and Selected Stories,* p. 343. For further discussion, see James R. Giles, "Some Notes on the Red-Blooded Reading of Kipling by Jack London and Frank Norris," *Jack London Newsletter,* 3 [1970], 56–62; and my "Sexual Conflict in *The Sea-Wolf:* Further Notes on London's Reading of Kipling and Norris," *Western American Literature,* 11 (1976), 239–48. Portions of the latter article have been incorporated in the present chapter.

18 For the influence of the JL-Strunsky relationship, see Pearsall, "Elizabeth Barrett Meets Wolf Larsen."

19 JL to Emma F. McLean, 12 December 1914, HEH, JL 12561.

20 Alfred Kazin, for example, refers to Larsen as "that Zolaesque Captain Ahab" [*On Native Grounds* [New York: Harcourt, Brace, 1942], p. 114), and Jay Martin describes JL as "continuing the heroic tradition of Melville in *The Sea-Wolf*" (*Harvests of Change: American Literature, 1865–1914* [Englewood Cliffs, N.J.: Prentice-Hall, 1967], p. 239).

21 James Ellis, in "A New Reading of *The Sea Wolf,*" *Western American Literature,* 2 (1967), 127–34, should be credited with successfully arguing that Larsen is a more complex figure than earlier critics had realized. Though I differ with Ellis on some points of emphasis and interpretation, his article is unquestionably useful. Closer to my emphasis is Samuel A. Shivers, "The Demoniacs in Jack London," *American Book Collector,* 12 [September 1961], 11–14, in which Wolf Larsen is presented as an example of "a being of tremendous energy and determination who at the same time is possessed of an intensely evil quality." Shivers goes on to compare Larsen with Milton's Satan, but his brief remarks somewhat oversimplify Larsen's complex character. More incisive and stimulating, though also necessarily brief, is Earle Labor's discussion of Larsen in *Jack London,* pp. 94–96. Labor points in the right direction by suggesting that "Larsen is a fascinating composite of Shakespeare's Hamlet, Milton's Satan, Browning's Caliban and Setebos, and Nietzsche's *Übermensch.* But more than this composite, he is the Captain Ahab of literary Naturalism; and he bridges the gap between the Byronic hero and the modern antihero" (p. 95). To Labor's list of precursors I would add only the Gothic hero-vil-

lain. In *"The Sea-Wolf:* London's *Commedia,"* *Jack London Newsletter*, 8 (1975), 50–54, Lawrence Clayton argues that the novel was influenced by Dante.

22 Frank Norris, *Moran of the Lady Letty* (New York: Doubleday, McClure, 1898), pp. 197, 215. According to Irving Stone (*Sailor on Horseback*, p. 37), as a boy JL had read Zola's *Germinal*, another atavistic novel of initiation. But the closer resemblance between *The Sea-Wolf* and *Moran*, which he had read as recently as 1899, argues that his interest in atavism stems chiefly from Norris. In any case, the idea was commonplace at the turn of the century.

23 Joseph Conrad, "Heart of Darkness," in *Youth and Two Other Stories* (1902; rpt. Garden City, N.Y.: Doubleday, Page, 1923), pp. 92, 116, 128, 96. I have found no certain evidence of JL's reading of "Heart of Darkness." But since in early 1903 (according to Johns's autobiography, p. 259) he was reading "Youth," which precedes "Heart of Darkness" in *Youth and Two Other Stories*, and since his early enthusiasm for Conrad is well established (see note 16), it seems highly unlikely that he would have overlooked it. In "Jack London's Heart of Darkness," *American Quarterly*, 10 (1958), 66–77, Sam S. Baskett proposes that "Heart of Darkness" influenced *Martin Eden* and *John Barleycorn*, but he does not mention its possible influence on *The Sea-Wolf*.

24 Melville, *Moby-Dick*, pp. 235, 405. Page references appear hereafter in the text, preceded by *"MD."*

25 Bruccoli, Introd. to *The Sea-Wolf*, p. xv.

26 Warner Berthoff notes that in JL's hands "the naturalistic novel stands revealed as one more renewal of the durable genre of the Gothic" (*The Ferment of Realism: American Literature, 1884–1919* [New York: Free Press, 1965], p. 246).

27 This resemblance has been noticed by Forrest Winston Parkay, "The Influence of Nietzsche's *Thus Spoke Zarathustra* on London's *The Sea-Wolf*," *Jack London Newsletter*, 4 (1971), 20.

28 Robert Forrey, "Male & Female in London's *The Sea-Wolf*," *Literature and Psychology*, 24 (1974), 139.

29 According to Charmian London, JL's period of depression following the dissolution of his first marriage was associated in his mind with Nietzsche's "long sickness," which ended with his death from tertiary syphilis (*The Book of Jack London*, II, 31–33). The resemblance between the deaths of Nietzsche and Lar-

sen has been noticed by Parkay, "The Influence of Nietzsche's *Thus Spoke Zarathustra*," p. 22. The larger subject of Nietzsche's influence on *The Sea-Wolf* has been much debated. Walcutt (*American Literary Naturalism*, p. 312) suggested that JL may not have known of Nietzsche at all until 1905, as Charmian London seemed to imply when she quoted him as saying: "Have been getting hold of some Nietzsche. I'll turn you loose first on his 'Genealogy of Morals'—and after that, something you'll like—'Thus Spake Zarathustra'" (*The Book of Jack London*, II, 31). But Charmian's diary (HEH, JL 217) makes it clear that she began her reading of Nietzsche as early as 4 October 1904, and there is ample evidence that JL had at least a second-hand acquaintance with Nietzsche's ideas when he wrote *The Sea-Wolf* in 1903. For arguments to that effect, see Roy W. Carlson, "Jack London's Heroes," pp. 153–88; Parkay, pp. 16–24; my article "Nietzsche and *The Sea-Wolf*: A Rebuttal," *Jack London Newsletter*, 9 (1976), 33–35; and Michael Dunford, "Further Notes on Jack London's Introduction to the Philosophy of Friedrich Nietzsche," *Jack London Newsletter*, 10 (1977), 39–42.

30 William Shakespeare, *The Tragedy of Hamlet, Prince of Denmark*, ed. Tucker Brooke and Jack Randall Crawford, rev. ed. (New Haven: Yale Univ. Press, 1947), III. i. 77–82. James Ellis has observed that Larsen resembles Hamlet in being "disgusted with his world" ("A New Reading of *The Sea Wolf*," p. 128).

31 For a similar instance of JL's echoing Hamlet's soliloquy, see his letter to Anna Strunsky, 26 December 1900: "To break or be broken, there they stand. But to be broken while not daring to break, there's the rub" (*Letters*, p. 118).

32 *Paradise Lost* was one of the books that JL took with him to the Klondike in 1897 (see Franklin Walker, *Jack London and the Klondike*, p. 135), and years later he declared that he could "still fall for the rolling wonder of the music of 'Paradise Lost'" (JL to Albert Mordell, 2 October 1916, HEH, JL 12844).

33 In "Male & Female in London's *The Sea-Wolf*," p. 136, Robert Forrey similarly describes JL's attempt to synthesize an "ideal self which is both sensitive and masculine, tender and tough," though he believes that the attempt remains unsuccessful. Forrey also points out (p. 140) another instance of blatant sexual symbolism when Humphrey's knife, acquired during his earlier struggle for his manhood with Mugridge, becomes an object of fascination to Maud: "The dirk . . . rested in its sheath on my

hip. It was very natural that it should be there,—how natural I had not imagined until now, when I looked upon it with her eyes and knew how strange it and all that went with it must appear to her" (136). The same observation was made earlier by Earle Labor, who suggested further that the dismasting of Larsen's ship is a figurative castration. Labor also notes the sexual dimension of Humphrey's maturation and refers to the idea of "equipoise" as the novel's main theme ("Jack London's Literary Artistry: A Study of His Imagery and Symbols in Relation to His Themes," Ph.D. diss. Univ. of Wisconsin 1961, pp. 326, 215–20). On the latter point, Howard Lachtman observes: "Though [Larsen and Van Weyden] seem poles apart, the two men together form a symbolic composite of human nature seeking to adjust, balance, control, and reconcile its perpetually warring elements" ("The Wide World of Jack London," Ph.D. diss. Univ. of the Pacific 1974, pp. 267–68). In "Jack London's *The Sea-Wolf:* Naturalism with a Spiritual Bent," *Jack London Newsletter*, 6 (1973), 99–110, Kathleen B. Hindman sees the triangular conflict among Humphrey, Maud, and Wolf as primarily intellectual and "spiritual." Undeniably it has those dimensions, but the intellectual conflict is rooted in sexual psychology. In 1903, of course, JL knew nothing of Freud's *The Interpretation of Dreams*, which was not translated into English until 1913. He did read Freud in his later years, however, and three of Freud's works (though not *The Interpretation of Dreams*) remain among his books at HEH.

34 Quoted by Foner, *Jack London: American Rebel*, p. 62.
35 Geismar, *Rebels and Ancestors*, p. 153.
36 JL to Mary Austin, 5 November 1915, *Letters*, p. 463.
37 JL to George P. Brett, 10 September 1903, *Letters*, p. 153.
38 JL to Anna Strunsky, 23 July 1904, and JL to Carrie Sterling, 15 September 1905, *Letters*, pp. 163, 180.

Chapter 5: Redemption of an Outcast

1 JL to George P. Brett, 8 December 1904, *Letters*, p. 167.
2 JL to George P. Brett, 5 December 1904, *Letters*, p. 166.
3 JL to George P. Brett, 21 February 1905, *Letters*, p. 168.
4 JL to Cloudesley Johns, 7 June 1905, HEH, JL 12200.
5 Charmian London's MS diary (HEH, JL 218) records the beginning of composition on June 26, and the final leaf of the holograph MS (HEH, JL 1407) is dated 10 October 1905.

6 MS notes, Merrill Library.

7 TS notes, HEH, JL 1406. A TS copy of the chronology and of the encyclopedia article JL drew on are among the notes at HEH.

8 Charles G. D. Roberts, *The Kindred of the Wild: A Book of Animal Life* (Boston: L.C. Page, 1902), p. 101. JL's copy of this book, and of two other books by Roberts, is now at HEH.

9 *Red Fox* remains among the volumes in JL's library (HEH). The book version was not published until September—too late for JL to have consulted it while writing Part Two of *White Fang*. But he was familiar with *Outing Magazine*, in which *White Fang* was already scheduled to be serialized the following year, and the coincidence of the serialization of *Red Fox* with the composition of *White Fang* strengthens the probability that JL was reading the monthly installments of Roberts's narrative as they appeared. According to the date-stamps on JL's MS, Part Two was composed in late July and early August, by which time all the pertinent episodes of *Red Fox* had appeared in print.

10 See, for example, JL to George P. Brett, 31 October 1906, or JL to Loen Weilskov, 16 October 1916, *Letters*, pp. 216, 475.

11 Charles Child Walcutt, *Jack London* (Minneapolis: Univ. of Minnesota Press, 1966), p. 22.

12 Earl Wilcox, "*Le Milieu, Le Moment, La Race:* Literary Naturalism in Jack London's *White Fang*," *Jack London Newsletter*, 3 (1970), 42, 43.

13 JL to George P. Brett, 5 December 1904, *Letters*, p. 166.

14 The same point has been made succinctly by Abraham Rothberg: "The first forty-nine pages are irrelevant, connected to the novel only by the slender thread of Kiche's presence in both, but in themselves are a superb short story" ("The House That Jack Built," Ph.D. diss. Columbia University 1952, p. 187). In "The Descent of White Fang," *Jack London Newsletter*, 7 (1974), 123, Lynn DeVore similarly calls this episode "one of the best short stories London ever wrote."

15 *White Fang* (New York: Macmillan, 1906), p. 10. Page references appear hereafter in the text. "The Pit and the Pendulum" seems to have been one of JL's favorite Poe tales. He mentioned it in his 1903 essay "The Terrible and Tragic in Fiction," and again in a letter to George Sterling, 7 March 1916, HEH, JL 13690.

16 Wilcox, "*Le Milieu*," p. 48. Wilcox does, however, acknowledge a "Hemingwayish" quality in JL's "clipped, austere sentence structure" (p. 47).

17 *The Republic of Plato*, trans. F. M. Cornford (New York: Oxford Univ. Press, 1945), pp. 227–31.

18 Walcutt observes that "White Fang as clearly as Buck enacts London's own myth of a man unloved by his mother, unknown to his father, reared in poverty and deprivation, yet growing stronger and craftier because of innate powers that assert themselves and enable him to survive under extreme adversity" (*Jack London*, p. 23).

19 Earle Labor makes the point that the whole novel "may be regarded as a companion piece and antithesis, not to *The Call of the Wild*, but to 'Bâtard'" (*Jack London*, p. 80).

20 The roots of these sensations in JL's own memories are manifested in a painful letter to Mabel Applegarth, 30 November 1898, in which he recalls his theft of a piece of meat at the age of seven, and then goes on to associate his hunger with his loneliness:

From the hunger of my childhood, cold eyes have looked upon me, or questioned, or snickered and sneered. . . . I have calloused my exterior and receive the strokes as though they were not; as to how they hurt, no one knows but my own soul and me.

So be it. The end is not yet. If I die I shall die hard, fighting to the last, and hell shall receive no fitter inmate than myself. But for good or ill, it shall be as it has been—alone. (*Letters*, p. 7)

Beneath the posturing and self-pity lie pains unmistakably real —and much like those suffered by White Fang.

21 DeVore also considers this movement a regression but an ideological one: an adoption of the "weak ideals of a 'slave morality.'" DeVore concludes: "Thus the movement from *Call* to *White Fang* is less aptly described, as some have done, as one from Nietzschean superman to melioristic humanism than one from romance to progressive disillusionment" ("The Descent of White Fang," pp. 122, 126). In this unconvincing article the thought is as muddled as the syntax.

22 In "Thematic Significance of the Jim Hall Episode in *White Fang*," *Jack London Newsletter*, 2 (1969), 49–50, James R. Giles justifies this episode as the climax of the environmental theme. Maybe so, but to me it seems contrived and off-key.

23 Earl Wilcox is in error, however, when he compares One Eye's recognition of the "remotely familiar sounds" (68) of his own offspring to Buck's "visions" of primitive life in *The Call* ("Le Milieu," p. 46). What One Eye remembers is his previous litters during his natural lifetime, not a preternatural existence in

an earlier era. JL makes the distinction clear when he says of One Eye's discovery: "It was not the first time in his long and successful life that this thing had happened. It had happened many times, yet each time it was as fresh a surprise as ever to him" (68).

24 Wilcox makes a similar point when he says of One Eye's encounter with the porcupine and the lynx: "The objective manner in which London views the scene might easily be that of a zoologist watching the entire incident in a glass cage" ("*Le Milieu*," p. 46).

25 JL to George P. Brett, 11 October 1905, photocopy in Merrill Library.

26 Geismar, *Rebels and Ancestors*, p. 182.

27 Wilcox, "*Le Milieu*," p. 52.

28 Andrew Sinclair, *Jack: A Biography of Jack London* (New York: Harper & Row, 1977), p. 122.

Chapter 6: Revolution and Romance

1 TS notes in Post-Klondike Notebook, HEH, JL 1004.

2 JL to George P. Brett, 21 November 1902, *Letters*, p. 139.

3 Among the books in JL's library (HEH) is W. Pembroke Fetridge, *The Rise and Fall of the Paris Commune in 1871* (New York: Harper, 1871), which gives a full account of the rampaging mobs, summary executions, and random violence. Among other details, some of the members of the Commune tried to escape by inflating a gas balloon, though they were stopped before getting off the ground.

4 JL to George P. Brett, 10 September 1903 and 3 April 1904, *Letters*, pp. 153, 155.

5 "Big Socialist Vote Is Fraught With Meaning," San Francisco *Examiner*, 10 November 1904, p. 3. The article has been reprinted under the title "Explanation of the Great Socialist Vote of 1904" in Foner, *Jack London: American Rebel*, pp. 403–6.

6 Upton Sinclair, *The Jungle* (New York: Doubleday, Page, 1906), p. 389.

7 For an account of JL's friendship with Sinclair, see Charles L. P. Silet, "Upton Sinclair to Jack London: A Literary Friendship," *Jack London Newsletter*, 5 (1972), 49–76. The MS of JL's review of *The Jungle* is dated 6 March 1906 (HEH).

8 JL to George P. Brett, 26 March 1906, HEH, JL 11067. According to Charmian London's diary (HEH, JL 219), JL began mak-

ing notes for *The Iron Heel* in mid-August and began composition on August 25. The novel was completed in early December.

9 *Jack London Reports*, ed. King Hendricks and Irving Shepard (New York: Doubleday, 1970), pp. 352, 357.

10 Preface to *War of the Classes* (New York: Macmillan, 1905), p. ix. In a letter to Charles H. Kerr & Company, 1 August 1913, JL wrote: "Some time, if you glance over THE IRON HEEL again, you will find the position that I took some years ago was more in the line of Direct Action and Syndicalism than was it in the line of reformism. In short, in THE IRON HEEL I distinctly pointed out the failure of the political socialist movement" (HEH, JL 11424). For useful examinations of JL's various (sometimes conflicting) pronouncements on his socialism, see Robert B. Holland, "Jack London: His Thought and Art in Relation to his Time," pp. 277–340; and Starling Price, "Jack London's America," pp. 277–322.

11 "The Class Struggle," in *War of the Classes*, pp. 29, 27, 47.

12 "Revolution," in *Revolution and Other Essays*, pp. 8–9.

13 *Revolution*, p. 7. This volume contains one other essay, "What Life Means to Me," which was written in November, 1905, and which develops some of the ideas and phrasing that JL later used in *The Iron Heel*.

14 In his MS notes for *The Iron Heel* (HEH, JL 844) JL considered alternate names for both Ernest and Avis. He toyed briefly with Elsa instead of Avis, and Selfridge instead of Cunningham.

15 *The Iron Heel* (New York: Macmillan, 1908), p. 25. Subsequent page references appear in the text.

16 JL refers to all of these writers, and to some of their books, in his working notes for *The Iron Heel*. A full analysis of this debt lies beyond the scope of the present study, but a good place to begin is in Joan London's biography and Foner's *Jack London: American Rebel*. For more detailed comments on specific sources, see Sam S. Baskett, "A Source of *The Iron Heel*," *American Literature*, 27 (1955), 268–70; and Katherine M. Littell, "Jack London Through the Socialist Looking-Glass," *Jack London Newsletter*, 10 (1977), 23–28. In his manuscript on the annotated books in JL's library, David Mike Hamilton describes the markings and notes in several of the books from which JL drew material for *The Iron Heel*.

17 MS notes for *The Iron Heel*. JL twice mentions Lincoln as the kind of self-educated man-of-the-people he wanted Ernest to be.

According to his wife's diary (11 August 1906), JL was reading Untermann's *Science and Revolution* (1905) only a few days before he began work on *The Iron Heel*.

18 According to Franklin Walker's notes (Walker Collection, HEH, HM 45282), this statement was made in a letter from Untermann to Joan London, 22 January 1938.

19 "The Question of the Maximum" was first published in *War of the Classes* (1905).

20 The anecdote appears in Cloudesley Johns's autobiography, pp. 337–41, HEH, HM 42387.

21 C. London, *The Book of Jack London*, II, 135. In her diary Charmian mentions discussions with Payne on 15 April, 24 May, and 9 August 1906 (HEH, JL 219).

22 The source, which JL referred to in a footnote in the novel (p. 70), was Jocelyn Lewis, "Was It Worth While?" *Outlook*, 18 August 1906, pp. 902–4.

23 C. London, *The Book of Jack London*, II, 16.

24 For Harris's original accusation, see "How Mr. Jack London Writes a Novel," *Vanity Fair*, 82 (14 April 1909), 454. For JL's replies, see *Letters*, pp. 280–81, 285–86.

25 JL's TS notes on Louise Michel, along with the clipping, are in HEH (JL 442). The suggestion that Anna Roylston was based on Jane Roulston appears in Joan London, *Jack London and His Times*, pp. 180–81. It might be observed further that the fictional heroine's first name, Anna, was that of JL's and Jane Roulston's mutual friend Anna Strunsky. The combined name Anna Roylston thus constitutes JL's tribute to *two* admired friends of his early socialist years.

26 W. J. Ghent, *Our Benevolent Feudalism* (New York: Macmillan, 1902), p. 28. This work has long been considered one of the major influences on *The Iron Heel* for its pessimistic vision of American capitalism leading society backward into a state of neofeudalism, in which a few industrial magnates would dominate the quiescent masses. JL did use some of Ghent's facts and endowed Ernest Everhard with some of his pessimism (Ernest cites Ghent's book on p. 219), but on balance JL owes little more to Ghent than to such other socialists as Austin Lewis. In *War of the Classes*, he published a review of Ghent's book that can best be described as lukewarm.

27 MS notes, HEH, JL 1050.

28 Sinclair, *The Jungle*, p. 191. JL quotes this passage in his review of *The Jungle* (rpt. Foner, *Jack London: American Rebel*, p. 523).

29 For comments on the two strains in the fiction of social protest, see Walter B. Rideout, *The Radical Novel in the United States, 1900–1954* (Cambridge, Mass.: Harvard Univ. Press, 1954), pp. 12–13; Joseph Blotner, *The Modern American Political Novel, 1900–1960* (Austin: Univ. of Texas Press, 1966), pp. 140–41; David Ketterer, *New Worlds for Old: The Apocalyptic Imagination, Science Fiction, and American Literature* (Bloomington: Indiana Univ. Press, 1974), pp. 122–33; and Gordon Beauchamp, "*The Iron Heel* and *Looking Backward:* Two Paths to Utopia," *American Literary Realism,* 9 (1976), 307–14. Nathaniel Teich, on the other hand, sees *The Iron Heel* occupying a middle position between utopian and dystopian modes ("Marxist Dialectics in Content, Form, Point of View: Structures in Jack London's *The Iron Heel,*" *Modern Fiction Studies,* 22 [1976], 85–99, esp. 95–96).

The resemblance between *The Iron Heel* and Wells's *When the Sleeper Wakes* has been noted by Andrew Sinclair in *Jack,* p. 131. The resemblance to Ignatius Donnelly's *Caesar's Column* has been noted by Walter Rideout in *The Radical Novel,* p. 42, and in his introduction to a new edition of *Caesar's Column* (Cambridge: Harvard Univ. Press, 1960), p. xxiv; and by Blotner in *The Modern American Political Novel,* p. 151. Two copies of *Caesar's Column* remain among JL's books at HEH.

30 Donnelly, *Caesar's Column,* ed. Rideout, pp. 28, 31, 88.

31 Possibly the shift to Chicago reflects JL's enthusiasm for *The Jungle.* In his review of that novel (rpt. Foner, *Jack London: American Rebel,* p. 517), he called Chicago "industrialism incarnate, the storm-center of the conflict between capital and labor, a city of street battles and blood." JL's notes for *The Iron Heel* include a reference to the "Chicago Anarchists" who were executed following the Haymarket bombing in 1886, and also a reminder to "be sure and bring in Chicago, the 'City of Blood' —where the proletarian revolt was drowned in blood" (MS notes, HEH, JL 844).

32 Donnelly, *Caesar's Column,* ed. Rideout, pp. 256, 257. Jon Pankake has also noted the resemblance between these two passages ("The Broken Myths of Jack London," p. 122).

33 See especially Teich, "Marxist Dialectics"; Dorothy H. Roberts, "*The Iron Heel:* Socialism, Struggle, and Structure," *Jack London Newsletter,* 9 (1976), 64–66; and Paul Stein, "Jack London's *The Iron Heel:* Art as Manifesto," *Studies in American Fiction,* 6 (1978), 77–92.

34 The only ones to view Avis as protagonist (rather than merely as narrator) are H. Bruce Franklin, *Future Perfect: American Science Fiction of the Nineteenth Century*, rev. ed. (New York: Oxford Univ. Press, 1978), p. 229; and Jon Pankake, "The Broken Myths of Jack London," pp. 128–30. Pankake precedes me in recognizing the importance of Avis's problem of identity, though both he and Franklin find her metamorphosis more convincing than I do.

35 Stein, "*The Iron Heel:* Art As Manifesto," p. 90.

36 Labor, *Jack London*, p. 104.

37 JL to George P. Brett, 15 December 1906, *Letters*, p. 235.

38 Quoted in Joan London, *Jack London and His Times*, p. 313. In his essay "The Question of the Maximum," as he speculated over whether the future would lead to socialism or to the advent of powerful industrial oligarchies, he considered the latter course "possible" but "not probable" (*War of the Classes*, p. 193). Similarly, when the apparent pessimism of *The Iron Heel* was attacked by some of the more conservative socialists, London complained: "I *didn't* write the thing as a prophecy at all. I really don't think these things are going to happen in the United States. I believe the increasing socialist vote will prevent—hope for it, anyhow. But I will say that I sent out, in 'The Iron Heel,' a warning of what I think *might* happen if they don't look to their votes" (C. London, *The Book of Jack London*, II, 139). Here he seems to maintain that the novel is not so much a prophecy as a cautionary tale, a lurid romance aimed at rousing the indifferent and the faithful from their lethargy.

39 The apocalyptic imagery has been noted by David Ketterer, *New Worlds for Old*, pp. 126–33; Jon Pankake, "The Broken Myths of Jack London," pp. 118–21; and D. Seed, "The Apocalyptic Structure of Jack London's *The Iron Heel*," *Jack London Newsletter*, 13 (1980), 1–11. JL resorted to similar imagery after the outbreak of World War I, declaring that civilization was going through a "pentacostal cleansing that can only result in good for mankind" (JL to Perriton Maxwell, 28 August 1916, HEH, JL 12773).

40 Images of crucifixion were commonplace in the literature of protest, the most famous one occurring in William Jennings Bryan's "cross of gold" speech. Similarly, in Edward Bellamy's *Looking Backward* (Boston: Houghton Mifflin, 1888), Julian West cries, "I have seen Humanity hanging on a cross!" (p. 326).

41 Rpt. in Walker, *Jack London: No Mentor But Myself*, pp. 35–36.

42 For a more balanced characterization of the working class, see JL's Preface to *War of the Classes*, where he insists that socialism must deal "with what is, not with what ought to be," and that "the material with which it deals is the 'clay of the common road,' the warm human, fallible and frail, sordid and petty, absurd and contradictory, even grotesque, and yet, withal, shot through with flashes and glimmerings of something finer and God-like, with here and there sweetnesses of service and unselfishness, desires for goodness, for renunciation and sacrifice, and with conscience, stern and awful, at times blazingly imperious, demanding the right" (pp. xvi–xvii).

43 JL's notes reveal that at an early stage of his planning for the novel, he did intend such a focus on Ernest: "Very concrete, begin most likely with him—the leader of the people—his surroundings, his home, etc. etc.—At the end, dying, the word is brought him that the world war is afoot . . . and the final liberation comes." At some point JL rejected this plan and decided to shift the focus to Avis, as is indicated by another set of notes: "She—first chapter—tells briefly of herself, date, place in life, father, etc. etc.—all with forerunning hints of her meeting with Ernest & the great part he was to play in her life, & the great change in it" (MS notes, HEH, JL 844).

44 Rideout, *The Radical Novel*, p. 42.

Chapter 7: Art and Alienation

1 JL to George P. Brett, 28 May 1907, *Letters*, p. 245.

2 Charmian London referred to *Martin Eden* for the first time in her diary (HEH, JL 220) on August 8, noting that she was bringing the typing of the new MS up to date; and on August 10 she wrote to Louis Augustin that JL was "just starting a new novel" (HEH, JL 9449). Although Charmian had stated accurately that he began the novel in Honolulu (*The Book of Jack London*, II, 170), Irving Stone erroneously reported that composition began on the voyage from Oakland to Hawaii (*Sailor on Horseback*, p. 239). Stone's error was repeated by Foner, *Jack London: American Rebel*, p. 97; O'Connor, *Jack London*, p. 259; and Sinclair, *Jack*, p. 145. Russ Kingman (*A Pictorial Life of Jack London*: [New York: Crown, 1979], p. 184), and Dale L. Walker (*Jack London: No Mentor But Myself*, p. 165) state correctly that the novel was begun in Honolulu. For a more detailed account, see

my article "The Composition of *Martin Eden*," *American Literature*, 53 (1981), 397–408.

3 JL to George P. Brett, 11 July 1907, *Letters*, p. 245.

4 JL to George P. Brett, 28 May 1907, *Letters*, pp. 243–45.

5 These and the following TS notes are in HEH (JL 1004, JL 443, JL 1276).

6 MS notes, HEH, JL 968.

7 After JL's return from the Klondike, while he was struggling to succeed as a writer, one of his stepsisters (he does not say which one) was not above offering him the same kind of unwelcome advice received by Martin Eden. As he wrote to Mabel Applegarth, "Duty said 'do not go on [with your writing]; go to work.' So said my sister, though she would not say it to my face" (30 November 1898, *Letters*, p. 7).

8 Charmian's diary (HEH, JL 221) records JL's illness, heavy drinking, and depression on the return voyage, during which he did little or no work on the novel. On 15 February 1908, the day after his return to Tahiti, he told Brett that he still had a chapter and a half to go (HEH, JL 11105), and the final leaf of the holograph MS is dated February 24 (HEH, JL 969).

9 Sam S. Baskett compares *Martin Eden* with *The Education of Henry Adams* and *The Great Gatsby* in "*Martin Eden:* Jack London's 'Splendid Dream,'" *Western American Literature*, 12 (1977), 199–214. The change of title came after the novel was completed. On 27 February 1908 JL wrote to Brett to say that "in case 'SUCCESS' is already a copyrighted title, I give you herewith three titles which I prefer in the following order: (1) SUCCESS (2) STAR-DUST (3) MARTIN EDEN" (HEH, JL 11106). Brett chose the third title, and JL later confessed that he liked the new title better (JL to Ninetta Eames, 26 October 1908, *Letters*, p. 264). The name Martin Eden, it might be noted, was that of a neighbor of the Londons at Glen Ellen (see Anders Kruskopf, "Martin Eden of Sonoma," *American-Scandinavian Review*, 31 [1943], 347–48).

10 *Martin Eden* (New York: Macmillan, 1909), p. 71. Further page references appear in the text. This first American edition contains a number of typographical errors which do not appear in the first English edition (London: Heinemann, 1910). Though I have not collated the entire text, I have checked my own quotations against both the Heinemann edition and the holograph MS. The following errors in the Macmillan edition are particularly worth correcting: at 71.23 (chapter 8), "again" should

read "gain"; at 101.12 (chapter 12), "organ" should read "orgasm"; at 305.29 (chapter 35), "sneer" should read "seer"; and at 353.1 (chapter 41), "did not pay" should read "did pay." The latter error was corrected by Sam S. Baskett in his notes to the 1956 Rinehart Edition.

11 For JL's account of his own early acceptance of the Horatio Alger myth, see *John Barleycorn* (New York: Century, 1913), where he recalls his effort to learn the electrician's trade: "I still believed in the old myths which were the heritage of the American boy. . . . A canal boy could become a president. Any boy, who took employment with any firm, could, by thrift, energy, and sobriety, learn the business and rise from position to position until he was taken in as a junior partner. After that the senior partnership was only a matter of time. Very often—so ran the myth—the boy, by reason of his steadiness and application, married his employer's daughter" (pp. 187–88).

12 Charles Child Walcutt says that JL "never wrote a novel of manners, never took the patterns of American society seriously" (*Jack London*, p. 44). This statement is true of much of JL's work but not of *Martin Eden*, which Walcutt describes, unconvincingly, as one of JL's worst novels (p. 41).

13 JL owned a copy of the 1912 Harper edition of *Sister Carrie* (now at HEH), which he brought with him on his 1912 voyage around Cape Horn and urged his wife to read (Diary, 15 June 1912, JL 226). Charmian did read it and was much impressed, but the diary is tantalizingly vague on whether JL read it himself. I have found no evidence that he had read it in an earlier edition before writing *Martin Eden*, but the resemblance between the Hansons and the Higginbothams is nonetheless suggestive. The Hansons' dreary flat looks down at night on the lights of grocery stores, its "lean and narrow life" betokened by its "discordantly papered" walls, "thin rag carpet," and installment-plan furniture. Martin, too, notices the baldly mercenary sign over his brother-in-law's grocery store, the cheap chromo on the wall of the apartment, the loose seam on the "slatternly carpet" (29), and the water-stained walls of his tiny bedroom. In both novels the sister is a once-lively woman worn down by constant toil and the sullen authority of her husband who, when he comes home, puts on his "dilapidated carpet slippers" (29)—in *Sister Carrie* the phrase is "yellow carpet slippers"— and retires behind his newspaper. Both couples, fearful of losing a source of income, urge their unwelcome boarders to get a job

—any job—as quickly as possible. (Quotations from *Sister Carrie* are from the Norton Critical Edition [New York, 1970], pp. 9, 22.)

14 Sam S. Baskett is a rare exception, finding Ruth "relatively life-like" (Introd. to *Martin Eden* [New York: Holt, Rinehart and Winston, 1956], p. xviii). Writing to Anna Strunsky in December of 1900 (HEH, AW Box 3-A) about the failure of his love for Ruth's prototype, Mabel Applegarth, JL reveals much the same balance between affectionate sympathy and severe judgment that he would maintain in *Martin Eden:*

> I have never told but one woman that I loved her. Did I love her? There was no love greater, so I thought. She was more than mortal. I remember, we were eating cherries one day. Lying on my back and looking up I saw that the black juice had discolored her lips. I hailed it with delight. An omen that we were drawing closer together, that she was stripping off her immortality. . . . I came out of the great rough ugly world and stumbled upon her as in a garden. Culture? I knew none—had dreamed of it perhaps, but dreamed dimly. But she was surrounded with it, saturated in it, was a product of it. Can't you imagine the result, remembering always that she was also woman? The inevitable. I thought it was the greatest thing in the world. In reality, it was the puppy love, which affects each according to the time and season and the blood which runs in his veins—the false dawn, the glimmer. . . .
>
> But see! Time passed. I grew. I saw immortailty [*sic*] fade from her. Saw her only woman. And still I did not dream of judging. Time passed. I awoke, frightened, and found myself judging. She was very small. The positive virtues were hers, and likewise the negative vices. She was pure, honest, true, sincere, everything. But she was small. Her virtues led her nowhere. Works? She had none. Her culture was a surface smear, her deepest depth a singing shallow. . . . I awoke, and judged, and my puppy love was over. I have not seen her for long; I hear of her rarely; and out of it all, pity only remains.

Seven years later JL still remembered the cherry-stain incident and used it in the novel in chapter 11.

15 Recall once again JL's objection to the excessive detail in *The Octopus* (Walker, *Jack London: No Mentor But Myself*, p. 35).

16 JL praised *Jude* in a letter to Anna Strunsky, 27 November 1900, HEH, AW Box 3-A; and on 19 November 1913 JL cabled to Mitchell Kennerley, Lawrence's publisher, his extravagant praise of *Sons and Lovers* (copy of telegram in HEH, JL 12269). Maxwell Geismar refers to the novel's "central theme of a declassed and isolated artist" (*Rebels and Ancestors*, p. 172), but.

he does not pursue the point. The only critics to give sufficient emphasis to Martin as an artist are Jon Pankake, "The Broken Myths of Jack London," pp. 170–90; Sam S. Baskett, "*Martin Eden:* Jack London's Poem of the Mind," *Modern Fiction Studies*, 22 (1976), 23–36; and A. M. Zverev, *Jack London (on the centennial of his birth)*, trans. Olga P. Orechwa (Carbondale, Ill.: Jack London Newsletter, 1980), pp. 57–65. Both Pankake and Baskett anticipate my analysis at several points; the translation of Zverev's monograph appeared after the present chapter was written.

17 For JL's reading of *The Nigger of the Narcissus*, see chapter 4, note 16. Earle Labor also touches on the relevance of Conrad's statement ("Jack London's Literary Artistry," p. 143); and in "Jack London's America," pp. 327–83, Starling Price perceptively expands on Labor's observation, giving special attention to the cinematic and spatial qualities of JL's imagination. For comments on the Conradian elements in *Martin Eden*, see Baskett, "Jack London's Heart of Darkness."

18 For some useful comments on this tendency, with special emphasis on *Martin Eden*, see Gordon Mills, "The Transformation of Material in a Mimetic Fiction," *Modern Fiction Studies*, 22 (1976), 9–22.

19 Melville, "Hawthorne and His Mosses" (1850), rpt. in *Moby-Dick*, ed. Hayford and Parker, p. 542.

20 Cf. Frank Norris in "A Plea for Romantic Fiction": "Let Realism do the entertaining with its meticulous presentation of teacups, rag carpets, wall paper and haircloth sofas, stopping with these, going no deeper than it sees, choosing the ordinary, the untroubled, the commonplace. But to Romance belongs the wide world for range, and the unplumbed depths of the human heart, and the mystery of sex, and the problems of life, and the black, unsearched penetralia of the soul of man" (*The Responsibilities of the Novelist* [Garden City, N.Y.: Doubleday, Doran, 1928], pp. 167–68).

21 Ralph Waldo Emerson, "The Poet," in *Essays: Second Series* (Boston: James Munroe, 1844; rpt. in facsimile Columbus, Ohio: Charles E. Merrill, 1969), p. 9.

22 See, for example, N. E. Dunn and Pamela Wilson, "The Significance of Upward Mobility in *Martin Eden*," *Jack London Newsletter*, 5 (1972), 1–8. Dunn and Wilson overstate the case

when they say that Martin has "deluded himself in thinking that his writing was for an ideal purpose rather than for his own glory" (p. 6). Granted that the creative act entails a large investment of ego, it does not follow that the act lacks idealism.

23 JL made this point on a number of occasions. To a reader addressed as "Miss Brekke," for example, he wrote on 7 October 1916: "Martin Eden was an individualist, I was a socialist. That is the reason why I continued to live, and that is the reason why Martin Eden died" (HEH, JL 11055). In such simplistic statements JL distorts both his own complex nature and that of his novel.

24 Cf. JL's own ambitions at a similar stage: "Once I am in a position, where I do not have to depend upon each day's work to keep the pot boiling for the next day, where I do not have to dissipate my energy on all kinds of hack, where I can slowly and deliberately ponder and shape the best that is in me, then, at that time, I am confident that I shall do big work" (JL to George P. Brett, 21 November 1902, *Letters*, p. 141).

25 Brissenden's "Ephemera" was based on George Sterling's poem "The Testimony of the Suns," a pessimistic meditation on the cosmos of which JL was particularly fond (JL to J. H. Greer, 4 August 1915, HEH, JL 11867). But the magazine controversy that follows the publication of "Ephemera" is based on a controversy surrounding Sterling's poem "A Wine of Wizardry" in the summer of 1907. After being successively praised and caricatured, Sterling professed to JL his through disgust with the whole episode and his certainty that his poem was a great one regardless of what any of the Hearst publications said (Sterling to JL, 6 August and 12 September 1907, HEH, JL 19061, 19062). On 27 September, JL replied with effusive sympathy: "you are head-and-shoulders in the stars compared with the puny earthmen who dare to yawp at your power of beauty! . . . You convert me more and more to your point of view on the magazines, and the fact that there are only swine for whom to create beauty" (*Letters*, p. 251).

26 Walcutt, *Jack London*, p. 41. In "Divided Self and World in *Martin Eden*," George M. Spangler describes Martin's plight—rightly, I think—as a lack of "wholeness of personality" (*Jack London Newsletter*, 9 [1976], 120). For convincing defenses of the characterization of Martin and the ending of the novel, see

Price, "Jack London's America," pp. 406–21, and Jonathan Spinner, "Jack London's *Martin Eden:* The Development of the Existential Hero," *Michigan Academician,* 3 (1970), 43–48.

27 Friedrich Nietzsche, *The Birth of Tragedy,* in *Basic Writings of Nietzsche,* trans. Walter Kaufmann (New York: Modern Library, 1968), pp. 37, 59–60. Despite JL's well-documented interest in Nietzsche and cultural anthropology, I have found no evidence of JL's reading of *The Birth of Tragedy* or *The Golden Bough,* but such ideas were in the intellectual air and are clearly pertinent to the novel.

28 The myths that JL synthesizes in this novel resemble the demonic imagery described by Northrop Frye in *Anatomy of Criticism* (Princeton, N.J.: Princeton Univ. Press, 1957), pp. 147–50. See also pp. 187–88 on the inevitable presence of the solar myth in romance, and pp. 192–93 on the treasure motive. In view of the choice of the name Eden for his protagonist, it is significant that JL described the effect of *Paradise Lost* as resembling that of "an ancient sun myth" (JL to Albert Mordell, 2 October 1916, HEH, JL 12844). For more on mythic imagery in *Martin Eden* and other novels, see James Glennon Cooper, "The Womb of Time: Archetypal Patterns in the Novels of Jack London," *Jack London Newsletter,* 9 (1976), 16–28.

29 JL himself, according to his wife, occasionally viewed death as a welcome attainment of rest: "Jack's 'dream of rest' had more than once, in my hearing, been associated with death itself. Never was he so happy, he who at the same time so exalted life, that he could not descant upon the repose of death. One of my earliest memories of him is such a remark as this: 'To me the idea of death is sweet. Think of it—to lie down and go into the dark out of all the struggle and pain of living—to go to sleep and rest, always to be resting. Oh, I do not want to die now—I'd fight like the devil to keep alive. . . . But when I come to die, it will be smiling at death, I promise you'" (C. London, *The Book of Jack London,* II, 74–75). Earle Labor notes that the sea at the end is the "eternal cradle, the mighty womb from which all life has emerged and to which it must ultimately return" ("Jack London's Literary Artistry," p. 147).

30 MS notes, HEH, JL 968. Franklin Walker somehow overlooked these notes and concluded erroneously that JL had originally planned to extend Martin's adventures to the South Seas but

changed his mind and abruptly terminated the novel with a sui-
cide (''Jack London: *Martin Eden*,'' in *The American Novel:
From James Fenimore Cooper to William Faulkner*, ed. Wallace
Stegner [New York: Basic Books, 1965], p. 139). Arthur Calder-
Marshall, in his introduction to *Martin Eden* (London: Bodley
Head, 1965), pp. 13–16, accepted Walker's theory and added
still further erroneous speculations. For an attempt to
straighten out the facts, see my article ''The Composition of
Martin Eden,'' pp. 405–8.

31 The copies of *Typee*, *Omoo*, and *Moby-Dick* are still among
JL's books at HEH. There is no copy of *White-Jacket*, but it, too,
probably accompanied the Londons on the *Snark*, since their
copies of the first three books are part of a uniform four-volume
edition (Boston: Dana Estes, 1900) of which *White-Jacket* is the
fourth member. Irving Stone says, on unspecified authority,
that JL read *White-Jacket* during the voyage from Hawaii to the
Marquesas (*Sailor on Horseback*, p. 244).

32 In her diary for 17 and 18 October 1907 (HEH, JL 220), Charmian recorded that JL was reading *Typee*, and on 7 November
she recorded that she was typing chapter 26, in which the passage in question appears. For an account of the Londons' climb
out of the leper colony at Molokai in early July, see Charmian
K. London, *Our Hawaii* (New York: Macmillan, 1917; 1922),
pp. 164–66.

33 For the pertinent passages in ''Typee,'' see *The Cruise of the
Snark*, pp. 147–48. For some helpful comments on the wilder-
ness as a source of high hopes and ultimate disillusionment dur-
ing various phases of JL's career, see Earle Labor, ''Jack
London's Symbolic Wilderness: Four Versions,'' *Nineteenth-
Century Fiction*, 17 (1962), 149–61.

34 ''American Fiction Lacking in Courage,'' New York *Sun*, 2
March 1912, clipping in Scrapbook 11, p. 72 (HEH).

35 Herman Melville, *White-Jacket*, ed. Harrison Hayford, Hershel
Parker, and G. Thomas Tanselle (Evanston and Chicago: North-
western Univ. Press and the Newberry Library, 1970), pp. 392–
93. The resemblance between these episodes in *White-Jacket*
and *Martin Eden* was first noted by Labor, ''Jack London's Literary Artistry,'' pp. 152–53.

36 Charmian London, *The Log of the Snark* (New York: Macmillan, 1913), p. 179.

37 JL to Alice Lyndon, 29 July 1909, *Letters*, p. 282. The following
year he told another reader that he considered *Martin Eden* "far
above my more popular books" (JL to E. C. Beckwith, 24
August 1910, *Letters*, p. 319).

Chapter 8: Three Frontiers

1 JL to Clarence Buzzini, 13 January 1915, HEH, JL 11297. The
first paragraph of this letter refers confusingly to "William Harnish," but "William" is evidently a typographical error. The
second paragraph, obviously referring to the same man, correctly says "Elam Harnish," and Buzzini's letter to JL mentions
only Elam.
2 Post-Klondike Notebook, HEH, JL 1004.
3 TS notes, HEH, JL 509.
4 *Revolution and Other Essays*, pp. 188–89.
5 TS notes, HEH, JL 509.
6 Wayne W. Westbrook, "Plucking the California Goose—Financier James R. Keene and Jack London's Burning Daylight," *Jack
London Newsletter*, 11 (1978), 50–55. Keene, however, was the
model for Daylight only in his New York exploit and part of his
San Francisco speculations—not, as Westbrook suggests, for the
whole of Daylight's career. JL's notes, in fact, suggest that
Keene was not the only model in the New York episode: "Deal
by which the business men try to rob him. Three others and he
went into the deal. Then, unexpectedly, they told him to bear
the market by selling. He calls up all three on 'phone, and all
three assure him to sell (Remember how Rogers lied to Lawson
on copper)" (TS notes, HEH, JL 509).
7 See pp. 266–68 of Cloudesley Johns's unpublished autobiography (HEH, HM 42387).
8 Sam S. Baskett ("Jack London's Fiction: Its Social Milieu," pp.
21, 88–94) notes the general accuracy of JL's portrayal of business activity in the Bay Area, though he does not suggest any
specific sources.
9 JL to Ed Winship (of *Sunset* magazine), 20 September 1911,
HEH, JL 14018. Sam S. Baskett has suggested that Daylight's
business ventures are exaggerated versions of JL's own ventures
in eucalyptus trees and the Millergraph machine ("Jack London's Fiction: Its Social Milieu," pp. 221–23), and Andrew Sin-

clair observes that JL was "only a good businessman in his fantasy of himself" (*Jack*, p. 198).

10 Details of these events are recorded in Charmian's diary (HEH, JL 222, 223).

11 Franklin Walker, for example, says that the Klondike portion of the novel "moves vigorously and effectively" but that Harnish is "both grotesque and sentimental in his adventures in California" (*Jack London and the Klondike*, p. 229). Three critics who have viewed the last half of the novel with qualified sympathy are Clell T. Peterson, "Jack London's Sonoma Novels," *American Book Collector*, 9 (October 1958), 15–20; Gordon Mills, "The Symbolic Wilderness: James Fenimore Cooper and Jack London," *Nineteenth-Century Fiction*, 13 (1959), 329–40; and Earle Labor, "Jack London's Symbolic Wilderness: Four Versions," pp. 156–58, and "From 'All Gold Canyon' to *The Acorn-Planter:* Jack London's Agrarian Vision," *Western American Literature*, 11 (1976), 83–101. At the other extreme, Maxwell Geismar dismisses *Burning Daylight* as "another bit of hack work, a poor novel about Alaska" (*Rebels and Ancestors*, p. 190).

12 Mills, "The Symbolic Wilderness," p. 334.

13 In his 1901 review of *The Octopus*, JL singled out Annixter for special praise, noting that Norris's crusty rancher was "deliciously afraid of "feemale women"" (rpt. Walker, *Jack London: No Mentor But Myself*, p. 36).

14 Andrew Sinclair points out the importance of the habit of yarning that JL acquired during his teenage years on the Oakland waterfront: "Jack certainly knew how to tell a good story at the bar of the First and Last Chance Saloon. He was not so much a liar as an improver upon the truth, the heir of Mark Twain and Bret Harte and the frontier tradition" (*Jack*, p. 12). The *Aegis* stories have been collected by James E. Sisson in *Jack London's Articles and Stories in the (Oakland) High School Aegis* (Cedar Springs, Mich.: The London Collector, 1971).

15 See, for example, Kenneth Lynn, *The Dream of Success: A Study of the Modern American Imagination* (Boston: Little, Brown, 1955), p. 112.

16 *Burning Daylight* (New York: Macmillan, 1910), p. 6. Further page references appear in the text.

17 Kevin Starr calls this "probably the most improbable scene he ever wrote" (*Americans and the California Dream: 1850–1915* [New York: Oxford Univ. Press, 1973], p. 218). But such

solemnly realistic standards are hardly appropriate to a novel whose effects depend on the comic exaggerations of the frontier tradition. JL's interest in Daylight's colorful frontier speech dates back to his earliest notes on the original Elam Harnish and continues in a page of notes headed "Vernacular of Daylight," on which he lists colloquialisms to be used in the novel. Such attention also appears in the holograph MS (HEH, JL 510). In chapter 1, for example, JL changed Daylight's "Come on, you all!" to "Surge along, you all!"

18 Cf. *John Barleycorn*, p. 96, for JL's own memories of drinking as "a social duty and a manhood rite."

19 See Leslie A. Fiedler, *Love and Death in the American Novel* (New York: Stein and Day, 1960).

20 Cloudesley Johns claims that he was the model for this elevator boy, since he had provided JL with information about the monopolistic practices of the railroads (Johns's TS autobiography, pp. 197–98, HEH, HM 42387).

21 Peterson notes that in both *Burning Daylight* and *The Valley of the Moon*, the horse symbolizes, among other things, "the mysteries of sex and love" ("Jack London's Sonoma Novels," p. 18).

Chapter 9: Urban Discontents

1 *Saturday Evening Post*, 12 November 1910, pp. 12–15, 38–42. Quotations below are from pp. 13, 14. This clipping and others cited hereafter are filed with the MS of *The Valley of the Moon* in HEH (JL 1369).

2 JL to George P. Brett, 30 May 1911, HEH, JL 11152.

3 Russ Kingman has suggested that the San Jose woman was based on Ina Coolbrith, the Oakland librarian who befriended JL during his boyhood (Introd. to *The Valley of the Moon* [Santa Barbara, Calif., and Salt Lake City, Utah: Peregrine Smith, 1975], p. viii). The librarian JL had chiefly in mind, however, was the author of the *Collier's* article.

4 *Saturday Evening Post*, 2 September 1911, pp. 18–19.

5 Ibid., 18 November 1911, pp. 9–11, 52–54; 16 September 1911, pp. 15–17, 48–50. JL's use of these articles has been noted by Franklin Walker, "Ideas and Action in Jack London's Fiction," in *Essays on American Literature in Honor of Jay B. Hubbell*, ed. Clarence Gohdes (Durham, N.C.: Duke Univ. Press, 1967), p. 268.

6 This rash of back-to-the-land articles was complemented by the vogue of wilderness novels. As Peter J. Schmitt has shown in *Back to Nature: The Arcadian Myth in Urban America* (New York: Oxford Univ. Press, 1969), such writers as James Oliver Curwood, Gene Stratton Porter, and Harold Bell Wright emphasized the revitalizing power of rural or wilderness experience to an increasingly urbanized generation. See especially chapter 12, "The Wilderness Novel."

7 Diary, 22 January 1911, HEH, JL 225.

8 Notes for "San Francisco Slum Study," HEH, JL 1152.

9 Franklin Walker, in the first chapter of his unpublished biography (HEH, HM 45284), noticed that Sarah's hysterics were based on those of Flora London. See also JL's own allusion to his mother's hysteria quoted in C. London, *The Book of Jack London*, II, 52.

10 Baskett, "Jack London's Fiction: Its Social Milieu," pp. 8–11, 179–86.

11 Diary, 5 July 1912, HEH, JL 226. Clarice Stasz notes Charmian's contributions to this novel in "Charmian London as a Writer," *Jack London Newsletter*, 11 (1978), 23.

12 *The Valley of the Moon* (New York: Macmillan, 1913), p. 291. Page references appear hereafter in the text.

13 JL to Bessie London, 8 January 1911, *Letters*, p. 329.

14 In his MS (HEH, JL 1368), JL first wrote the second paragraph of chapter 1 thus: "Which was true. I liked dancing better than anything." He then wrote several words of the next paragraph before crossing out the entire passage and beginning the second paragraph, "Twenty feet away, a stout, elderly woman. . . ."

15 Gordon Mills, for example, says inaccurately that *The Valley* treats the wilderness theme "from the point of view of a working man" ("The Symbolic Wilderness," p. 332). Maxwell Geismar attributes to JL the racist rant of the anarchist Bert Wanhope, one of the novel's least attractive characters (*Rebels and Ancestors*, p. 207). In *Americans and the California Dream*, p. 220, Kevin Starr exaggerates the novel's racism by failing to distinguish between the points of view of Saxon and Billy. And Clell T. Peterson is similarly imprecise when he calls Billy "the hero" of the novel and then quotes one of his uglier racist remarks ("Jack London's Sonoma Novels," p. 16).

16 *The Long Day* was written by Dorothy Richardson and published anonymously (New York: Century, 1905). JL's review

appeared in the *Examiner* for 15 October 1905 and is reprinted in Walker, *Jack London: No Mentor But Myself*, pp. 79–86. JL's account of the laundry episode is on pp. 84–85. When JL was a boy, his stepsister Ida London also worked in a laundry (see Kingman, *A Pictorial Life*, p. 32).

17 JL paid special tribute to this scene in his review of *The Octopus* (rpt. Walker, *Jack London: No Mentor But Myself*, p. 36).

18 JL himself lived in a similar cottage at 807 Pine Street, West Oakland, in the late 1880s. A surviving photograph shows even the white picket fence (see Kingman, *A Pictorial Life*, p. 34).

19 For a useful historical perspective on JL's racism, see chapter 5 of Robert B. Holland's dissertation, "Jack London: His Thought and Art in Relation to His Time," pp. 224–76.

20 Howard Lachtman has stressed this dimension of the novel in his "Reconsideration: *The Valley of the Moon*," *New Republic*, 6 September 1975, pp. 27–29.

21 The importance of the Turner thesis is stressed by Abraham Rothberg, "The House That Jack Built," pp. 268–70.

Chapter 10: A Broken Clock

1 C. London, *The Book of Jack London*, II, 255.

2 Diary for 1913, HEH, JL 227. Unless otherwise cited, subsequent quotations from the diary are from this volume.

3 Diary for 1912, HEH, JL 226.

4 The data on Allan Dunn's early career come from *Who's Who in America*, 8 (1913–1914).

5 The inscribed volume is still among the books in JL's library, now at HEH.

6 JL's words to his wife (Diary, HEH, JL 227) form the basis of the scene in *The Little Lady* in which Dick confesses to Paula that his jealousy has revived his love for her: "I am proud that I am a lover. At my age, a lover!" (363). In her biography, however, Charmian carefully conceals the real cause of her husband's outburst. She cannot resist quoting his flattering words, but she moves them forward several months (to the time of the Wolf House fire) and claims they were prompted by a sudden illness which she says caused JL to fear for her life (*The Book of Jack London*, II, 255). Subsequent page references to *The Little Lady* (New York: Macmillan, 1916) will appear in the text.

7 *Letters*, p. 374.

8 Diary, 11 March 1908, HEH, JL 221.

9 Diary, 12 March, 30 October, 18 September 1911 (JL 225).

10 Quoted from MS in HEH, dated 20 January 1909 (JL 992). The article was published in the *Australian Star*, 4 February 1909, p. 1.

11 Forrest's ranch and house are not, however, exact replicas of JL's ranch and Wolf House. Forrest's estate of 250,000 acres, which extends "west from the Sacramento River to the mountaintops" (77), is vastly larger and more prosperous than JL's 1400-acre holdings in the Sonoma Valley; and the Big House, though resembling Wolf House on the inside, has a stucco exterior and "Hispano-Moresque" design (13) that was modeled after a picture of the mansion of Phoebe A. Hearst at Pleasanton, California (C. London, *The Book of Jack London*, II, 287–88).

12 The link between the two Dunns in the mind of Charmian, at least, is illustrated by a letter she received from Robert Dunn on 1 November 1915, at the top of which she noted, with appropriate emphasis: "*This* Dunn was in Korea with Jack" (HEH, JL 5803). I have drawn biographical data about Robert Dunn from *Who's Who in America*, 19 (1936–1937).

13 Edwin B. Erbentraut makes this point in "The Symbolic Triad in London's *The Little Lady of the Big House*," *Jack London Newsletter*, 3 (1970), 82–89. In a brief but incisive discussion of *The Little Lady* in "From 'All Gold Canyon' to *The Acorn-Planter*," pp. 99–100, Earle Labor says: "His alter ego, the artist-writer Evan Graham, possesses exactly those qualities lacking in Forrest. . . . 'Grace, light, delight': these are contrasted against the deadly efficiency of Forrest, who is basically a sterile clockwork figure" (100). This judgment of Forrest seems a bit severe (Labor also refers to his "damnable efficiency" and calls him "an agronomical Ethan Brand, governed by head but lacking in heart"); but Labor was the first to point out that Dick is not simply an idealized portrait of the author. For another provocative critique of Forrest, this one from a feminist point of view, see Clarice Stasz, "Androgyny in the Novels of Jack London," pp. 128–32. A Freudian analysis by Robert Forrey, less convincing than his earlier article on *The Sea-Wolf*, is "Three Modes of Sexuality in London's *The Little Lady of the Big House*," *Literature and Psychology*, 26 (1976), 52–60.

14 C. London, *The Book of Jack London*, II, 255. In the novel Paula makes an identical confession: "Yes, I am positively aching to

be out again over the world with Dick. . . . If we could only start to-morrow! But Dick can't start yet. He's in too deep with too many experiments and adventures on the ranch here" (211).

15 JL to Roland Phillips, 14 March 1913, *Letters*, pp. 374–75. When JL was ready to begin the novel, on 4 April 1914, he wrote again to Phillips in much the same hyperbolic vein: "I have spent a week mulling over my next novel, which I shall entitle: 'THE LITTLE LADY OF THE BIG HOUSE.' This is the story I wrote you about last year. In it is the old, eternal triangle, in this case two men and a woman, the two men forty years of age, and the woman thirty-six years of age, and in a setting that never before in the history of all the literature of all the world was ever put into print" (HEH, JL 13166). Irving Stone spliced a line from this letter onto a few (misquoted) sentences from the 1913 letter and then assigned the entire spurious letter an erroneous date, the "fall of 1914" (*Sailor on Horseback*, p. 313).

16 JL to Albert Farr, 28 July 1914, HEH, JL 11677. The rebuilding was never undertaken, but JL's enthusiasm for the ranch persisted. "I wish you could see my ranch now," he crowed to George Brett in 1915. "It is beginning to come along. I have raised two crops on soil that was worked out for forty years and that never, in the entire history of California, ever grew more than one crop a year. I have so many farming triumphs to brag about that I shall not brag about them until the day comes when we have you here on the ranch and can brag to you personally" (12 November 1915, HEH, JL 11226). Though such a burst of enthusiasm often prefaced an attempt to wheedle another advance out of Brett, though JL experienced plenty of failures along with his triumphs, and though he spent more of his last years away from the ranch than on it—still his delight in his farming experiments was genuine and lifelong. Writing without sufficient knowledge of the facts—and sometimes ignoring or distorting the facts they did know—such critics as Kenneth Lynn and Kevin Starr have contributed to a misunderstanding of this period of JL's life. For a helpful corrective, see Labor, "From 'All Gold Canyon' to *The Acorn-Planter*."

17 On the MS (HEH, JL 890), JL changed "the hub of the ranch activity" to "the hub of the ranch organization," thereby increasing the emphasis on Dick's oversystematized life.

18 The barrenness of the ironically named Forrests has been discussed by Peterson, "Jack London's Sonoma Novels," p. 20, and by Labor, *Jack London*, pp. 143–44.

19 In the final sentence I have rejected the first edition reading, "failures. . . . their," in favor of the singular noun and pronoun, "failure. . . . his," which JL used in the original MS and which agrees better with the singular "any farmer" in the preceding sentence.

20 JL to Frank Garbutt, 21 September 1914, HEH, JL 11805.

21 JL to Joan London, 7 March 1916, *Letters*, p. 467.

22 JL to Mattie N. Hines, 28 August 1916, HEH, JL 12004.

23 JL to L. B. Goodyear, 29 October 1915, HEH, JL 11859.

24 Diary, 8, 9, 10 December 1914, HEH, JL 228.

25 JL to Alexander G. Cotter, 18 June 1915, *Letters*, p. 452.

26 In quoting this passage, I have restored the correct MS reading, "the Noseless One," in place of the erroneous "Noiseless One" of the first edition.

27 Labor, *Jack London*, p. 144.

Epilogue

1 McClintock's comments on JL's interest in Jung first appeared in "Jack London's Use of Carl Jung's *Psychology of the Unconscious*," *American Literature*, 42 (1970), 336–47, rpt. as chapter 6 of *White Logic: Jack London's Short Stories* (Grand Rapids, Mich.: Wolf House Books, 1975), pp. 151–74.

2 In his table of contents, McClintock refers to the decline as "1906–1911," but in the preface he gives the years as "1906–1912" and describes JL as "gradually incapacitated by his philosophical pessimism and other personal problems" (*White Logic*, p. xi). I find no such incapacity.

3 Joan London, *Jack London and His Times*, and Foner, *Jack London: American Rebel*. Foner, in particular, weakens his case when, in the notes appended to the revised edition of his book (New York: Citadel, 1964), pp. 148–49, he conflates *The Little Lady* and *The Mutiny of the Elsinore*, speaking of Pike, Pathurst, and Jacobs (from *The Mutiny*) and the Forrests and Evan Graham (from *The Little Lady*) as if all of them were characters in the same novel! By thus attributing to *The Little Lady* the racism of *The Mutiny*, Foner is able to misjudge the former as "probably the worst novel London ever wrote" (p. 147).

4 JL to Mabel Applegarth, 30 November 1898, *Letters*, p. 7.

5 McClintock, *White Logic*, pp. 20–33.

6 JL's comment on Benjamin De Casseres reveals something of this ambivalence toward Nietzsche: "This man [De Casseres] is really and truly the American Nietzsche. I, as you know, am in the opposite intellectual camp from that of Nietzsche. Yet no man in my own camp stirs me as does Nietzsche or as does De Casseres" (JL to George P. Brett, 21 February 1912, *Letters*, p. 361).

7 JL's failure to mention *Moby-Dick* may imply a desire to conceal the heaviness of his debt to it. He similarly failed to mention Donnelly's *Caesar's Column* in his notes for *The Iron Heel* or anywhere else that I have been able to discover.

8 "A Classic of the Sea," an essay on R. H. Dana's *Two Years Before the Mast*, in *The Human Drift* (New York: Macmillan, 1917), p. 102.

9 For some useful comparisons of the major JL biographies and how they treat various controversies of JL's life, see Clarice Stasz, "The Social Construction of Biography: The Case of Jack London," *Modern Fiction Studies*, 22 (1976), 51–71. See especially pp. 60–64 on the biographers' typically negative characterizations of Charmian, though Stasz overcorrects them in an effort to defend her against all aspersions.

10 For an objective examination of the events surrounding JL's death and the evidence for and against a possible suicide, see Andrew Sinclair, *Jack*, pp. 236–42.

11 E. M. Forster, *Aspects of the Novel* (New York: Harcourt Brace & World, 1927), pp. 136, 143.

12 C. London, *The Book of Jack London*, II, 269.

Chronology of Jack London's Life

1876   January 12, born out of wedlock in San Francisco to Flora Wellman of Massillon, Ohio; father was almost certainly William Henry Chaney, a "professor" of astrology; September 7, Flora married John London, named her child John Griffith London.

1877–   Lived in series of dingy houses, flats, and small farms in
1885   rural areas of East Bay and finally in Oakland.

1885–   Attended grammar school, frequented Oakland Public
1892   Library; delivered newspapers, worked in cannery; bought sailboat, sailed on Bay; joined oyster pirates, then associated informally with Fish Patrol.

1893   January–August, sailed to North Pacific on seal-hunting schooner *Sophia Sutherland*; November 12, won first prize in newspaper contest for "Story of a Typhoon off the Coast of Japan"; worked in jute mill.

1894   Shoveled coal in power plant; April 6, left on eight-month tramping journey throughout U.S. and Canada; June 29, began serving thirty-day sentence in Erie County Penitentiary after arrest for vagrancy outside Niagara Falls, New York.

1895   January, entered Oakland High School; wrote stories and sketches for high school *Aegis*; fell in love with Mabel Applegarth.

1896   Dropped out of high school, crammed for University of California entrance examinations; attended university at Berkeley for fall semester.

1897   Enrolled at Berkeley for second semester but withdrew for financial reasons; became frequent soapbox speaker

for socialist cause; worked on writing; spring, worked
at Belmont Academy Laundry; July 25, sailed for Klondike; spent winter in cabin at mouth of Stewart River.

1898   Spent spring in Dawson; June 8, left Dawson, sailed
skiff down Yukon River to sea, arrived home early
August; wrote Northland stories; early December, "To
the Man on Trail" accepted by *Overland Monthly*.

1899   Seven more Northland stories published by *Overland
Monthly*; July, "An Odyssey of the North" accepted by
Atlantic Monthly.

1900   April 7, married Bessie Maddern; April, first book, *The
Son of the Wolf*, published by Houghton Mifflin; late
August, began *A Daughter of the Snows* and collaboration with Anna Strunsky on *The Kempton-Wace Letters*.

1901   January 15, daughter Joan born; completed *A Daughter
of the Snows* in March, continued work on *Kempton-
Wace Letters*.

1902   February, moved from Oakland to Piedmont; fell in
love with Anna Strunsky; July 30, sailed for England,
lived in East End of London, wrote *The People of the
Abyss*; October 20, daughter Bess born; returned home
in mid-November, completed *Kempton-Wace Letters*,
began *The Call of the Wild*.

1903   January, completed *The Call of the Wild*; early May,
began *The Sea-Wolf*; June and July, began love affair with Charmian Kittredge, separated from Bessie,
moved to Oakland.

1904   Early January, completed *The Sea-Wolf*, left for Korea
to report the Russo-Japanese War; June 30, returned
from Korea; fall, wrote *The Game*.

1905   Late spring, bought 130-acre Hill Ranch near Glen Ellen
in Sonoma County; June 26, began *White Fang*, completed it October 10; October 18, left for socialist lecture tour through Midwest and East; November 18,
divorce from Bessie granted, married Charmian Kittredge in Chicago the following day.

1906   February 15, returned from lecture tour, began
construction of ketch *Snark*; early April, began *Before
Adam*, completed it June 7; August 25, began *The Iron*

Heel, completed it early December; late December, began tramp sketches collected in *The Road*.

1907   February 5, completed tramp sketches; April 23, sailed for Hawaii in *Snark*, arrived May 18; early August, began *Martin Eden*; October 7, left Hawaii in *Snark*, arrived Marquesas December 6; December 19, left Marquesas, arrived Tahiti December 27.

1908   February 2–14, sailed to California and back on *Mariposa*; February 24, completed *Martin Eden*; April–November, cruised in South Seas, toured Solomon Islands; early August, began *Adventure*; November 20, entered hospital in Sydney, Australia, for treatment of tropical ailments.

1909   April 8, sold *Snark*, sailed for South America on freighter *Tymeric*; April 22, completed *Adventure*; May 19, arrived Ecuador; June 5, began *Burning Daylight*; August 29, arrived home in Glen Ellen.

1910   January, began plans and purchases for Wolf House; early February, completed *Burning Daylight*; late February–early March, spent three weeks at Carmel, wrote *The Scarlet Plague*; June 19, daughter Joy born, died thirty-eight hours later; September, worked on *The Assassination Bureau, Ltd.*; October, bought sailboat *Roamer*, cruised on Sacramento and San Joaquin rivers; October 22, began *The Abysmal Brute*, completed it December 14.

1911   June–August, took wagon trip to northern California and southern Oregon; September, worked on *Assassination Bureau*; early December, began *The Valley of the Moon*; December 21, left for New York.

1912   March 1, sailed from Baltimore on *Dirigo* around Cape Horn; July 17, completed *The Valley of the Moon*; August 4, arrived Glen Ellen; September–December, wrote *John Barleycorn*.

1913   January 8, began *The Mutiny of the Elsinore*, completed it late August; August 22, Wolf House destroyed by fire; mid-September, began *The Star Rover*.

1914   Early March, completed *The Star Rover*; April 3, began *The Little Lady of the Big House*; April 17, left for Mexico to report American intervention at Vera Cruz; contracted acute dysentery, then pleurisy; June 18, arrived Glen Ellen; December 8, completed *The Little Lady*.

1915   February 8, began *Jerry of the Islands*; February 24, sailed for Hawaii; June, completed *Jerry*, began *Michael, Brother of Jerry*; July 23, returned to Glen Ellen; October 12, began *Hearts of Three*; December 7, completed *Michael*; December 16, sailed for Hawaii.

1916   Spring, completed *Hearts of Three*; August 3, returned to Glen Ellen; November 22, died of uremia complicated by self-administered dose of morphine.

Books by Jack London

Following is the initial publication information on London's works. A number of these titles are of course still in print by different publishers, in English and several other languages. For more comprehensive bibliographies of works by and about Jack London, see Hensley C. Woodbridge, John London, and George H. Tweney, *Jack London: A Bibliography* (Georgetown, Calif.: Talisman Press, 1966; rpt. with supplement, Millwood, N.Y.: Kraus Reprint Co., 1976); Dale L. Walker and James E. Sisson III, *The Fiction of Jack London: A Chronological Bibliography* (El Paso: Texas Western Press, 1972); and Joan R. Sherman, *Jack London: A Reference Guide* (Boston: G.K. Hall, 1977).

The Son of the Wolf: Tales of the Far North. Boston: Houghton Mifflin, 1900. [short stories]

The God of His Fathers and Other Stories. New York: McClure, Phillips, 1901. [short stories]

Children of the Frost. New York: Macmillan, 1902. [short stories]

The Cruise of the Dazzler. New York: Century, 1902. [juvenile novel]

A Daughter of the Snows. Philadelphia: J.B. Lippincott, 1902. [novel]

The Kempton-Wace Letters. New York: Macmillan, 1903. [epistolary polemics in fictional form, written with Anna Strunsky]

The Call of the Wild. New York: Macmillan, 1903. [novella]

The People of the Abyss. New York: Macmillan, 1903. [sketches of slum life]

The Faith of Men and Other Stories. New York: Macmillan, 1904. [short stories]

The Sea-Wolf. New York: Macmillan, 1904. [novel]
War of the Classes. New York: Macmillan, 1905. [socialist essays]
The Game. New York: Macmillan, 1905. [novella]
Tales of the Fish Patrol. New York: Macmillan, 1905. [juvenile stories]
Moon-Face and Other Stories. New York: Macmillan, 1906. [short stories]
White Fang. New York: Macmillan, 1906. [novel]
Scorn of Women. New York: Macmillan, 1906. [play]
Before Adam. New York: Macmillan, 1907. [novel]
Love of Life and Other Stories. New York: Macmillan, 1907. [short stories]
The Road. New York: Macmillan, 1907. [sketches of tramp life]
The Iron Heel. New York: Macmillan, 1908. [novel]
Martin Eden. New York: Macmillan, 1909. [novel]
Lost Face. New York: Macmillan, 1910. [short stories]
Revolution and Other Essays. New York: Macmillan, 1910. [essays]
Burning Daylight. New York: Macmillan, 1910. [novel]
Theft. New York: Macmillan, 1910. [play]
When God Laughs and Other Stories. New York: Macmillan, 1911. [short stories]
Adventure. New York: Macmillan, 1911. [novel]
The Cruise of the Snark. New York: Macmillan, 1911. [travel sketches]
South Sea Tales. New York: Macmillan, 1911. [short stories]
The House of Pride and Other Tales of Hawaii. New York: Macmillan, 1912. [short stories]
A Son of the Sun. Garden City, N.Y.: Doubleday, Page, 1912. [short stories]
Smoke Bellew. New York: Century, 1912. [short stories]
The Night-Born. New York: Century, 1913. [short stories]
The Abysmal Brute. New York: Century, 1913. [novella]
John Barleycorn. New York: Century, 1913. [autobiography centering on experience with alcohol]
The Valley of the Moon. New York: Macmillan, 1913. [novel]
The Strength of the Strong. New York: Macmillan, 1914. [short stories]
The Mutiny of the Elsinore. New York: Macmillan, 1914. [novel]
The Scarlet Plague. New York: Macmillan, 1915. [novella]

The Star Rover. New York: Macmillan, 1915. [novel]
The Acorn-Planter: A California Forest Play. New York: Macmillan, 1916. [play]
The Little Lady of the Big House. New York: Macmillan, 1916. [novel]
The Turtles of Tasman. New York: Macmillan, 1916. [short stories]
The Human Drift. New York: Macmillan, 1917. [miscellany]
Jerry of the Islands. New York: Macmillan, 1917. [novel]
Michael, Brother of Jerry. New York: Macmillan, 1917. [novel]
The Red One. New York: Macmillan, 1918. [short stories]
On the Makaloa Mat. New York: Macmillan, 1919. [short stories]
Hearts of Three. New York: Macmillan, 1920. [novel]
Dutch Courage and Other Stories. New York: Macmillan, 1922. [juvenile stories]
The Assassination Bureau, Ltd. New York: McGraw-Hill, 1963. [novel completed by Robert L. Fish]
Daughters of the Rich. Ed. James E. Sisson. Oakland, Calif.: Holmes Book Co., 1971. [one-act play]
Gold. Ed. James Sisson. Oakland, Calif.: Holmes Book Co., 1972. [play written with Herbert Heron]

Index

Works by Jack London are listed separately and designated by (JL); works by other writers are listed under the name of the writer. Characters are listed separately, followed by the abbreviated titles of the novels in which they appear. The following abbreviations are used:

JL	Jack London
DS	*A Daughter of the Snows*
CW	*The Call of the Wild*
SW	*The Sea-Wolf*
WF	*White Fang*
IH	*The Iron Heel*
ME	*Martin Eden*
BD	*Burning Daylight*
VM	*The Valley of the Moon*
LL	*The Little Lady of the Big House*

Abysmal Brute, The (JL), xii–xiii, 188

Adams, Henry: 242; *The Education of Henry Adams*, 130, 270 n9

Adventure (JL), xii

Alger, Horatio, Jr., 130, 172, 271 n11

"Apostate, The" (JL), 101

Applegarth, Mabel, 124, 129, 236, 238, 272 n14

Armstrong, LeRoy: "The Man Who Came Back," 188–94 *passim*

Assassination Bureau, Ltd., The (JL), 187

Atherton, Gertrude, 28

Atlantic Monthly, 7, 18

"Bald-Face" (JL), 172

Bamford, Frederick Irons, 104–5

Barnum, P. T., 180

Baskett, Sam S., 193, 250 n27, n29, 259 n23, 265 n16, 270 n9, 272 n14, 272–73 n16, 273 n17, 277 n8, n9

"Bâtard" (JL), 35, 90, 263 n19

Beauchamp, Gordon, 267 n29

Before Adam (JL), xi, xii, 121

Bellamy, Edward: *Looking Backward*, 99, 100, 107–8, 118, 268 n40

"Benefit of the Doubt, The" (JL), 188

Berthoff, Warner, 259 n26

Bible: Ecclesiastes, 70, 72, 222; Genesis, 84; Ruth, 137

Bierce, Ambrose, 76–77

Bill (WF), 82–84, 93

Bishop, Del (DS), 22, 23

Bloom, Harold, xiii

Blotner, Joseph, 267 n29

Bond, Marshall and Louis, 35

Brett, George P.: as JL's editor, 8–9, 33, 53–55, 79–80, 100, 101, 124; chooses title of ME, 270 n9; JL's letters to, quoted, 8–9, 33–35, 54, 77, 79–80, 99, 189–90, 283 n16; mentioned, 59

Brewster, Maud (SW), 58–78 passim, 114, 117, 169, 185, 236, 260–61 n33

Brissenden, Russ (ME), 127, 128–29, 130, 153–54, 157, 274 n25

Brown, Sarah (VM), 193, 196–97, 202, 280 n9

Brown, Saxon. See Roberts, Saxon

Brown, Tom (VM), 193, 196–97, 202, 209, 210

Browning, Elizabeth Barrett, 114

Browning, Robert; 20, 24; "Caliban Upon Setebos," 59, 258 n21

Bruccoli, Matthew J., 61, 257 n15

Bryan, William Jennings, 268 n40

Buck (CW), 35–52, 85, 90, 91, 98, 158

Burning Daylight (JL): xi, 165–86, 235, 239; genesis, composition, and sources, 165–69, 277 n6; as Western comedy, 169–74, 278 n14, 278–79 n17; mythic elements, 170, 183–86; Western heroism, 174–78; sexual conflict, 175, 181–86; comedy of manners, 181–83; mentioned, 18, 188, 221

Burning Daylight. See Harnish, Elam

Butler, Charles (ME), 128, 130–31, 152, 172, 177

Calder-Marshall, Arthur, 275–76 n30

Caldwell, Professor (ME), 141, 150

Call of the Wild, The (JL): xi, 33–52, 53, 59, 91, 158, 236, 237, 243, 248–49 n16; genesis and composition, 33–35, 254 n5; publication, 34; remuneration for, 34, 253 n3; choice of title, 34–35; sources and influences, 35–38, 254 n7, n8, n15, 256 n31; primordial experience, 38; naturalism, 38–39; romantic primitivism, 39–40; as escape fiction, 40; value of work, 41–43; value of love, 41, 43–44; Southland vs. Northland, 43–46; orphanhood, 43–45; father-son conflict, 45–52; influence of Moby-Dick, 45–52; compared with WF, 79–80, 81–82, 84–86, 91, 98; mentioned, ix, xiii, 54, 78, 100, 129, 263 n21

Carlson, Roy W., 250 n29, 253 n20

Cather, Willa, 240, 251 n38

Century Illustrated Monthly Magazine, 55, 77

Cervantes, Miguel de: Don Quixote, 22

Charles (CW), 36–37, 41, 42, 85

Cheese-Face (ME), 144, 147, 158

Children of the Frost (JL), 18

"Class Struggle, The" (JL), 102

Clayton, Lawrence, 256 n26, 258–59 n21

Clemens, Samuel L. (Mark Twain): 240, 278 n14; Adventures of Huckleberry Finn compared with CW, 39–40

Collier's Weekly, 190, 216

Connolly, Lizzie (ME), 128, 129, 143, 154

Conrad, Joseph: xii, xiii, 237, 257 n16; "Heart of Darkness," 41, 59, 60–61, 257 n16, 259 n23; The Nigger of the Narcissus, 57, 140,

Conrad, Joseph (*cont.*)
  257 n16; *Lord Jim*, 57, 257 n16;
  Nostromo, 257 n16; *Victory*, 257
  n16
Coolbrith, Ina, 279 n3
Cooper, James Fenimore, 170, 201
Cooper, James Glennon, 275 n28
Corliss, Vance (*DS*), 18–31 *passim*,
  41, 76, 252 n12
Cosmopolitan Magazine, 8, 9,
  189, 214
Crane, Stephen: 56–57, 59, 196,
  240; "The Open Boat," 57; "The
  Bride Comes to Yellow Sky,"
  171; *Maggie*, 196
Cranston, Mary Rankin, 190–91
Crissey, Forrest, 191
Critic, The, 56
Cruise of the Dazzler, The (JL), xii,
  57
Cunningham, Avis. *See* Everhard,
  Avis
Cunningham, John (*IH*), 104, 106,
  118
Curwood, James Oliver, 280 n6

Dante, 258–59 n21
Darwin, Charles, and Darwinism:
  37, 90; *The Descent of Man*, 59.
  See also Social Darwinism; Spencer, Herbert
Daughter of the Snows, A (JL): xi,
  16, 17–32, 33, 34, 41, 171, 182,
  237; genesis and composition,
  18–19; JL's evaluation of, 19;
  publication of, 19; style, 19–21;
  artistic weaknesses, 19–23; literary stereotypes in, 22–23; as
  comedy of manners, 22–29; sexual conflict, 23–32, 252–53 n19,
  253 n20; as red-blooded realism,
  26–29; racism in, 29–31; mentioned, x, 38, 57, 76, 137
Davis, Richard Harding, 4, 217
Debs, Eugene, 101, 103
De Casseres, Benjamin, 285 n6

DeVore, Lynn, 262 n14, 263 n21
Dickens, Charles, 22
Dinsmore, Frank, 166–67
Donnelly, Ignatius: *Caesar's Col-
  umn*, 108, 109–12, 118, 237, 267
  n29, 285 n7
Dowsett, John (*BD*), 167, 180
Dreiser, Theodore: 134, 138, 240;
  Sister Carrie, 131, 133, 271–72
  n13; Cowperwood trilogy, 179
Dunn, Allan, 212–15, 217, 218–19
Dunn, N. E., 273–74 n22
Dunn, Robert, 217–18, 282 n12

Eames, Ninetta. *See* Payne, Ninetta
  Eames
Eden, Marian (*ME*), 128
Eden, Martin (*ME*): as artist, 16,
  138–59, 237, 270 n7, 272–73 n16;
  as tragic hero, 156–64, 239; compared with Elam in *BD*, 165, 177,
  181, 183; compared with Billy in
  VM, 191; mentioned, 271 n13,
  273–74 n22, 274 n23, 274–75
  n26, 275–76 n30
Ellis, James, 258 n21, 260 n30
Emerson, Ralph Waldo, 15, 151
Erbentraut, Edwin B., 282 n13
Everhard, Avis (*IH*): 104–22 *passim*,
  137, 195, 265 n14; as narrator and
  protagonist, 112–13, 114–17, 268
  n34, 269 n43
Everhard, Ernest (*IH*), 102–22 *passim*, 137, 265–66 n17, 266 n26,
  269 n43

Faulkner, William, 4, 5, 7, 78, 141
Faust, 68–69
Fetridge, W. Pembroke: *The Rise
  and Fall of the Paris Commune in
  1871*, 264 n3
Fiedler, Leslie A., 176
Fielding, Henry, 22
Fisk, Jim, 167
Fitzgerald, F. Scott: *The Great
  Gatsby*, 270 n9

Fitzgerald, Zelda, 238
Flink, Andrew, 255 n20
Foner, Philip S., 235, 253 n3, 265 n16, 269 n2, 284 n3
Forrest, Dick (*LL*), 212, 217–34 *passim*, 239, 281 n6, 282 n11, n13, 282–83 n14, 283 n17
Forrest, Paula (*LL*), 212, 217–18, 221–34 *passim*, 281 n6, 282 n13, 282–83 n14
Forrey, Robert, 65, 260–61 n33, 282 n13
Forster, E. M., 243
Francois (*CW*), 41–44 *passim*, 50, 85
Franklin, H. Bruce, 268 n34
Frazer, James G.: *The Golden Bough*, 47–48, 156, 275 n27
Freud, Sigmund: *Totem and Taboo*, 47–48, 49; *The Interpretation of Dreams*, 260–61 n33
Frye, Northrop, 275 n28

Game, The (*JL*), xi, 79
Geismar, Maxwell, 47, 77, 96, 272–73 n16, 278 n11, 280 n15
Ghent, W. J.: 103; *Our Benevolent Feudalism*, 105–6, 266 n26
Gilder, Richard Watson, 55, 77
Giles, James R., 257–58 n17, 263 n22
God of His Fathers, The (*JL*), 18
"Gold Hunters of the North, The" (*JL*), 166
Gould, Jay, 167
Gower, Ronald, 250 n29
Graham, Evan (*LL*), 212, 215, 217–19, 221–31 *passim*, 233, 282 n13
Gray Beaver (*WF*), 85, 90, 95–96, 97

Hal (*CW*), 36–37, 41, 42, 85
Hale, Annette and Edmund (*VM*), 194
Hall, Jim (*WF*), 91, 263 n22
Hall, Mark (*VM*), 190

Hamilton, David Mike, 256 n31, 265 n16
Hardy, Thomas: 95; *Jude the Obscure*, 138, 272 n16
Harnish, Elam (*BD*): 30, 165–86; as Western comic hero, 172–78; as business tycoon, 178–81; as humorous romantic hero, 181–83; as mythic hero, 183–85
Harpham, Geoffrey, 250 n29
Harris, Frank, 105
Harrison (*SW*), 55, 64
Harte, Bret, 23, 170, 278 n14
Hastings, Jack and Clara (*VM*), 190
Havens, F. C., 167–68, 178
Hawthorne, Nathaniel, 7, 240
Hazard, Jim (*VM*), 190
Healy, John J., 22
Hearst, William Randolph, 216–17
Hearts of Three (*JL*), xiii
Hemingway, Ernest, 262 n16
Henley, William Ernest, 185
Henry (*WF*), 82–84, 93
Higginbotham, Bernard (*ME*), 127, 128, 133–35, 139, 149, 159
Higginbotham, Gertrude (*ME*), 127, 128, 133–35, 139, 159
Higgins, Mercedes (*VM*), 203–6, 209, 210
High School Aegis (Oakland), 17, 172
Hindman, Kathleen B., 260–61 n33
Hirsch, E. D., Jr., xiii
Holland, Robert Belton, 248 n5, 250 n29, 250–51 n37, 265 n10, 281 n19
Homer, 16
Hopper, Jimmy, 190
Houghton Mifflin Company, 18
Howells, William Dean: 15, 147, 149, 240; *A Traveler from Altruria*, 108; *The Rise of Silas Lapham*, 130, 131–32, 171, 179
"Hyperborean Brew, A" (*JL*), 172

Ibsen, Henrik, 20, 27–28; *A Doll's House*, 27

Iron Heel, The (JL): xi, 99–122, 137, 195, 235–39 *passim*, 285 n7; genesis and composition, 8–9, 99–100, 264–65 n8, 265 n14, 267 n31, 269 n43; sources and influences, 101–12, 265 n16, 265–66 n17, 266 n25, n26; as utopian and dystopian fiction, 107–12; influence of *Caesar's Column*, 108, 109–12; social conflict, 112, narrative method, 112–13; Avis as protagonist, 113–17; Ernest as inadequate hero, 113–14; realism and romance, 117–19, 121–22; apocalyptic imagery, 119–20; evolutionary socialism, 119–22; JL's evaluation of, 265 n10, 268 n38; mentioned, xii, 18, 123

Jackson (*IH*), 104, 105, 113, 114, 115
James, Henry, 10, 15, 240
J. B. Lippincott Company, 19, 33
Jennings, Ann S., 225 n19
Jerry of the Islands (JL), xiii
Jim (*ME*), 135, 139
John Barleycorn (JL), 46, 178, 240, 259 n23
Johns, Cloudesley: 5–6, 55, 248 n16, 279 n20; quoted, 168; JL's letters to, quoted, 3, 7, 10, 14, 18, 19, 80
Johnson (*SW*), 55, 64, 72–73
Jung, Carl, 235

Kama (*BD*), 175–76
Kazin, Alfred, 38, 258 n20
Keene, James R., 167, 168, 178, 277 n6
Kempton-Wace Letters, The (JL and Strunsky), 19–20, 33
Ketterer, David, 267 n29, 268 n39
Kingman, Russ, 269 n2, 279 n3
Kipling, Rudyard: xiii, 10, 16, 59, 158, 185, 237, 252 n15; *Captains*

Courageous, 26, 57, 252 n15, 257–58 n17; *The Jungle Book*, 37–38, 59, 237
Kittredge, Charmian. *See* London, Charmian Kittredge
Kruskopf, Anders, 270 n10

Labor, Earle, ix, 35, 38, 48, 114, 234, 241, 248 n5, 254–55 n16, 258 n21, 260–61 n33, 263 n19, 273 n17, 275 n29, 276 n33, n35, 278 n11, 282 n13, 283 n16
Lachtman, Howard, 260–61 n33, 281 n20
Lafargue, Paul, 103
Larsen, Death (*SW*), 58, 73–74
Larsen, Wolf (*SW*): 55–78 *passim*, 172, 236, 239, 243, 259–60 n29, 260 n30, n32; as Gothic hero-villain, 67–68; and Faust, 68–69; and Hamlet, 69–70; and Captain Ahab, 70–74; and Milton's Satan, 74–75; mentioned, 90, 114
"Law of Life, The" (JL), 83
Lawrence, D. H.: *Sons and Lovers*, 138, 272 n16
Leach, George (*SW*), 55, 68
Letton, Nathaniel (*BD*), 167
Lewis, Austin, 103, 266 n26
Lewis, Sinclair, xiii
Lippincott, J. B. *See* J. B. Lippincott Company
Littell, Kathrine M., 265 n16
Little Lady of the Big House, The (JL): xi, 210, 211–34, 235, 239; theme of middle age and loss, 211–12, 219; genesis, composition, and sources, 211–21, 232–33, 281 n6, 282 n11, 283 n15; love triangle, 221–23; Dick's overregimented life, 223–28; Forrests' childlessness, 224–25; Paula's fragmented character, 228–29; flawed ending, 231–34; JL's evaluation of, 232–33

London, Bess Maddern (first wife of JL), 54, 107

London, Charmian Kittredge (second wife of JL): 187–88, 190, 220, 238–39, 253 n3, 269 n2, 271 n13, 276 n32, 285 n9; JL's letters to, quoted, 13; begins love affair with JL, 54; reads MS of *SW*, 55; as model for Maud in *SW*, 58; JL's courtship of, 79, 80; as model for Avis in *IH*, 107; emotional breakdown, 169; marital stresses, 169, 193–94, 211–19, 238–39; birth and death of daughter, 188; as model for Saxon in *VM*, 191, 193–94; contribution to *VM*, 194; attraction to Allan Dunn, 212–15, 281 n6; reaction to *LL*, 232–33; quoted, 3–4, 14, 104, 164, 243–44, 259 n29, 275 n29; mentioned, 123, 165

London, Eliza. *See* Shepard, Eliza London

London, Flora Wellman (mother of JL), 12, 14, 193

London, Ida. *See* Miller, Ida London

London, Jack (John Griffith London): literary reputation, ix–xi; as novelist vs. short story writer, x–xiv, 17–19, 33–34, 80, 123; literary motivation, 3–12; socialism, 6, 12, 99–107, 235–36, 274 n23; creative ecstasy, 11, 46–47, 146, 147–49; double vision, 11–16, 236–40; as sailor, 12, 53–56, 123, 161–62; childhood, 12–13; racism, 12, 29–31, 199–201, 242; role-playing, 12–14; rationalism and materialism, 12–15; on spiritualism and supernatural, 12, 14–15; idealism, 12–16; literary apprenticeship, 17–18; heightened literary ambition, 33–34; charges of plagiarism, 35–36, 81, 105, 249 n24; as rancher, 165–66,

168–69, 187, 211–12, 220–21, 282 n11, 283 n16; question of artistic decline, 235–36, 238–39; place in American fiction, 239–41; weaknesses and strengths, 241–44

—literary views: on novel vs. short story, x, 18–19, 33–34, 80; on originality, xiii, 10, 162; on writing as a career, 3–5, 247 n1; on artistry vs. hack work, 3–12, 151–54, 274 n24; on bowdlerization, 7–8, 248–49 n16; on revision, 8–9; on didacticism, 10; on style and technique, 10; on tragedy, 11; on romance vs. realism, 15–16, 144–51; on his strength as a writer, 123–24; on plagiarism, 249 n24

—themes and subjects of novels: prizefighting, xi, xii–xiii; fantasy and supernatural, xi–xii; physical brutality, xi, xii, 13, 16, 27, 36, 55–56, 57–58, 59–61, 90, 96, 111–12, 197–98, 206; race, xii, 29–31, 199–202; conflict, xiv, 11–16, 38–40, 112–13, 236–40, 250 n29; creative ecstasy, 11, 27, 46–47, 71, 146, 147–49; death, 11–12, 69–70, 71–72, 73–74, 76, 120, 154–64, 177–78, 204, 233–34, 275 n29; White Logic, 11–12, 46, 178, 239; wilderness vs. civilization, 16, 23–31, 38–40, 42–52, 89–91, 93–98, 169–86 *passim*, 187–91, 209–10; sexual conflict and balance, 16, 23–32, 65–67, 75–76, 98, 175, 181–86, 202–10, 252 n12, 252–53 n19, 253 n20, 260–61 n33; comedy of manner, 22–29, 129–38, 181–83; nature of women, 23, 26, 27–29, 182–85; atavism, 26, 39, 59–61, 259 n22; red-blooded initiation, 26–29, 37–38, 41–51, 56–58, 59–61,

London, Jack (*cont.*)
  64–67; American West, 28–29, 169–78, 199–202, 210, 278 n14, 278–79 n17; social Darwinism, 29–30, 119, 121, 179–80; naturalism, 38–39, 59–61, 82, 90, 91–98, 120–21, 195–98, 240–41, 250 n37; work, 41–43; love; 43–44, 145–46, 170–71, 181–86, 194, 206–7, 221, 230–31; orphanhood, 43–45, 89–90, 159–60, 263 n18, n20; White Silence, 45–48, 93–94, 239; father-son conflict, 45–52; ritual and myth, 45–52, 119–22, 155–63, 170, 174, 177–78, 183–86, 199–201; Gothicism, 61–65; 67–69; socialism, 99–122, 151, 179, 209, 235–36, 274 n23; art, 123–30, 138–59, 164; success, 129–38, 151–56; working-class life, 133–35, 139, 188–89, 191–93, 195–98; suicide, 154–64, 231–34; farming, 168–69, 185–86, 190–91, 209–10, 220–21, 224, 226–27, 234; marriage, 183, 185–86, 193–94, 202–10, 211–34, 238–39; middle age, 218–19, 229–30

London, Joan (daughter of JL), 235, 265 n16

London, John (stepfather of JL), 193

London, Joy (daughter of JL), 188

Longfellow, Henry Wadsworth, 159

Louis (*SW*), 55, 62–63, 72

Lucile (*DS*), 24, 25, 27, 31, 252–53 n19

Lynn, Kenneth, 278 n15, 283 n16

McClintock, James I., ix, x, 28, 235, 237, 284 n2

McClure, S. S., 18, 19

McLean, Alexander, 58

McLean, Dan, 58

Macmillan Company, 8, 33, 34; mentioned, 100, 101, 124, 248 n16

Maeterlinck, Maurice, 150

Major, Charles: *When Knighthood Was in Flower*, 222

Martin Eden (JL), xi, 16, 117, 122, 123–64, 165, 170, 172, 178, 181, 192, 196, 235–39 *passim*, 243; genesis, composition, and sources, 124–29, 160–64, 259 n23, 269–70 n2, 270 n8, n9; as novel of success, 129–38, 151–56; as novel of manners, 132–38; education of an artist, 138–56; socialism, 151, 274 n23; motivation of Martin's suicide, 154–64; mythic elements, 155–63; Martin as orphan, 159–60; JL's evaluation of, 164, 277 n37; mentioned, ix, 5, 18

Martin, Jay, 258 n20

Marx, Karl, and Marxism, 113, 119, 120, 122, 179. *See also* Socialism

Mason, Dede (*BD*), 168–70, 179, 181–86

Melville, Herman: 7, 36, 38, 149, 161–63, 237–38, 240, 243, 258 n20; *Pierre*, 139; *Typee*, 161–62, 276 n31; *Omoo*, 161, 276 n31; *White-Jacket*, 161, 163, 276 n31; mentioned, xiii, 10, 59

—*Moby-Dick:* and *CW*, 45–46, 48–49, 51–52; and *SW*, 58–59, 61, 62–64, 69, 70–74; and *WF*, 83–84, 88–89, 91, 92; influence on JL, 237–38, 285 n7; mentioned, ix, 38, 161, 249 n24, 276 n31

Mercedes (*CW*), 36–37, 41, 42

"Mercy of the Sea, The" (JL), 53–57

Meredith, Anthony (*IH*), 112, 114, 118, 120, 121

Michael, Brother of Jerry (JL), xiii

Michel, Louise, 105, 266 n25

Miller, Ida London (stepsister of JL), 128, 280–81 n16

Miller, Judge (*CW*), 35, 41, 43, 85

Mills, Gordon, 170, 250 n29, 255 n17, 273 n18, 278 n11, 280 n15

Milton, John: 237: *Paradise Lost*, 59, 74–75, 221, 258 n21, 260 n32, 275 n28

"Minions of Midas, The" (JL), 100

Morehouse, Bishop (*IH*), 104, 113, 119, 120

Morris, William: *News from Nowhere*, 108

Morse, Ruth (*ME*), 117, 127–59 *passim*, 164, 236

Mortimer, Mrs. (*VM*), 190–91, 279 n3

Mugridge, Thomas (*SW*), 55, 57, 64, 66, 68, 75, 257 n11, 260 n33

Mutiny of the Elsinore, The (JL), xii, 9, 212, 284 n3

Naturalism: 240–41, 250 n37; in *CW*, 39; in *SW*, 59–61; in *WF*, 82, 90, 91–98; in *IH*, 120–21; in *VM*, 195–98

Nietzsche, Friedrich: and *DS*, 253 n21; and *SW*, 59, 69, 77, 259 n21, 259–60 n29, 263 n21; and JL's "long sickness," 79, 259–60 n29; and *IH*, 103, 118; and *ME*, 156–57, 275 n27; and *BD*, 177, 180; and *VM*, 204, 205; as JL's ideological opponent, 77, 237, 285 n6; *The Birth of Tragedy*, 156–57, 275 n27; *The Genealogy of Morals*, 259–60 n29; *Thus Spake Zarathustra*, 259–60 n29

"Night's Swim in Yeddo Bay, A" (JL), 172

Noel, Joseph, 188, 193

Norris, Frank: 4, 39, 59, 149, 240–41, 250 n37; *The Octopus*, 15, 121–22, 138, 170, 171, 198, 272 n15, 278 n13, 281 n17; JL's review of *The Octopus*, 15, 121–22, 272 n15, 278 n13, 281 n17; *Moran of the Lady Letty*, 26, 57–58, 59–60, 257–58 n17, 259 n22; *Blix*, 28; *A Man's Woman*, 28, 171; *McTeague*, 131, 138, 139;

The Pit, 171, 241; "A Plea for Romantic Fiction," 273 n20

O'Connor, Richard, 27, 269 n2

"Odyssey of the North, An" (JL), 7, 18, 58

On the Makaloa Mat (JL), 235

"Other Animals, The" (JL), 254 n15

Outing Magazine, 81, 262 n9

Overland Monthly, 17, 168

Pankake, Jon, 254–55 n16, 267 n32, 268 n34, n39, 272–73 n16

Parkay, Forrest Winston, 259 n27, 259–60 n29

Partington, Blanche, 215

Payne, Edward B., 104, 194

Payne, Ninetta Eames, 194

Pearsall, Robert Brainard, 252 n12, 258 n18

People of the Abyss, The (JL), 33

Perrault (*CW*), 41–44 *passim*, 85

Petterson, Clell T., 257–58 n17, 278 n11, 279 n21, 280 n15, 283 n18

Phillips, Roland, 189, 214, 219–20

Plato: *Republic*, 87–89

Poe, Edgar Allan: 11, 56, 61, 240; "The Pit and the Pendulum," 82, 262 n15; "To Helen," 145

Porter, Gene Stratton, 280 n6

Price, Starling, 248 n5, 265 n10, 273 n17, 274–75 n26

"Question of the Maximum, The" (JL), 103

Racism, 12, 199–202, 242

Realism: xiv, 15–16, 251 n38, 273 n20; in *IH*, 117–18; in *ME*, 129–38, 146–51; in *BD*, 171, 178–86; in *VM*, 195–98. *See also* Naturalism

"Red One, The" (JL), 235

"Revolution" (JL), 101, 102, 104

Richardson, Dorothy: *The Long Day*, 196, 280–81 n16
Rideout, Walter B., 267 n29
Road, The (JL), 123
Roamer (yacht), 188, 190, 194
Roberts, Billy (*VM*), 190–210 *passim*
Roberts, Charles G. D.: *The Kindred of the Wild*, 81; *Red Fox*, 81, 262 n9
Roberts, Dorothy H., 267 n33
Roberts, Saxon (*VM*), 190–210
Romance and romanticism: xiv, 15–16, 239–41, 250 n37, 273 n20; in *CW*, 39; in *IH*, 117, 119–22; in *ME*, 144–51
Roosevelt, Theodore, 4
Rothberg, Abraham, 262 n14, 281 n21
Roulston, Jane, 105, 266 n25
Roylston, Anna, 105, 266 n25

St. Vincent, Gregory (*DS*), 18, 22, 29, 30
San Francisco *Examiner*, 55, 101
Saturday Evening Post, 34, 54, 188, 189, 191, 193
Scarlet Plague, The (JL), xi–xii, 187, 188
Schmitt, Peter J., 280 n6
Scott, Weedon (*WF*), 84, 85, 90, 91, 93, 94
Sea-Wolf, The (JL): xi, 100, 169, 185, 236–39 *passim*, 243; genesis and composition, 53–55; sources and influences, 55–59, 257 n11, 257–58 n17, 258 n18, n20; influence of *Moby-Dick*, 58–59, 61, 62–64, 69, 70–74; naturalism and atavism, 59–61; influence of Norris's *Moran*, 57–58, 59–60; influence of "Heart of Darkness," 60–61; Gothicism, 61–65, 67–69; sexual conflict, 65–67, 75–76, 260–61 n33; influence of *Hamlet*, 69–70, 74; influence of *Paradise Lost*, 74–75; JL's evaluation of, 77; mentioned, 26, 48, 79, 122, 129
Seed, D., 268 n39
Sewell, Anna: *Black Beauty*, 36
Shakespeare, William: 151, 237, 249 n24; *Romeo and Juliet*, 11; *Hamlet*, 59, 69–71, 74, 76, 156, 258 n21, 260 n30, n31; *King Lear*, 69; *Much Ado About Nothing*, 170
Shepard, Eliza London (stepsister of JL), 128
Shivers, Samuel A., 258 n21
Silet, Charles L. P., 264 n7
Silva, Maria (*ME*), 128, 134, 159
Sinclair, Andrew, 98, 236, 277–78 n9, 278 n14, 285 n10
Sinclair, Upton: 6, 101–2; *The Jungle*, 101–2, 107, 267 n31
Sisson, James E., III, 253 n3
Smith, Beauty (*WF*), 85, 90, 93, 94
Smith, Henry Nash, 28
Smoke Bellew (JL), 189
Smollett, Tobias, 22
Snark (ketch), 123, 129, 161, 165
Social Darwinism, 29–30, 119, 121, 179–80
Socialism: 6, 12, 235–36; in *IH*, 99–122; in lectures and essays, 100–104; in *ME*, 154, 274 n23; in *BD*, 179; in *VM*, 209
Son of the Sun, A (JL), 189
Son of the Wolf, The (JL), 18
Sophia Sutherland (schooner), 53, 56
Spangler, George M., 274 n26
Spargo, John, 103
Spencer, Herbert: 30, 139, 144, 150, 179, 180, 237; stylistic influence of, 10; as agnostic, 14
Spinner, Jonathan H., 255 n18, 274–75 n26
Spitz (*CW*), 37, 42, 45, 46–51, 85, 158
Star Rover, The (JL), xii, 9

Starr, Kevin, 278–79 n17, 280 n15, 283 n16

Stasz, Clarice, 251 n42, 253 n22, 280 n11, 282 n13, 285 n9

Steffens, Lincoln, 103

Stein, Paul, 114, 267 n33

Sterling, George: reads MS of *SW*, 55; as model for Brissenden in *ME*, 128–29, 274 n25; as model for Mark Hall in *VM*, 190; mentioned, 167

Stone, Irving, 253 n3, 256 n25, 259 n22, 269 n2, 276 n31, 283 n15

"Story of a Typhoon off the Coast of Japan" (JL), 17

Strawn-Hamilton, Frank, 127

Strunsky, Anna: 33, 266 n25; collaboration with JL on *The Kempton-Wace Letters*, 19–20; influence on *DS*, 19–20, 252 n11, n12; as model for Maud in *SW*, 58, 258 n18; as model for Avis in *IH*, 107; JL's letters to, quoted, 5–6, 12

Swinburne, Algernon C.: 139; "The Garden of Proserpine," 159–60

Teich, Nathaniel, 267 n29, n33

"Terrible and Tragic in Fiction, The" (JL), 56

Theft (JL), 187

Thornton, John (*CW*), 35, 36, 38, 41, 43, 44, 45, 49, 50, 85, 90, 91

"Thousand Deaths, A" (JL), 7

"To the Man on Trail" (JL), 17

Trotsky, Leon, 119

Turner, Frederick Jackson, 210

Twain, Mark. *See* Clemens, Samuel L.

"Typee" (JL), 161

Untermann, Ernest, 103, 265–66 n17

Valley of the Moon, The (JL): xi, 187–210, 211, 212, 221, 234, 235, 239, 240; genesis, composition,
and sources, 188–94, 279 n3, 280 n9, n14; Saxon as protagonist, 194–95, 280 n15; scenes of working-class life, 195–98; race and religion, 199–202; sexual conflict and marriage, 202–10; weaknesses of Book Three, 209–10

Van Weyden, Humphrey (*SW*), 55–78 *passim*, 114, 185, 236, 260–61 n33

Veblen, Thorstein, 106–7

Walcutt, Charles Child, 39, 81, 155, 241, 252–53 n19, 253 n21, 255–56 n23, 259–60 n29, 263 n18, 271 n12

Walker, Dale L., 253 n3, 269 n2

Walker, Franklin, ix, 35–36, 248 n5, 251 n1, 255 n17, 257–58 n17, 275–76 n30, 278 n11, 279 n5, 280 n9

Wanhope, Bert (*VM*), 198, 199, 201, 202–3, 280 n15

Wanhope, Mary (*VM*), 192, 195–96, 199, 202–3

Ward, Susan, 249 n23

War of the Classes (JL), 101, 269 n42

Wasserstrom, William, 28

Waterloo, Stanley: *The Story of Ab*, 249 n24

Watson, Charles N., Jr., 250 n36, 255–56 n23, 257–58 n17, 259–60 n29, 269–70 n2, 275–76 n30

Wellman, Flora. *See* London, Flora Wellman

Wells, H. G.: 99, 100, 108–9, 118; *When the Sleeper Wakes*, 100, 108–9, 267 n29; *Anticipations*, 108

Welse, Frona (*DS*): 18–31 *passim*, 76, 182, 252 n12, 252–53 n19; as "new woman" and Western heroine, 27–29

Welse, Jacob (*DS*), 20, 22, 29–30, 171, 253 n21

Westbrook, Wayne W., 167, 277 n6
Weyden, Humphrey Van. *See* Van Weyden, Humphrey
Wharton, Edith, 138, 240, 242
"What Life Means to Me" (JL), 104, 265 n13
White Fang (JL): xi, 37, 79–98, 236, 237, 238; genesis, composition, and sources, 79–81, 254 n15, 261 n5, 262 n9; compared with *CW*, 79–80, 81–82, 84–86, 91, 98; naturalism, 82, 91–98; Part One as separate story, 82–84; influence of *Moby-Dick*, 83–84, 88–89, 91; prose style, 85–86; "wall of light," 86–89; orphanhood, 89–90, 263 n18; socialization, 90–91; weakness of ending, 91, 263 n22; mentioned, xiii, 99, 100, 101

White Fang (*WF*), 80–97
White Logic, 11–12, 46, 178, 239
White Silence, 45–49, 93–94, 239
"White Silence, The" (JL), 46, 48
Wickson (*IH*), 107, 110
Wilcox, Earl, 82, 97, 254–55 n16, 255–56 n23, 262 n16, 263–64 n23, 264 n24
Wilson, Pamela, 273–74 n22
Winship, Ed, 104
"Wonder of Woman" (JL), 46
Wright, Harold Bell, 280 n6

Young, Egerton R.: *My Dogs in the Northland*, 35–36

Zola, Émile: 39, 59, 93, 250 n37; *Germinal*, 121, 259 n22
Zverev, A. M., 272–73 n16

JACKET DESIGNED BY TOM ESSER
COMPOSED BY THE COMPOSING ROOM, KIMBERLY, WISCONSIN
MANUFACTURED BY BANTA COMPANY, MENASHA, WISCONSIN
TEXT AND DISPLAY LINES ARE SET IN TRUMP MEDIEVAL

Library of Congress Cataloging in Publication Data
Watson, Charles N., 1939–
The novels of Jack London.
Bibliography: pp. 291–293.
Includes index.
1. London, Jack, 1876–1916—Criticism and
interpretation.   I. Title.
PS3523.046Z9954   1982   813'.52   82-70548
ISBN 0-299-09300-X